MASTERING

SOCIO

C000097435

MACMILLAN MASTER SERIES

Banking
Basic English Law
Basic Management
Biology
British Politics
Business Communication
Chemistry
COBOL Programming
Commerce
Computer Programming
Computers
Data Processing
Economics
Electrical Engineering
Electronics
English Grammar
English Language
English Literature
French
French 2

German
Hairdressing
Italian
Keyboarding
Marketing
Mathematics
Modern British History
Modern World History
Nutrition
Office Practice
Pascal Programming
Physics
Principles of Accounts
Social Welfare
Sociology
Spanish
Statistics
Study Skills
Typewriting Skills
Word Processing

MASTERING
SOCIOLOGY

GERARD O'DONNELL

MACMILLAN

First published 1985

Published by
MACMILLAN EDUCATION LTD
Houndmills, Basingstoke, Hampshire RG21 2XS
and London
Companies and representatives
throughout the world

Printed and bound in Great Britain by
Anchor Brendon Ltd, Tiptree, Essex

British Library Cataloguing in Publication Data
O'Donnell, Gerard
Mastering sociology
1. Sociology
I. Title
301   HM51
ISBN 0–333–34496–0
ISBN 0–333–38731–7 Pbk
ISBN 0–333–38732–5 Pbk export

To Sara, Duncan (Young Social Scientist of the Year 1982)
and Rory, my expert advisers

CONTENTS

CONTENTS

CONTENTS

PREFACE

Mastering Sociology is a systematic introduction to the study of society; combining a comprehensive coverage of the various sociology ordinary level GCE syllabuses in the text, with a wide range of extracts from a variety of source materials which both extend the text, allow the students to experience something of the flavour of the originals, and can provide a base for the kind of data response and stimulus questions which are becoming increasingly popular.

Unusual and valuable features of the book are specimen questions with examples of the kind of outline marking schemes used by GCE examiners and specimen answers of a length and content calculated to get high marks in Sociology at 'O' level, but within the capability of good candidates. These schemes and answers, together with examples of actual recent questions set by all the Boards currently offering Sociology at 'O' level, makes the book particularly appropriate to the self taught student, while enhancing its value as a class text.

All areas of the AEB, Oxford Local, Welsh Board, Cambridge Local* 'O' Level and London 'O/A' Level syllabuses are covered; although the book in general follows the sequence of the new AEB syllabus introduced in 1982. [*In respect of Cambridge Local, this explicitly requires students to engage in cross-cultural comparison where this is appropriate. It is not possible to include much cross-cultural material in *Mastering Sociology* — examples will be found in *The Human Web* (John Murray) by Gerard O'Donnell or *Human Societies* — Hambling & Mathews (Macmillan).]

In preparing the book particular regard has been paid to the proposed amalgamation of the GCE and CSE in the new GCSE and the development of Joint 'O' level/CSE examination (e.g. The East Anglian, London Regional and University of London joint examination operational from 1986). To this end text material should be within the capability of most students while source material will often stretch the most able and provide a base for 'A' level work.

As you start this book your examination may seem a long way off, but it is useful to bear in mind some points about the examination so that you can get used to practising them as you answer the sample questions set at the end of each section.

ACKNOWLEDGEMENTS

The author and publishers wish to thank the following who have kindly given permission for the use of copyright material: Addison-Wesley Publishing Company for extracts from *People at Work* by Pehr G. Gyllenhammer. Copyright 1977 by Addison-Wesley Publishing Company, Reading, Massachusetts; George Allen & Unwin (Publishers) Ltd for an extract from *Political Representation and Elections in Britain* by P. G. J. Pulzer; Edward Arnold (Publishers) Ltd for an extract from *The British Police* by Simon Holdaway; Associated Newspapers Group for a cartoon by MAC published in the *Daily Mail*; B. T. Batsford Ltd for extracts from *Sociology in Britain* by E. Krausz; Basil Blackwell Ltd for extracts from *Girl Delinquents* by Anne Campbell and *Methods of Sociological Enquiry* by Peter Mann; Calouste Gulbenkian Foundation (Lisbon) for extracts from *Broadcasting and Youth* (1979); Child Poverty Action Group for an extract from 'Family in the Firing Line'; Comedia Publishing Company Ltd for an extract from *1984 – Autonomy, Control and Communication* edited by C. Aubrey and P. Chilton; The Controller of Her Majesty's Stationery Office for extracts from *Social Trends*, from *Report on Education No. 97* and from *People in Britain*, Social Studies in the Census (Office of Population Censuses and Surveys, 1981); Heinemann Educational Books for extracts from *Cycles of Disadvantage* by Rutter and Madge; Hodder & Stoughton Ltd for an extract from *The Changing Anatomy* by Anthony Sampson; Holt Saunders Ltd for extracts from *Deviance, Reality and Society* by S. Box; Hutchinson Publishing Group Ltd for an extract from *Basic Political Concepts* by Renwick and Swinburn; Longman Group Ltd for extracts from *Population* by R. Kelsall, from *Education* by Ronald King and from *Elections* by I. McLean; Open Books Publishing Ltd for extracts from *Fifteen Thousand Hours* by M. Rutter *et al.*; Oxford University Press for extracts from *Change in British Society* by A. H. Halsey (2nd edition 1981); Penguin Books Ltd for extracts from *Inside the Inner City* by Paul Harrison (Pelican Books, 1983), *Voters, Parties and Leaders* by J. Blondel, *Techniques of Persuasion* by J. A. C. Brown, *Communities in Britain* by R. Frankenberg, *Class in a Capitalist Society* by J. Westergaard and H. Resler, *Just Like a Girl* by S. Sharpe, *Housewife* by A. Oakley, *Maternal Deprivation Re-assessed* by M. Rutter, *Marriage* by L. Mair, and *Human Groups* by W. Sprott; Routledge & Kegan Paul for extracts from *Symmetrical Family* by Michael Young and Peter Willmott; *The Rules of Disorder* by Peter Marsh, Elizabeth Rosser and Rom Harré; Souvenir Press Ltd for an extract from *You Can Teach Your Child Intelligence* by David Lewis.

THE EXAM AND PREPARING FOR IT

1. In answering the sample examination questions set in the earlier sections of the book it must be borne in mind that while it is necessary to subdivide the book into syllabus headings in order to present the subject coherently, the areas of sociological study are interdependent. A particular question may require information drawn from a number of sections (e.g. family, class and education). When you have finished the book, try working through some of your earlier efforts, drawing this time on all the knowledge that you have acquired during the course.

2. Write clearly. Boards do vary in the importance which they attach to structure. London states: 'Candidates are reminded of the necessity for good English and orderly presentation in their answers'; AEB is less concerned with style provided the meaning is clear. In all cases, write in essay form – do not write notes as your answer, although you may wish to make a few notes on your paper before commencing your real answer. (Put a neat line through these and the examiner will ignore them.) Remember the examiner will have hundreds of papers to mark in two or three weeks – he or she will not spend a lot of time trying to work out what you mean or in deciphering your handwriting; the repetition of points to try and make a scrappy answer look longer will not impress and flowery description is a waste of time.

3. If the question is broken into sections look for the number of marks awarded to each part. It is a waste of time to devote several lines to an answer that can gain only 1 mark; the examiner will only expect a few words. A common (and disastrous) error is to write almost all you know about a particular topic in answer to a section attracting few marks and then fail to repeat relevant information in the major section which is intended to attract that information.

4. A mere recital of the names of sociologists gains no marks at any level. At 'O' level you are not expected to know detailed sociological theory (ethnomethodology, etc.) – you *should* know the different approaches to sociological enquiry and it is useful to be able to give examples of specific research. (Oxford Board specifically states: 'Candidates should be prepared to make reference to any relevant sociological studies or surveys of which they have knowledge when

answering questions set on any part of the syllabus'.) You should be able to make balanced judgements about the structure and institutions of society but mere unsubstantiated opinion is worthless. You should know something of the various methods of research used by sociologists and be able to interpret and analyse evidence presented in a variety of ways – that is one reason why graphs, tables and extracts are included in the book.

5. Sheer length gains no marks. Time will limit your length in any case – a good answer to an essay question may be 500–600 words long; but a well-constructed concise essay may be able to present all the relevant facts in less.

6. Work out how much time you can afford to spend on each question; when the time is up to move on to the next question – you can return to complete unfinished answers if you have time. Three good answers will almost certainly gain less marks than five average ones.

7. Spend some time reading through the paper carefully and choose those questions you know most about (not those that sound easy). Some people find it best to write up their second best answer first – so that they become more confident as they progress.

8. Do not answer more questions than you need – some boards exclude all surplus answers written after the required answers, others mark them all and take the best answers up to the required number – you are always wasting valuable time.

9. Answer the question asked, not the one you hoped would be asked. If you have read 'model' or 'specimen' answers, do not be tempted to regurgitate them verbatim; extract from them the material relevant to the question asked.

10. A reading list is not included in this book because experience shows that few 'O' level candidates have the time (or inclination?) to read more widely than the textbook.

    However you will enjoy and appreciate sociology more if you *do* extend your reading – dipping into *New Society* a weekly magazine, and in particular its pull-out supplement 'Society Today' which appears about once a month (some sample extracts are included in this book) and is directed at GCE candidates; and read more of some of the books from which extracts are taken.

11. The 1950s and 1960s in Britain saw the first major invasion of Britain by Sociology. In these years many standard, popular sociology texts were introduced which gave (and still give) valuable insights into sociological concepts. *Coal is Our Life*; *Family and Kinship in East London*; *The Fishermen* remain useful books but students do need to be aware of how dated some of these studies now are and compare them critically with the realities of the 1980s.

PART I

WHAT IS SOCIOLOGY ?

SOCIOLOGICAL TERMS AND CONCEPTS

1.1 CULTURE AND SOCIAL ORDER

The word 'sociology' was used first by a Frenchman, Auguste Comte, in 1838 to describe what he called 'the science of the associated life of humanity'. Many people before Comte had studied aspects of society in a systematic way but Comte sought to establish Sociology as a distinct discipline; in fact he regarded it as the most important science, at the top of a hierarchy of science of increasing complexity. On the other hand some people do not regard Sociology as a science at all, but as a way of wrapping up the obvious in complex terms.

In Chapter 2 we shall have a look at Sociology as a 'science'; in this chapter the intention is to establish what it is that sociologists study – the 'associated life of humanity' referred to by Comte.

Most animals live in groups in order to protect themselves, raise their offspring and to improve their efficiency in providing themselves with food and shelter; because they have to co-operate, certain rules and expectations develop.

If a group of chickens fought constantly over their food they would often injure each other but this is avoided by the establishment of a pecking order or 'hierarchy' in which the right of the more aggressive chickens to eat first is established.

People live much more complex lives than chickens and it is more important for them to co-operate with others, certainly few people would wish to live in a society dominated by the most aggressive individuals. When co-operation takes place it is necessary for the people concerned to agree on certain ideas and share a similar pattern of behaviour. In Britain it is accepted that the first person to start a bus queue has a right to get on the bus first and people arriving later will usually be deterred from pushing in by the expectation that others in the queue will disapprove.

Most animals live in groups

When a group of people establish a way of life in which there are generally accepted modes of conduct and beliefs their behaviour and morality is described as their *culture*.

A culture will include speech, dress, food and general behaviour; but perhaps more importantly it will include thought processes.

A country will generally share a cultural pattern and so we may refer to the British culture or French culture but there will usually be differences between the behaviour and beliefs of groups within any single country based on such facts as class, age or ethnic background. In Britain it is usual to distinguish between 'working class' and 'middle class' cultures.

An American sociologist Oscar Lewis has suggested that a distinctive 'sub-culture' is found in the slums of large cities. This 'culture of poverty' has its own distinctive beliefs and behaviour including a mistrust of authority, hatred of the police, feelings of inferiority linked to an idea that it is impossible to influence events, and a belief in male superiority.

The term 'community' is sometimes used to describe all the people that share a similar culture, but it usually refers to a closer sense of identification between individuals in terms of co-operation and a sense of belonging. For most practical purposes it is better to think in terms of a community as sharing a territory well known to all its members whether this is a monastery or a set of city streets and to distinguish this social grouping from a 'culture'.

A community implies shared needs in terms of such factors as schools, safe roads, housing and protection; there is therefore a need for co-operation. A common culture is one way in which such co-operation is ensured, although different cultures within a society may bring variety and colour to our lives, provided that there are certain shared values to prevent disorder.

1.2 SOCIALISATION

There are a number of ways in which social order can be maintained, including the use of force. However the most effective way of ensuring that the people within a society work together without disorder is for them to be brought up to expect to behave in a particular and broadly similar way.

From the moment that we are born we start to learn; first in the family then the neighbourhood and school. In this way we are 'socialised', brought up to accept certain forms of behaviour as appropriate for us and to expect other people to behave in a particular way.

We learn our 'gender' behaviour – the way that little boys and little girls are expected to behave; our 'class' identity – the way that we should behave if we are to be accepted into a certain social status group; our 'property values' – which will ensure that our attitude to ownership will be appropriate to the society in which we live.

What we learn during the first few years of life will usually prove critical in determining our future. Jesuits summed up this situation centuries ago – 'give me the boy at seven and I will have the man'. Most research however indicates that the most critical years for socialisation begins not at seven but at birth; one researcher, John Bowlby, established that the most critical years for the formation of emotional stability were from birth to age three.

Naturally, the socialisation process will reflect the needs of the society; it may be harsh and disciplined in order to produce a tough war-like people as among the people of Sparta in Ancient Greece or gentle and permissive as among the Arapesh of New Guinea where there were few economic or social pressures.

An interesting example of a deliberate attempt to influence the socialisation process was the replacement of houses and trees by guns and soldiers in books for little Japanese children before the Second World War.

1.3 CONFORMITY AND DEVIANCE

Most people within a society will behave as they are expected to behave – 'conform'. If most people do not conform to the expected patterns of conduct, then either the society will break up in chaos, or a new pattern of conduct will emerge which will become the new 'conformity'. Most societies will also have some people who do not conform to the expected, they differ – 'deviate' – from the normal. These 'deviants' may be individuals who reject some or all of the beliefs of the society, and who may also behave in a way which is unacceptable to the majority within the society. The deviants may also however be part of a group, all of whose members accept different beliefs or practice different behaviour from that common in the general society – in this case they are members of a 'deviant sub-culture'. The individual deviant may be a holy hermit or a child-molester; the member of the deviant 'sub-culture' may be part of a permanent community in a large city that makes its living from crime, or a transient member of a gang of Hell's Angels.

Deviance depends not upon a given action but upon the acceptability of a certain action in a certain circumstance. For example the injection of a drug by a nurse in a hospital may be socially approved, the injection of the same drug by a young person 'for kicks' may be condemned and punished.

As a society changes, its view of what is deviant will also change. It is now socially acceptable for young women unaccompanied by men to drink in public houses. A few years ago such behaviour would have labelled the girl concerned as a prostitute – a deviant from the accepted morality of British culture. But prostitution as an occupation has not been regarded as deviant in all cultures, for example there were sacred prostitutes in the temples of ancient Babylon.

What is deviance?

An action that might be quite acceptable to one group of people may be severely sanctioned by another. A girl who shoplifts may be seen as deviant by her middle-class teacher but not by her peer group. How are we to decide whether her continued shoplifting implies the stronger influence of her peer group's values upon her or her failure to realize the negative view take of it by her teacher?... But an individual who fails to adjust his behaviour would be more likely to be judged stupid than criminal.

Another problem relates to what is seen as constituting an adverse reaction from, or a sanction by, others in the group. Such a reaction does not generally take the form of expulsion from the group, for social psychological research has shown that deviant members are often a valuable part of group dynamics. Marsh's (1978) work on soccer fans shows that the 'nutter' of the group fulfills an important function in underlining normal conduct: his behaviour is not only tolerated but even encouraged by other members. The breaking of a social rule may provoke a number of immediate reactions. It has been suggested that anger, embarrassment and humour are three typical reactions to rule violation. However, they are also reactions to behaviour other than rule breakage. Humour may be a reaction to joke telling and anger to failing a driving test – neither of these is a breach of any rule. Another problem exists with respect to discovering what the social rules are. . . . It is virtually impossible for someone to sit down and enumerate the rules of behaviour for, say, a dinner party. It is only when a breach occurs that we feel something has gone wrong – for example, when there is a long and embarrassing silence in the conversation, or when someone gets so drunk that he loses control over his behaviour. . . . It seems, that the search for an absolute and universal definition of delinquency has to be abandoned. Laws change; labels change; and the same action may have a multitude of descriptions applied to it. [A. Campbell, *Girl Delinquents* (Oxford: Blackwell, 1981) abridged.]

1.4 ROLES AND STATUS

By definition however most people are not deviant, they behave in the way that people expect them to behave. Consciously or unconsciously they act a part, they adopt a 'role'. In fact as people grow older they act many parts and so have to adapt to a variety of roles; they retain the basic role they have learnt in terms of personality but add to these new 'bit parts' as gang members or mothers or students. These 'multiple roles' may conflict and cause tension and uncertainty; a man may be promoted at work and have to adopt the role of manager over his former workmates, although he still wants to be able to act his role as their mate. A woman may wish to start a job when her child is small but have difficulty in reconciling her role as a mother with her role as a worker. Society will expect her to be a good timekeeper as an employee but expect her to stay with her small child if it is sick.

Once learnt it is often difficult to unlearn our role and when people have to act a role which would not normally be expected of them it is called 'role reversal'; in some British communities today there may be jobs for women, but no jobs for men and the men who have grown up expecting to be the breadwinners find themselves unwilling house-husbands. They may seek other outlets to prove their masculinity; it has been suggested that this may be one of the many underlying factors contributing to violence in Northern Ireland.

All the roles we adopt in relating to other people are called our 'role set' and the people that we relate to in each situation are called our 'role others'.

Many of the roles we adopt are 'ascribed', that is they are determined in advance or without regard to our wishes – we have the status of a child or we become an Earl when our noble father dies. Other roles are 'achieved', that is we earn them in some way; we rob banks and earn the role of criminal or stand for Parliament and achieve the role of MP.

The roles we act will be important factors in determining our 'status' in our society. Our status is our position in a hierarchy; it is the degree to which we command the respect of others in the community. We may have higher status than others within a society by virtue of the supposed worth attached to the job we do; or we may have higher status if we have won a Victoria Cross thus demonstrating our bravery; or we may simply have higher status among our immediate friends because of some special skill we possess or trait of character that they admire.

Our status may relate to the degree that we behave in a manner approved of by our society. Or it may relate to a social position over which we have little control. Social class in Britain is an example of this if we are a member of the 'working class' (with a manual job) we will have less status than if we are 'middle class' (with a 'white collar' job). We may be able to achieve middle-class status through education but if we are born into a middle-class family our position will be protected by our family's ability to acquire greater opportunities for us in terms of education and contacts.

Learning a role

'A prisoner had reached the final stage of adjustment to the camp situation when he changed his personality so as to accept the values of the Gestapo.' They copied their terms of abuse, they copied their games, and they tried, with their miserable resources and such bits as they could steal, to dress like their captors. 'When asked why they did it they admitted that they loved to look like one of the guards.'

This surely displays the power of social prestige. To begin with the Gestapo conduct was odious and contemptible. Their victims then became inured to a new life. They are back again as children, ill-treated perhaps, but now that they have lost touch with the outer world for ever, this is a new life and as children they take on the standards of their ruthless 'fathers'. This, according to Dr Bettelheim, is exactly what was intended.

Civil Prisons. The last example of groups of men under stress is the civil prison community. Here the stress is very different from what it is in the other two types of imprisonment. The deprivations are different from those in the prisoner of war camps and not so severe as those in concentration camps. The prisoners are in public disgrace, though their own attitudes will vary from individual to individual according to the crimes he has committed. Some doubtless feel guilty, for some it is just in the luck of the game, while others – homosexual offenders, for example – feel that their 'crime' is no crime at all. Nevertheless, in so far as they associate with one another they form a primary group. . . . The leaders are those who act up to the norms of the group. The code has two main principles; loyalty to other prisoners and hostility to prison officials.

Any newcomer must accept the code or he will be ostracised by his companions. . . . The prestige system of any society is bound to influence all who are members of it. After all, the criminal has his position in society to keep up. Society has condemned him. He must therefore find some other backing. The experienced prison inmate finds that there is nothing absolutely intolerable about prison life. He feels no guilt. Everyone knows what everyone else has done, and no one has cause to look down their noses. Prison life is a kind of life, it's no use moaning, let's make the best of it. [W. Sprott, *Human Groups* (Harmondsworth: Penguin, 1958) abridged.]

1.5 NORMS AND VALUES

Although people will occupy different status positions within a society and act out differing roles there will be a certain behavioural pattern that will be regarded as 'normal' in any particular situation. This standard behaviour that we expect people to use is called a 'norm' for short by sociologists and it is the acceptance by most people of the norms of a society that allow the society to function reasonably smoothly.

If you went to see your doctor in his surgery and he was wearing nothing but underpants, boots and a bow-tie your confidence in him might be a bit shaken but the structure of your society would not be in danger of damage. However if people came to expect to help themselves to anything they liked provided the owner was weaker than they, then our society could not continue in the form we know.

Most people in our society would not consider engaging in such actions as indiscriminate stealing or killing because both would be against the 'moral values' of our culture. When a 'norm' reinforces one of the society's 'moral values' sociologists refer to it as a 'more' and the moral value itself simply as a 'value'. One such more in our society is the responsibility of parents to care for their children and treat them in a humane way.

Child-battering breaks a more of modern British society although violence against one's own children, short of permanent damage, would have been acceptable a hundred and fifty years ago. On the other hand many British motorists drive at more than seventy miles an hour on motorways when they think it safe to do so, or a father buys his seventeen-year-old son half a pint in a pub. They are breaking the law but not one of our society's mores. Law and more are therefore not the same thing.

Some 'values' such as a respect for life are general to most cultures but there will be wide variations in many other respects such as property rights. Even the interpretation of respect for life will vary widely; in Britain there would be widespread support for a defensive war but in the forests of Paraguay the German-speaking Mennonites have established a flourishing community which has as a central 'more' a refusal to take up arms in any circumstance.

Less important norms are called 'folkways'; people who break them may be considered eccentric, as would a doctor holding surgery in his underwear, but they would not be regarded as doing anything morally wrong. Folkways may be transient – the fashionable length for females' skirts is an example of such a temporarily accepted mode of correct conduct – or they may be more permanent and are then referred to as 'customs'. In Britain friends usually greet each other by shaking hands or just saying 'hello'. In Italy they may well embrace and kiss each other on both cheeks.

1.6 CONFLICT AND CONSENSUS

Of course if everyone accepted all the values of a society and followed all its norms there would be no change in that society's culture; however societies do change, some more rapidly than others, despite social pressures to ensure uniformity of behaviour.

There are two major ways of looking at the process of social change; one way is that favoured by the 'Functionalists'. Emile Durkheim – a Frenchman born in 1858 – did not invent the term 'functionalist' but it was he who emphasised that the most important aspect in integrating a society was a 'consensus', or agreement, about the principles on which the society was based. Durkheim felt that there was a 'collective conscience' in a society reflected by the shared values and norms that it possesses. Functionalists believe that a society's culture reflects that society's needs, that each aspect of culture has a 'function' in ensuring the smooth operation of the society. The functionalist would therefore consider that a society adapts its norms to changing needs because once a norm or value ceases to be useful in assisting the society to operate it becomes 'dysfunctional' and is rejected by the society.

If change occurs too quickly the society cannot adapt quickly enough and people become confused by the lack of rules. They enter a state of 'normlessness' called 'anomie' and escape from their confusion by alcoholism and other forms of drug-taking, aggression and suicide. Durkheim's most famous study was one into the causes of suicide in which he related the suicide rates in various countries to the degree of integration of individuals within the culture of the country concerned.

While the 'functionalist' tends to emphasise the importance of change as a gradual process, others tend to regard change as a much more explosive process resulting from inherent conflict within societies. In his *Manifesto of the Communist Party* Marx stated 'the history of all hitherto existing society is the history of class struggles'. This 'conflict theory' of social change has had a great deal of influence on sociologists.

Essentially what 'conflict theory' suggests is that the norms of a society must be meaningful to the individuals within the society or they will be 'alienated', or isolated, from them and rebel against them. As there is only a certain amount of wealth, power and other desired factors available within any society such conflict becomes almost inevitable.

Religion is a good example of an element within a society that may integrate and unite believers but also be a source of conflict, for example between Protestants and Catholics or Hindus and Muslims.

CHAPTER 2

SOCIOLOGICAL METHOD

2.1 MAJOR RESEARCH METHODS

There are two main reasons for carrying out research into society. One is 'descriptive', to discover the facts: What is gypsy life really like? How many people are poor? The second reason is 'explanatory', to find the causes of particular forms of group behaviour: Why are people prejudiced against certain ethnic groups? Why are young people more likely than older people to be involved in crime? Often research will seek to discover answers to both types of question: how? and why?

To explain an aspect of society we can start with a 'theory' – perhaps people are prejudiced against certain ethnic groups because they are frightened of them? We then have to *test* our theory by establishing some 'hypothesis', some supposed relationship between cause and effect – perhaps people fear immigrants because they think they are likely to reduce their own chance of finding a home? Having established our hypothesis we then have to test it.

It is at the testing stage that arguments arise as to whether sociology is a science. Certainly a social science such as sociology is much less certain than a natural science such as chemistry or meteorology. One deals with a subject matter – man – with an almost indefinite number of variables; the others deal with inanimate objects with a much more limited range of possibilities. However chemists and weather-men are often wrong – there can be no certainty in any science; the essential aspect of a science is that a scientific *method* is used. The scientist must be 'objective', he himself need not be neutral in his views on the subject matter but he must ensure that his investigation is carried out in such a way that any personal views do not influence his research.

In testing his hypotheses the sociologist has to avoid personal bias that may influence the result; he must also try and avoid bias on the part of the group being studied. The group members may be eager to suggest reasons for their behaviour, because they hope for financial advantage or because they wish to please the researcher.

In all sociological research there is a need for 'data' – selected information on which tests may be conducted – and this data can be divided into two types. 'Quantitative', anything that can be put into number form, the number of people in a particular age group or social class for example. 'Qualitative', which has to do with matters not capable of being related into a statistical form such as ideas that affect behaviour.

Although both forms of data may be used in the same research there are two main types of research technique appropriate to qualitative data research and two types appropriate to quantitative research. *Quantitative* research techniques can be divided into 'surveys' of various kinds and 'experiments'. *Qualitative* research techniques include 'participant observation' and 'in-depth interviewing'.

Sociological research can take place over a period of time so that trends can be observed and links established between cause and effect; the follow up results being compared with information collected earlier. Such research over a long period is called a 'longitudinal study'. The problems of longitudinal studies include expense, contacting the original sample after a lapse of years and sorting out the degree to which effects relate to the original possible causation and to what degree they are the result of experiences meanwhile. A good example of a longitudinal study is *From Birth to Seven* by Davie, Butler and Goldstein published in 1972 which was the result of a survey carried out on 17 000 children born during one week of 1958, into the effect of social class position on the children's development. The children were subsequently investigated again at the ages of 11 and 15.

Sociology as a science

Sociology today is both enjoying, and suffering from a tremendous wave of interest both inside and outside the universities. Within the universities it has become one of the most popular subjects with undergraduates and outside the universities the general public has become accustomed to hearing and reading about sociological problems and sociological investigations. But this popularity carries with it the dangers of both amateurism and slap-dash workmanship. Sociology itself is a difficult subject since its field of enquiry is so broad. Yet it is fascinating because we live in societies and our data are all around us all the time.

... To claim for sociology that it is a *scientific* study of society, would seem to be claiming too much. No sensible sociologist would deny that to attempt to study scientifically the society in which he lives is difficult. Not only is the field for study extraordinarily complicated, but also the sociologist is a part of it himself, with all his personal values, biases and prejudices.

The difficulty is to know where to start on a truly scientific approach, and, sad to relate, some people never bother and are happy to put forward their own highly-biased views as sociological 'findings'. This is both misleading and at times mischievous, and does the subject great harm. . . . Where then to start on this difficult task? Some critics of sociology have claimed that it is a study of the obvious. . . . On the other hand, there are people who feel that sociology is wasting its time trying to explain the unexplainable. Human motivations and behaviour patterns appear far too complicated for scientific generalisations. If sociologists really knew anything which could be used for the good of society, why is our crime-rate rising all the time? Why do they not get to the root causes of race riots and wildcat strikes and stop them? . . . Simple points can be raised at once to some of the critics—to those who claim that sociology is all so obvious it could be said that we certainly do all live in societies, but how many of us have any systematic under-standing of their workings? To take one simple case, British society has certain forms of social stratification but who would have the courage to claim that we all of us understand how our social class system works?

The critics who use the argument of too much complexity are proved wrong every minute of the day. If life were utterly com-plex it would be unlivable—no one would ever know what to do next or what was likely to happen next. It is the very orderliness of so much of our social life which refutes the complexity criticisms in driving my car I have, at the peril of serious accident, relied on the other motorists and pedestrians I encountered to keep certain rules of social behaviour just as I have done myself. [P. Mann, *Methods of Sociological Enquiry* (Oxford: Blackwell 1976) (abridged).]

2.2 QUESTIONNAIRES

Questionnaires can be used in all kinds of research. The questionnaire is simply a list of questions, and its advantage is that it can be relatively cheap to administer and can provide the means by which large numbers of people can be questioned. The most obvious form of the questionnaire is that used for the National Census started in 1801 which is normally held every ten years. This provides the government with the information it needs to provide future services such as those for the elderly; schools; housing and transport, as well as future taxation policy!

The questions on the questionnaire have to be carefully worked out so that they are unambiguous and able to be understood by the target group. It is also important that a question should not suggest a particular response.

A trial run or 'pilot study' is often first carried out on a small number of people so that confusing or misleading questions can be rephrased.

Postal questionnaires are often used when the information requested is straightforward, but they have the disadvantages of not being returned and of being misunderstood. The presence of a researcher on the other hand may result in untrue responses as the person being interviewed may seek to impress or shock the interviewer, they are also more costly to administer than the postal variety.

In 1955 Geoffrey Gorer produced the results of a survey 'Exploring English Character' carried out largely by questionnaire. Although interesting, its reliability is suspect as it was based on answers returned in response to a survey published in the *People* newspaper. One has to ask whether readers of the *People* were typical of English people generally and whether the sort of people who would bother to send in answers to a questionnaire of this kind were even typical of the *People* readers

2.3 INTERVIEWS AND OBSERVATION

Interviewing people may seem the obvious way to find things out, but people are often reluctant to disclose their true behaviour or thoughts, particularly on emotive issues such as sexual conduct or religion. The language of the interviewer can also provide a barrier either in arousing hostility or mistrust, or simply in not being sufficiently understood by the respondent.

The 'structured' interview has a precise format, with definite questions in a clear sequence. It can be of use in providing factual information quickly, for example on the use of local leisure or transport facilities. The 'unstructured' interview allows the interviewer to ask questions out of sequence, re-phrase questions and encourage the person being interviewed. This form of interview is potentially more useful in determining such qualitative aspects as depth of feeling but has certain disadvantages – it needs a more skilled interviewer who can put the person interviewed at ease without suggesting a particular kind of response. Tape recordings are now often used for unstructured interviews, allowing a greater free flow of information.

Another common form of obtaining information is that of observation; simply watching and recording what we see. We must be careful that the behaviour we are witnessing is typical of the norm within that situation; that it is not being influenced by our presence and that we are understanding what is in fact happening. Many sociologists have been able to join the groups that they wish to study and have become participants, actively involved in the group being studied. This technique is known as 'participant observation'. The advantages are a much deeper understanding of the group and its behaviour; a danger is that identification with the group may lead to unconscious bias in its favour, or that the very fact of the sociologist's presence will influence the behaviour of the group so that it does not behave as it normally would.

Participant observation is a favourite device of 'ethnography' – a form of study that seeks to capture a total picture of how a group operates without any preconceived notions of how or why it behaves as it does.

2.4 SAMPLING

Earlier in this chapter, Geoffrey Gorer's study of English character was noted in that the people who participated were probably unrepresentative, being self-selected. Most surveys are of groups too large for everyone to be questioned individually. It is necessary to select, or 'sample', some individuals for questioning rather than others, so that the numbers are large enough to fairly represent the group but be reasonably easy and economic to handle.

The normal way to carry out surveys is now based on 'random sampling' techniques. This eliminates any possibility of bias and is based on mathematical calculations that ensures that an appropriate number of people are selected on a random base from within the target group. The list of all the

People are often reluctant to disclose their true behaviour

"If an election were held tomorrow, which party. . .?"

members of the group from which the random sample is to be drawn is known as the 'sampling frame'. A simple example might be to take every tenth person on the electoral register in a constituency to forecast a by-election result. It is not haphazard in the way of many advertising agency surveys, where people are stopped at random in the street.

Where the sample is based very accurately on representatives from each 'strata', or layer, within the group it is known as a 'stratified sample'. This means that a sample is drawn in correct proportion from each identifiable section within the group being studied. For example if seventy-two per cent of the group to be studied were men and ten per cent were under eighteen the same percentage figure for each strata would apply in the sample group as well.

A 'quota' sample is a cheaper method of operating a stratified sample. A specified percentage, or 'quota', of each category in the target group is decided upon, but instead of particular individuals being selected by using a mathematical calculation the interviewer can seek out anyone who fits the category being studied. The disadvantage is one of bias. For example the interviewer may wish to interview fifty girls between the ages of fifteen and twenty. If home calls are made on a normal weekday between 10 a.m. and 4 p.m. most of those interviewed are likely to be unemployed or truanting. Both the simple random sample and the stratified random sample would have identified individuals and would thus have been more likely to draw upon a representative cross section of the age group.

Random sampling

Many students are deeply suspicious of opinion poll findings. (So, indeed, are many politicians, especially when the polls claim that public opinion differs from the politicians' estimates of it.) Let us look at the two criticisms which are most frequently made of opinion polls.

'Nobody has ever approached *me* in an opinion poll. How am I to know that the results they get are a fair sample of what the population as a whole thinks?' When opinion polling first started people thought they would have to contact a vast number of voters in order to get a fair idea of the views of the electorate as a whole. This idea was shattered by the notorious *Literary Digest* poll of 1936. The *Literary Digest*, an American magazine, contacted over two million Americans by telephone to ask how they intended to vote in the presidential election of that year. Their result predicted an easy win for the Republicans: but in fact F. D. Roosevelt scored a sweeping Democratic victory. Contacting two million people had proved neither necessary nor sufficient for an accurate prediction. The *Literary Digest* went wrong because it failed to ensure that the people it approached were representative of the whole population. Everybody it telephoned, needless to say, possessed a telephone. But telephones, in 1936, were mostly owned by the rich, and the rich mostly voted Republican. But the poor, who had no telephones, strongly favoured the Democrats.

At the same time other pollsters, sampling only about 2,000 voters, had correctly predicted that the Democrats would win. They, like all modern opinion pollsters, had taken great care to make sure that their sample was representative: that the proportion of women, old people, working-class voters, and so on was the same in the sample as in the population as a whole. If you have got a fair sample you can make a reliable prediction. Nowadays there are two main ways of getting a fair sample. One is to send interviewers out with strict instructions as to the sorts of people they must interview. If 60 per cent of the electorate is working-class, say, then 60 per cent of those the interviewer selects must also be working-class. This is called "quota sampling". The other way, called "random" or "probability" sampling, is to take the electoral register as a basis, draw names from it in a strictly controlled way (electoral number 23 and every 37th number thereafter, for instance) and send interviewers to the people selected in this way and to them alone. In this way again a fair sample can be obtained ... We cannot eliminate the margin of error entirely; but with sufficiently accurate sampling we can get it down to a matter of two or three per cent either way. This margin is known as "sampling error", and it is highly relevant to the second main criticism which is made of opinion polls. [I. McLean, *Political Realities – Elections* (London: Longman, 1976) (abridged).]

2.5 PRIMARY AND SECONDARY SOURCES

The information that sociologists use in their research can be divided into 'primary' and 'secondary' sources. Primary sources include data collected by researchers, official documents, eyewitness accounts, diaries and other information collected firsthand. Secondary sources are second-hand sources of information; this book is mainly a secondary source of information and as such should be read particularly critically, as one of the dangers of using secondary sources is that wrong information can be passed on if the writer has made a mistake.

Mistakes can also be made in primary source material; data may be collected wrongly, selected in a biased fashion or exaggerated in its importance. Information which depends on opinion rather than fact is particularly hard to verify.

The Census of Population taken on a Sunday evening in April every ten years is a good example of a reliable primary source. Great care is taken to ensure accuracy; the questions are factual and the people who carry out the count – the 'enumerators', have no reason to bias the results; indeed they would be prosecuted if they did. Questions asked in the census have to be approved by both Houses of Parliament so that it is unlikely that any ambiguous questions will be asked. Everyone has to answer most census questions so there is no possibility of sampling error; although a more detailed form requiring more information has been issued on a sampling basis since the census of 1961.

2.6 THE USES AND PRESENTATION OF RESEARCH

Some research has an obvious use; it is necessary to know the number of children being born in order to plan school building programmes or be able to estimate the number of people requiring prison accommodation in ten years time. The research may not simply lead to the closing down of schools or the building of more prisons but suggest alternatives: Should redundant schools be used to provide facilities for unemployed teenagers? Are there sensible alternatives to putting people into prison?

Some research may seek answers to specific problems: Is loneliness a factor in suicide?; why do working-class children perform less well on average at school than middle-class children? Having established that there is a cause and effect – a 'causal relationship' between two factors – it may be possible to alter the effect by changing the situation that caused it.

The cause and effect in sociological studies are called 'variables' because they can be changed, or varied. The cause is the 'independent variable' and the effect is the 'dependent variable' because it 'depends' on – is influenced by – the independent factor.

An example of the use of this type of research was the introduction of 'social priority area' schools in 1968 because it was established that certain categories of children such as those from one-parent families or ethnic minorities were more likely to perform badly at school. The schools in areas with more than a certain proportion of children in the target groups were given more and better paid staff than those elsewhere, together with improved facilities.

Some research may not seek to identify and solve any problems but will help us to understand why particular behaviour occurs and so may prove useful to those concerned in providing particular services. For example, one study sought to see what influence housing policies had on the family as an institution and ultimately resulted in some local authorities trying to move communities *together* from 'slums' to new housing rather than moving individuals so that people were living among strangers.

In presenting the results of their research sociologists have to be careful to present it in such a way that it cannot be misinterpreted; that any bias they may have brought to the study is clear, and that enough information is given for the audience to be able to draw alternative conclusions if there is a possibility of differing interpretations.

The research needs to contain a clear statement of what is being studied; the research procedures, including the nature of the sample; the way the data was collected and how the data was analysed; the results of the study and what implications the researchers think can be made from the results.

OUTLINE EXAMPLE OF AN APPROACH TO A GCE QUESTION ON SOCIOLOGICAL METHOD

Question:

It has been suggested that scientific method includes the following six process:

(1) identifying a problem,
(2) selecting appropriate methods to study the problem,
(3) collecting relevant data,
(4) analysing the data,
(5) interpreting the data,
(6) reporting findings and conclusions.

Take any sociological study that you are familiar with and show how it fits in (or does not fit in) with the six stages quoted above. Make sure that you refer clearly to one particular piece of research.

Survey:

The Sexual Behaviour of Young People by Michael Schofield

PROCESS	METHODS AND FINDINGS
1. **Identifying the problem** ('Key variables' – Boys/Girls Working/Unemployed Social Class/Age/ Religion)	In 1964 the BMA produced a report on Venereal Disease in Young People and this seemed to indicate a link between 'promiscuity' (several parties over a period) and venereal disease. However the limited evidence available was based on those who reported to VD clinics and those with unwanted pregnancies. It was decided to carry out an impartial survey of all types and classes of young people.

2. **Selecting appropriate methods of study.**	*Considered and rejected*	Psychological tests: Self-administered Questionnaires; Group Discussion.
(Nuffield grant – but limited finance)	*Decided upon* –	Questionnaires administered by specially recruited interviewers

a) The information was to be obtained direct from target group
b) There was to be a series of random samples
c) Questions on sexual behaviour to be preceded by questions on background and leisure
d) The sample was sufficiently large to establish 'norms'
e) Care was taken to exclude all moral injunctions or value judgements.

3. **Collecting relevant data** (Questions tried out on groups of teenagers first. Some questions tried out on 300 before final form. 10 young graduates recruited for interview: 5 males to interview boys; 5 females to interview girls)	*Schedule*	261 items (231 direct questions and 50 statements for agreement or disagreement as 'attitude inventory')

Probably first study of this kind based on random sampling – 1873 interviews, either in research office or home, as person interviewed wished.

Problems:
a) Self-esteem; those interviewed wanted to tell the interviewer what they thought the interviewer wished to hear.
b) Needed a representative selection therefore could not just use Youth Clubs (only 25 per cent of target group attended).
c) People wary of 'salesmen' and refusals could not be replaced – no giving up until 6 call backs made.

4. Analysing the data	a) *Classifying*	e.g.	Each interviewer checked their coding of questions with a supervisor whilst it was still fresh in their minds.
	b) *Tabulation*	e.g.	Information put on 13,111 punch cards (7 for each individual) fed into a computer and analysed.
	c) *Comparing*	e.g.	The 'Correlation', or establishing a connection between a number of 'variables' with sexual experience (e.g. Money, church attendance, wages, time home in the evening).
	d) *Processing*	e.g.	Measuring the intensity of family influence on a 6 point scale ('Anchored' even if not exact)

5. Interpreting the data (Drawing conclusions)	Relating the discriminating features of the sexually experienced to such factors as facilities available to them, physical development, conformity, permissiveness. Among the discriminating features of the boys in this category were – scepticism of adult moral standards, a desire to leave school early, earlier puberty, more easily influenced by other teenagers, going out more in the evenings.
6. Reporting findings and conclusions. (This might include 'Theory Building' in	Includes dealing with possible sources of error e.g. bias caused by refusals. It was not possible to compare the findings with a past period as no comparable research existed; however it was suggested that the difference between young peoples'

some research projects, although not in this.) sexual behaviour at that time was probably not very different from that of similar groups in the past.
The main finding and conclusion was: 'These results suggest that promiscuity, although it exists, is not a very prominent feature of teenage sexual behaviour. Consequently the risks of VD are not very great.'

QUESTIONS FROM PAST 'O' LEVEL G.C.E. PAPERS

Recent questions from the following GCE boards are given at the end of each Section:
   Associated Examining Board (O Level)
   Cambridge University Local Examinations Syndicate (O Level)
   University of London (O/A Level)
   University of Oxford Delegacy of Local Examinations (O Level)
   Welsh Joint Education Committee (O Level)

1. **Either:** (a) What steps should a researcher take if he wishes to ensure that his sample is representative of the population involved in a social survey?
   Or: (b) What are the main considerations to be borne in mind when conducting social research by post?

Associated Examining Board

2. Read the following passage and then answer the questions.
   'Observation has been a basic part of scientific method for hundreds of years. Very often the researcher may be a participant observer and his involvement in the group raises some interesting problems. Non-participant observation of a children's play session can reduce the mass of information to a more manageable quantity by the use of time-sampling.'

(a) Explain the meaning of *participant observer*.
(b) State any **two** possible problems associated with participant observation.
(c) State any **two** ways in which *non-participant observation* might take place.
(d) Describe what is meant by time sampling.

Welsh Joint Examining Board

3. Explain the importance of any **four** of the following in social surveys:
(a) Random sampling.
(b) Interviewer bias.
(c) Pre-coded questions.
(d) Sampling frame.
(e) Pilot study.

Associated Examining Board

4. 'A child is born into a world that already exists. From the point of view of society, the function of socialization is to transmit the culture and motivation to participate in established social relationships to new members. We may view this society from several perspectives. . . . First, there is the perspective of *norms* and *values*. A second perspective is that of *status* and *role*. Another perspective focuses on *culture and group sub-divisions*. Still another perspective is that of *social change*.'

(From: The Child and Society by F. Elkin.)

After reading the above passage explain, with the use of appropriate examples, what is meant by:
(a) norms
(b) values
(c) status
(d) role
(e) culture and group subdivisions
(f) social change

Welsh Joint Examining Board

NOTE: For this section in the Welsh Board paper four lines are allowed for the answers to each item (a) to (f)

PART II
THE FAMILY

DEVELOPMENT AND CHARACTERISTICS OF THE MODERN FAMILY

3.1 WHAT A FAMILY IS

Defining 'a family' is not so simple as most people might immediately assume; there are many forms of family. In British society a basic family usually consists of a man and woman who have a steady relationship with each other and who also have children; children are essential to the idea of 'family', but they need not necessarily be 'consanguine' – that is, related by blood to the adults with whom they live – although they usually are. A simple group of this kind is called a 'nuclear' family. Nearly all 'nuclear' families are related to one or more other nuclear families through parent-child relationships; mother will often have parents and brothers and sisters living and so will father. This family is called the 'extended family' and can include all known relations.

Larry/BBC

A clear father/husband figure is not present either in this picture of an extended family or in the 'realistic' cartoon opposite!

In 1984 a survey carried out by the Harris Research Centre found that 79 per cent of people questioned thought that the typical 'household' in Britain consisted of a husband, a wife and two or three children; in fact only 14 per cent of 'households' fitted that description.

Of coure not all 'households' consist of families; and despite the description of a family by Burgess and Locke (page 29) a family need not 'constitute a single household' – most 'extended families' in Britain today do not.

A good definition of a family was given by Burgess and Locke in their book *The Family* (1953) – 'The family is a group of persons united by the ties of marriage, blood, or adoption; constituting a single household, inter-acting and intercommunicating with each other in their respective social role of husband and wife, mother and father, brother and sister; creating a common culture'; however this definition is not sufficiently broad to cover all types of family.

Marriage: romantic v. 'convenience'

Marriage in societies where a person's prospects in life depend primarily on his status by birth and on that of the people to whom he is allied by kinship or affinity has a very different significance from that which industrialized societies attach to it. In the latter societies we worry about the compatibility of spouses, and the degree of incompatibility that should be considered sufficient to justify their separation. Except for those who hold religious con-victions in relation to marriage vows, the prime consideration in such discussions is the welfare of the children of unsuccessful marriages, whose emotional life, we have learned in recent years, may be blighted by the dissensions of their parents. In these societies a person makes his own way in a profession or employment; many people are handicapped by the class they are born into, but only a few gain or lose by the individual status of their parents. To be married is by no means indispensable, since the domestic labour that was once supplied by wives is now provided by machines, and the economic support that once came from husbands can now be pro-vided by a woman's own earnings. Many women do not wish to bear children, and there are only a few who find in this the sole reason for existence.

In societies based on a subsistence economy all this is different. There is no wage-labour, and the production of food is the work of kin groups organized as teams. It is expected that everyone should marry as soon as possible:
... Women are expected, and expect, to bear as many children as they can. Marriage is a matter of the allocation of women to hus-bands, sometimes, but not always, taking individual choice into consideration. Personal compatibility is not a matter for much concern; spouses spend little time together in any case. Marriage is primarily of importance as a knot in the network of kinship links that bind such a society together. It is the formally recognized means of recruiting new members to a line of descent, and it creates alliances between such lines. The making of marriages depends in part on the claims that men are entitled to make on one another's daughters; in part on the kind of alliance that men, seeking wives for themselves or their sons, believe will be advantageous; and to a small

degree, and more in some societies than in others, on the individual preferences of a man and a woman. Marriage is a matter of serious concern to a much larger number of people than the spouses themselves. Hence it is hedged about with rules and ceremonies to a much greater extent than it is in those societies, which Radcliffe-Brown long ago reminded us are exceptional, that make an ideal of 'marriage for love'. [Lucy Mair, *Marriage* (Harmondsworth: Penguin, 1971).]

3.2 WHY FAMILIES?

In nearly all cultures the family is the most important social group although its functions will vary.

In a few societies one of the functions of the family is political, family networks are the major channels of power. In Britain today this function is virtually limited to the Royal Family, although economic power is still a factor, with a few families of major property owners and bankers exercising considerable influence.

In some societies protection is still a major function of the family; in Southern Europe for example the protection of the honour of its females is still considered an important role of the male members of a family. Care of the sick, elderly, disabled or unemployed are all ways in which families have protected their members.

In many societies one of the family's functions is economic, as a unit both of production and consumption. In Britain the family is still a major unit of consumption; requiring items such as housing, holidays, television sets and cars; but industrialisation has removed joint working from most families, although it still does occur, for example, among farmers and Asian shopkeepers.

The family has a function in most societies of regulating sexual conduct, but although important this is not an essential function of all family systems. In one study of 250 societies it was found that sixty-five allowed unmarried and unrelated people complete sexual freedom; so even if promiscuity is increasing in Britain it would not necessarily mean that the family was decreasing in importance. There are some societies, for example, where the connection between intercourse and birth is either not understood or disregarded, the husband simply regarding any child born to his wife as his own. This aspect of family life was summed up by Malinowski, an anthropologist. (Anthropology is the study of man and his development; particularly it is the study of primitive societies and of previous civilisations.) 'Marriage is the licensing not of sexual intercourse but of parenthood.'

In virtually all societies however the family is the main unit for rearing children, taking a major role in socialising them to play their part in society. Idealistic attempts have been made to abolish the family by

The nuclear family does seem to be the simplest structure for doing what it has to do

various groups, for example by Russia in 1917, but the family has re-emerged as the basic social unit, handing on the norms and values of society from generation to generation.

In Israel communes called *kibbutzim* arrange for children to be looked after collectively so that men and women are free to work on equal terms. However in recent years there has been an increase in the amount of time that parents and their children spend together.

The crucial role that the family plays in the socialisation of most people has been illustrated by the work of John Bowlby and others (see Chapter 1.2) particularly the need of young children for a warm, intimate and continuous relationship with a mother or 'mother-substitute' – who could be male.

In *A Sociological Portrait* (ed. Paul Barker, 1972) Geoffrey Hawthorne puts the case for the family very simply – 'The fact remains that the nuclear family does seem to be the simplest conceivable structure for doing what it has to do, and even if we do not know much about how it does it . . .that must be a very powerful restraint on change'.

Child care

The main reasons for regarding continuity as an essential requisite of mothering are the well-established associations between 'broken homes' and delinquency and the short-term disturbance which often follows a young child's separation from his parents (Yarrow, 1964). Both of these findings suggest that breaks in the parent-child relationship *may* have adverse effects, but as breaks are frequently associated with other adverse factors it remains to be established whether it is the separation as such which is the deleterious influence ... That transient separations are not necessarily a bad thing is evident from the high rate of separations in normal individuals. Douglas, Ross and Simpson (1968), in a national sample of some five thousand children, showed that by four and a half years of age, a third of children had been separated from their mother for at least one week. Furthermore, they showed that there was only a weak association between brief separations and delinquency (41 per cent separations in delinquents as against 32 per cent in controls). Of course, all children must separate from their parents sometime if they are to develop independent personalities, so the question is not *whether* children should separate from their mothers but rather *when* and *how* separations should occur. The finding that certain sorts of happy separation may actually protect young children from the adverse effects of later stressful separation (Stacey, Dearden, Pill and Robinson, 1970) also emphasizes the importance of considering the circumstances of a separation when deciding whether it is likely to be beneficial or harmful.

Perhaps an even more crucial point is the equation of 'separation' with 'discontinuity' in a relationship. Bowlby argued that the young pre-school child is unable to maintain a relationship with a person in their absence and that for this reason even brief separations disrupt a relationship. Experience with normal children suggests that this is not always so, at least in favourable circumstances. Of course, young children do find it more difficult, but it seems probable that environmental conditions as well as age influence a child's ability to maintain a bond during a person's absence.... Nevertheless his early dictum was widely accepted and led to a very marked reluctance by some Children's Officers to remove children from even appalling home circumstances. It also led to foster homes being preferred as a placement over children's homes in spite of the fact that discontinuity of mothering is often just as great in foster homes (Dinnage and Pringle). Actually, there is no satisfactory evidence in support of the dictum 'better a bad family than a good institution'. Taken at its face value it seems to imply some mystical quality present in the family and suggests that the quality of mothering provided is irrelevant. This is such an obvious nonsense (and certainly not intended by Bowlby) that it scarcely warrants serious consideration.

Furthermore, the care in even the best institutions often falls well short of the average home although it is superior to the worst homes. As Bowlby (1951) rightly noted, it does seem peculiarly difficult for an institution to provide parental care of the quality and quantity expected in a family setting. The observation undoubtedly means that the greatest caution should be exercised in placing a child in long-term institutional care, but equally a bad home should not be automatically preferred to a good institution. It is necessary in each case to examine the quality of parental care provided (including its stability) ... It is important to note that mothers fulfil many roles in the family and have an important influence on their children's development in a myriad of ways.

Obviously, the young child needs care and protection to ensure that he comes to no harm. As he grows older discipline and guidance are necessary. Food is essential to life and when young the infant cannot feed himself. In all these circumstances the mother is often a dominant influence in the home. Throughout childhood and adolescence both parents constitute models of behaviour for the child to follow (or reject). Play has a crucial function in psychological development (Millar, 1968) and although much play is with other children, play with parents is also influential in many ways. Some of the class-related differences between parents may be important for children's later development (Bernstein and Young) ... The development of children is so bad in the worst families – such as those where baby battering occurs (Helfer and Kempe; Skinner and Castle), where there is chronic discord and lack of affection between two psychopathic parents (Rutter), or where parental social adjustment is at its worst (West), that even an institutional upbringing may be preferable. The outcome for children reared in institutions is certainly worse than that of the general population (Ferguson), but the outcome for many children from the best institutions is reasonably satisfactory (Conway; Tizard, Cooperman, Joseph and Tizard). The frequency of deviant behaviour in institutional children is well above population norms (Yule and Raynes), but equally it is below that of children in the most disturbed and loveless homes (Rutter, 1971). The generally good adjustment of kibbutzim children who sleep and spend their day in an institution (although remaining in contact with their parents) also argues against the suggestion that mothering must take place in the child's own home.

Nevertheless, there is something in the dictum in that it is clear that the quality and amount of maternal care provided in the *average* institution is much worse than the *average* family. [Michael Rutter, *Maternal Deprivation Reassessed* (Harmondsworth: Penguin, 1982) (abridged).]

3.3 DIFFERING FAMILY PATTERNS

There are three basic ways in which a family may be constituted: *mono-gamy* – one man married to one woman; *polygyny* – one man married to several women; *polyandry* – one woman married to several men. Poly-andry is very rare and although about 25 per cent of the world's people live in societies where polygyny is accepted it is becoming less common as industrialisation and the modern wage economy, plus the extension of compulsory education, makes the acquisition of additional wives and children more of an economic liability than an economic asset. Polygamy is the term used to cover both polyandry and polygyny.

There are usually good economic, sexual and social reasons for the existence of any particular family pattern, for example in societies where polygyny is practised there are usually more girls than boys.

In all societies whatever the family pattern there are two aspects of the family co-existing (see section 3.1). There are spouses (husbands and wife or wives) and their siblings (children with the same parents) – this group is called the 'nuclear' family. In a polygamous society there will be several nuclear families each having one parent in common.

Each nuclear family will usually be related to many other people including aunts, uncles, grandparents, nephews and nieces, all these people in 'kinship' with each other are the 'extended family'.

In some societies the extended family may all live together, share their property and operate as a unit; in which case they are known as a 'joint family'.

In other societies the extended family may not operate as a unit but will still be very important to its members – assisting each other if unem-ployed or ill, helping to look after each others' young children, caring for its elderly members – this pattern of help is called a 'mutual support system'. In some cases the nuclear family may have little or no connection with the other members of its extended family. There are also other ways of classifying family organisation:

Patriarchal – Wealth and prestige comes from the father and he controls the family.

Matriarchal – The mother controls the family.

Egalitarian – Authority in the family is more or less equally divided.

or

Patrilineal – Descent is through the father, the father's surname is taken and sons inherit.

Matrilineal – Descent is through the mother.

Bilineal – Descent is through father and/or mother.

or

Patrilocal – Families settle in or near the home of the husband's parents.
Matrilocal – Families settle in or near the home of the wife's parents.
Neolocal – Families live away from the locality of both the husband's and
wife's parents.

or

Exogamous – Marriage normally to people outside the immediate circle
of relatives or immediate community
Endogamous – Marriage normally restricted to one's own kin or social
group.

The norm of the modern British family can therefore be said to be monogamous, with a growing tendency towards being nuclear, egalitarian,
neolocal, and exogamous. Still patrilineal but becoming bilineal in some
respects!

Gender differences in the family

I Domesticity: Within the Family

As a consequence of industrialization, the home means 'family'
rather than 'work'. Our language contains the phrase 'a family man',
but there is no corresponding phrase for women. It would be socially
redundant: the family *means* women. Women bear children, women
rear children, women are in the home as housewives: if the home
means the family, then the family *is* women.

What kind of family is this?

Compared with other family systems throughout history and in
different cultures, it is small, mobile and non-productive. On one
level it is functionless: it has no broad economic or political or social
significance. But on another level, its functions are crucial:

The family produces people. It does this in two ways – by socia-
lizing children, and by stabilizing adult personalities in the socially
approved moulds of wife–mother–housewife and husband–father.
The production of people is not a new function for 'the' family as
such, but its significance in the case of the modern family is enlarged
through the family's loss of its other, pre-industrial functions.
Because women are the childbearers, the modern emphasis on people-
production also affects women directly. This connection is clarified
when the importance of gender – femininity and masculinity – in the
structure of the modern family is understood.

Gender differentiation between the roles of female and male is
the axis of the modern family's structure. 'Marriage is rooted in the
family rather than the family in marriage.' Husband and wife are

not the same sort of role, nor are father and mother, nor are house-wife and non-housewife. The modern family stresses two sorts of bond: a cross-sex bond (marriage) and a cross-generational bond (the parent–child relationship). They share the same pattern of gender role-differentiation, and a clue to the nature of this differen-tiation is given by linguistic usage. The following are the conventional couplets: husband and wife, mother and father, man and wife. In each case a reversal sound odd: wife and husband, father and mother, wife and man. The last couplet has the oddest ring, because a reversal of terms destroys the meaning of the phrase, which is man (person) and wife (female-person-in-the-possession-and-under-the-control-of-man). As it indicates, marriage is a situation of inequality: in mar-riage, women are not equal with men. This is because marriage defines a woman's place in society as it does not a man's. 'Differen-tiation' is a neutral word. The contrast between the roles of female and male in the family is not simply one of differentiation but of opposition. The order of terms in the couplet 'husband and wife' indicates a patriarchal structure. [A. Oakley, *Housewife* (Harmonds-worth: Penguin, 1974).]

3.4 FAMILY FORMS IN BRITAIN TODAY

Before the Industrial Revolution (which started about 1750), most people lived fairly near their relatives and did not travel much; the extended family was an important unit.

In rural areas however people might still live at a distance from their neighbours, and one sociologist – Laslett – has suggested that kin living in 'close geographical proximity may even be somewhat commoner in the contemporary industrial city than it was among the peasantry'.

Industrialisation started an exodus from the countryside into the towns. Young people often set out independently to make their way in the world and many extended families split up. For a time many people lived as part of nuclear families isolated from their kin.

As children grew up and married they often settled near their parents and siblings and extended families once more became the norm; although it must be remembered that immigration of young people from countries like Ireland, and a continued input from the countryside always meant that there were numerous isolated nuclear families.

Today however the nuclear family is becoming the main operating unit in Britain particularly among the young middle class, and for most people the extended family is becoming less important. Although immigration from the Indian sub-continent has increased the importance of extended families in some areas, it seems unlikely that the extended family will re-emerge in importance as many of its functions have been taken over by the Welfare State.

Fig. 3.1 *people in households: by type of household and family in which they live*

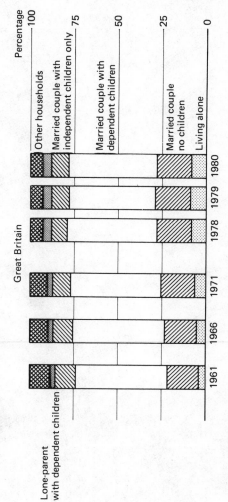

SOURCE *Social Trends No12* (London: HMSO, 1981).

The proportion of people living as members of 'lone-parent' or 'single-parent' families in Britain doubled between 1961 and 1981 to 5 per cent and in 1982, 20 per cent of children under 16 were not living with both natural parents. However eight out of every ten people lived in a family unit headed by a married couple.

THE CHANGING NATURE
OF THE MODERN
BRITISH FAMILY

4.1 THE CHANGING ROLE OF THE FAMILY

Industrialisation reduced the economic role of the family; parents and children can now rarely work together. Increasing educational opportunities have reduced this feature of family life still further; sons more rarely follow their Dad down the pit, or get fixed up at the shipyard through an uncle's influence. The introduction of Labour Exchanges in 1909 had already reduced the need for such family patronage.

Old Age Pensions, introduced in 1908, home helps, and residential homes for the elderly reduce the need for the family to care for the retired. Compulsory insurance against illness from 1911 and the National Health Service have made it unnecessary for the family to act as a shield in times of disablement and illness. Unemployment benefit, supplementary benefits, council housing, free school meals, health visitors, home helps and social workers have all helped to reduce the social care role of the family.

In 1870 the first Education Act began to eat away at the educative function of the family, and the raising of the school leaving age and an increase in nursery education has continued this process. The pre-school playgroup movement tries to retain family ties, however, and there has been a resurgence of interest throughout the education service in endeavouring to increase parental involvement.

The family has however maintained its primary role in the socialisation of the young child, but the decrease in family size has telescoped this function into a period of less than ten years for most married couples.

4.2 CHANGING RELATIONSHIPS WITHIN THE FAMILY

The changes that have taken place in the functions that the family performs have had a consequent influence on relationships within the family.

Wives and children are no longer completely dependent on their husbands and fathers and are therefore less subject to their control. In 1978 for the first time the number of working wives exceeded 50 per cent of all married women, compared with 10 per cent in 1931, while the Welfare State provides a safety net for those who leave home. The occupation of the husband is still however the major factor in determining the family's standard of living and class position. It has been suggested that it is the more upper-class fathers that are now in a position of holding the greatest economic power over their children, as working-class fathers now have little economic bargaining power. For example, middle- and upper-class children are more likely to remain in education after the statutory school leaving age and are therefore in a position of economic dependency. If children from poor homes do go to higher education their major award will make them relatively self-supporting. Children from richer homes will be dependent on their parents, usually their father, making up their grant.

Many children are now better educated than their parents and are less likely to hold them in awe or seek their advice, even although life experience might be a better source of wisdom than academic achievement.

The decline in the authoritarian role of parents and the growing equality between men and women has increased the degree of partnership within the home. In the 1950s Burgess and Locke were already saying that the family had moved from 'institution to companionship' and described this family form as the 'companionship family' and by 1973 Young and Willmott in *The Symmetrical Family* were describing the new family, with reservations, as 'egalitarian'.

The 'Symmetrical Family'

The new family could be labelled simply egalitarian. But that would not square with the marked differences that still remain in the human rights, in the work opportunities and generally in the way of life of the two sexes. The term which is best, in our view, is the one used by Gorer, the 'symmetrical family', although the emphasis we want to give is not the same as his. He said that, 'In a symmetrical relationship A responds to B as B responds to A; the differences of temperament, of function, of skills are all minimized.' We think it is closer to the facts of the situation as it is now to preserve the notion of difference but ally it to a measure of egalitarianism. In this context the essence of a symmetrical relationship is that it is opposite but similar. If all segregation of roles ever disappeared (apart from that minimum prescribed by the dictatorship of a biology from which there is for most people no escape) then one might properly talk about egalitarian marriage. But to be fair to what has happened in this century a term is needed which can describe the majority of families in which there is some role-segregation along with a greater degree of equality ... If husbands did any 'work' at all at home the tasks that they, and their wives, thought proper to them were those to which male strength and male manual skill lent themselves. It was not a man's place to do woman's work any more than the other way round. All that has now changed. Wives are working outside the home in what is much less of a man's world than it used to be.

Husbands also do a lot of work in the home, including many jobs which are not at all traditional men's ones – which is one reason why the distinction between work and leisure is now a great deal less clear for men than it used to be. It never was very distinct for women. There is now no sort of work in the home strictly reserved for 'the wives'; even clothes-washing and bed-making, still ordinarily thought of as women's jobs, were frequently mentioned by husbands as things they did as well. The extent of the sharing is probably still increasing ... But taking all forms of help into account it was still true that fewer semi-skilled and unskilled workers contributed at all in this sort of way ... They shared their work; they shared their time. But if the trend was towards it, most married couples were obviously still a long way from the state of unisex that some young people had arrived at. There were many roles which were still primarily the prerogative of one sex or another, particularly in the classes which were not so far on in the process of change. In 1970 the general rule in working-class families with cars was still that the husbands were the drivers and the wives passengers, like the children. But this role, too, was well on the way to being shared. [M. Young and P. Willmott, *The Symmetrical Family* (London: Routledge & Kegan Paul, 1973) (abridged).]

4.3 MATERNAL AND PATERNAL ROLES

The decreasing importance of the extended family, the reduced child-bearing period, greater educational opportunities, the decrease in the economic power of fathers and the development of the Welfare State have altered the nature of most modern British families.

Traditionally the mother would stay at home and care for the children while the father went to work. Men would not expect to do domestic tasks such as cleaning, shopping, cooking and child care; a working wife would also cast doubts about a man's masculinity and his ability to fend for his family.

In 1956 Dennis, Henriques and Slaughter produced their well-known work on the life of coal-miners. *Coal is Our Life*, and this very much reinforces the traditional stereotype of mother, 'maternal', and father 'paternal', roles. The husband spending most of his leisure time with his workmates and the wife with her mother and female friends. Such separate marriage roles are called 'segregated conjugal roles'.

However at roughly the same time Young and Willmott produced their important work on family life in Bethnal Green and the suburb of 'Green-leigh', to which people from Bethnal Green were being moved as part of a slum-clearance programme. *Family and Kinship in East London* con-firmed the traditional roles so far as older people were concerned but young fathers were spending more time with their children than had been the case. By 1963 John and Elizabeth Newson in *Patterns of Infant Care* had concluded that 'the modern father's place is in the home' and that both the mother and the father were becoming increasingly home-centred.

It is important to remember that although it is possible to state 'hard data' such as the average number of children in a family now compared with a hundred years ago exactly, it is not possible to measure changes in relationships and attitudes in the same way. However, it is clear that fathers generally are taking a much more active role in homemaking and family care than formerly. There is less formal punishment and more comradeship between parents and children than in the past with families spending more of their time together in the home, on holiday and on trips in the family car, and mothers are increasingly combining full-time or part-time work with their home-centred activities thus enhancing their status as contributors to the household budget. Maternal and paternal roles are starting to 'converge'.

Changing family patterns

The State has contributed indirectly towards the liberation of women, especially through the expansion of health services and education. But the loneliness of mothers with young children is still well attested and the absence of communal provision for such women remains an unsatisfied need. Meanwhile, more direct emanci-pating influences have come from developed methods of birth con-trol and, most important, the gradual movement of women, including married women, into employment. In the first two decades of this century less than 10 per cent of married women in Britain went out to work: in 1951 the percentage was 21.74: by 1966 it had risen to 38.08, and by 1976 to 49. The slow spread of affluence has also played its part in combination with the invention of power appliances to relieve some of the drudgery of housework. Suburbanisation and geographical mobility have provided escape for some from the matrilocal matriarchies of the traditional urban working-class com-munities—a point which reminds us that women's liberation has discriminated so far in favour of younger as against older women. So we could go on through a catalogue of economic and technical changes, and their consequences, which have made possible the trend towards *The Symmetrical Family* of Young and Willmott.

The correlative history, which is rather less noticed, is that of husbands and fathers. This too is a social transformation deserving its own detailed history. It would begin with young men of the Victorian upper-middle classes moving into marriage with prejudices mitigated at least to the point of co-operating in planned parenthood. Later, working men returning from the First World War had to accommodate, in many cases, to wives who had acquired a more independent outlook from having worked in the munitions factories, and from having run their homes unaided. Literacy and the wireless pushed back horizons between the Wars. Unlike previous wars, the Second World War did not tip the demographic balance in favour of men by killing more men than women: the number of men and women remained roughly in balance, the reserve army of women disappeared.

Still more important, seventy years ago, working men typically lived in local occupationally homogeneous communities. Such communities evolved essentially male public organizations—the pub, the betting shop, the football club; organizations which loosened marriage bonds and took resources away from women and children. But the newer patterns of inter-war industry around London and Birmingham, in the Home Counties and the Midlands, took their toll of the older male domination—reducing class solidarity perhaps and inviting more romantic love certainly. Particularly after the Second World War, hours of work were reduced, holidays lengthened, home ownership became more common, children were less ever-present, and men were drawn into a more intimate and longer spousehood than their predecessors had ever known. Privatization was a key description of the affluent worker in Luton by the 1960s. It involved a closer, more co-operative, domesticity for millions of men. [A. Halsey, *Change in British Society* (Oxford: Oxford University Press, 1981).]

4.4 THE NUCLEAR FAMILY – ITS ADVANTAGES AND DISADVANTAGES

The nuclear family is sometimes called the 'conjugal family' to emphasize the fact that the family type referred to is that of a man, his wife and their children – 'conjugal' means 'to do with marriage'. However, the use of the term 'conjugal family' can be misleading. The man and woman may be living together unmarried; there may be only one parent whether by death, divorce, desertion or choice; the children may be adopted.

The nuclear family has become increasingly important during the past thirty years for a number of reasons:

1. Increased educational opportunities have led to young people becoming qualified for a wider variety of jobs and this has necessitated

leaving their home neighbourhoods. They have often adopted a different lifestyle to their parents and have less in common with them.

2.   The run down of traditional industries has resulted in a population movement, particularly of the young and mobile, from such areas as the North-west to the developing areas such as the South-east.

3.   Slum clearance and the building of replacement estates elsewhere together with an increasing desire for home-ownership has led to young families being separated from their extended family to a greater degree than in the past.

4.   The small modern family is more easily cared for without external help than was the family of a hundred years ago. However this is not a recent phenomenon, as the average number of live births per married woman had already declined from about six in 1870 to about two in 1925.

5.   The services of the Welfare State can be used to replace the functions previously provided by the extended family (but these same services often help to keep the nuclear family together in times of crisis).

6.   Greater physical mobility, such as car ownership, communications such as television, and access to possible means of contact in an emergency – the telephone – makes the removal from neighbourhood and extended family less daunting psychologically than formerly.

Goode in *World Revolution and Family Patterns* sees the emergence of the nuclear family as the main operating unit as a consequence of the needs of modern industrial society; certainly its mobility increases job opportunities and promotion prospects. The isolation of the nuclear family has tended to encourage its members to know each other as companions and to carry out activities together more, decreasing contact not only with the extended family but with other non-domestic acquaintances as well. This turning in of the nuclear family upon itself has been called 'privatisation'.

This privatisation can be an advantage in enhancing relationships within the family but it can lead to isolation, particularly of the young mother, graphically described by Hannah Gavron in *The Captive Wife*. The social isolation of the privatised nuclear family may also strain relationships because of the lack of outlets in times of stress.

Old people are now more likely to feel useless and end their days in isolation; young married couples no longer have access to a willing baby sitter; infants no longer have an opportunity to experience the early social contacts provided by granny and cousins. In many ways independence has been exchanged for security.

THE STABILITY OF
THE FAMILY

5.1 CONFLICT WITHIN THE FAMILY

Some sociologists, such as Parsons and Bales, have concluded that the
family is growing more important and stronger in our community today
because of the increasing emphasis on children and partners as individuals;
isolation increasing the partners' importance to each other. But this isolation has made the tasks of husband and wife more difficult and as difficulties increase more people can be expected to fail to overcome them.

Husband and wife must be friends as well as partners. Economic responsibility is sharply focused on the adult male while the children are
young. The young wife is isolated with young children all day at home
often having been educated to expect that she herself will achieve success
in the workplace rather than prepared for domesticity. The scene is set for
tension, frustration and despair.

In the past, husband and wife had established roles to play. Now both
are much less certain of what is expected of them – there is a degree of
'anomie'. Both partners may have conflicting wishes. The wife may expect
the husband to be the strong authoritarian figure which she has been socialised to associate with masculinity, but at the same time want a comrade of
equal status who will change the baby and do the shopping. The husband
may expect feminine domesticity, but also a partner with whom he can
argue world events on equal terms or who can go to work to supplement
the family income. Role conflict may be a major source of family conflict.

Children, too, have greater difficulty in knowing what to expect of
parents, particularly when the value systems of home and school do not
correspond in terms of discipline. Extended education brings continued
dependence, at the same time as children are maturing physically earlier
and being subjected to more commercial pressures. Television introduces
other life-styles to young people and may increase the natural rebelliousness of youth to adult authority.

The differing views of young and old are often referred to as the 'generation gap'

"I know it's a bit late, but looking at our Nigel, I think I'm starting a post-natal depression."

There are increasing examination pressures on the young and children may despise their less well educated parents (see section 4.2). The family may at times seem oppressive and restrictive of the freedom of expression that the modern emphasis on the importance of the individual has aroused as an aspiration. Sir Edmund Leach in 1967 went so far as to say: 'The family with its narrow privacy and tawdry secrets is the source of all our discontents.'

The difference in views of young and old is often referred to as the 'generation gap', however this can be over-estimated. Certainly parents today have more time to spend with their children, and argument has replaced physical punishment in many homes. A report by the advertising agency McCann Erickson in 1976–77 found that the attitudes and aspirations of parents and their children were surprisingly similar.

5.2 THE LAW AND THE FAMILY

Prior to 1870 the legal status of women was the same as for children and lunatics, they were in effect the property of their husbands. In 1882 the *Married Woman's Property Act* gave married women the right to keep their own earnings, to contract life insurance and to own personal property up to the value of £20. In 1882 Women could sue in the law courts, and could be sued.

In 1918 the Suffrage Acts gave the women the vote and in 1923 the *Matrimonial Causes Act* awarded equal rights of Divorce. The *Matrimonial Proceedings and Property Act* of 1970 made it possible for a divorced wife to be given a share in the home as of right. In 1970 too the *Equal Pay Act* was introduced and by 1975 all women should have been receiving the same pay as men doing similar work. Women are now in law fully equal to their husbands.

While women have been gaining equality, the rights of children have also improved by acts insisting upon their education; controlling adoption; protecting them in employment and making arrangement for them to be taken away from their family and put in the care of local authorities if they are in physical or moral danger.

The law has not only assisted in changing the status of women and children within the family, it has increasingly assisted in the dissolution of marriage. Between 1715 and 1852 only 244 divorces were granted; the procedure was expensive and lengthy. In 1857 it was made possible to sue for divorce by going before only one court and it was no longer necessary to obtain a private Act of Parliament, but the procedure was still expensive.

Until 1920 and the introduction of the 'Poor Person's Rules' divorce was really only possible for the more well-to-do; possibilities for divorce were further increased during the Second World War when a Legal Aid Scheme was introduced for the forces. This was extended to civilians in 1949.

Until 1937 the only ground for divorce was adultery but a further *Matrimonial Causes Act* then extended the grounds to desertion, cruelty and incurable insanity.

More generous legal aid was made available from 1961, and in 1969 the *Divorce Law Reform Act* (operational from 1971 except in Scotland, where the law did not change until 1977) introduced a new and easier conception of divorce based on the 'irretrievable breakdown of marriage'.

There is a variety of other ways in which the law may affect the family. A man may be punished for failing to support his family by not accepting suitable employment. In 1969 the *Family Law Reform Act* reduced to eighteen years the age at which a person could marry without parental consent. In general, changes in the law relating to the family – like most law changes – reflect the changing attitudes and values in society.

5.3 DIVORCE AND REMARRIAGE

Changes in the law have certainly had an impact on the divorce rate as a glance at the statistics will show; but other factors may be of greater importance in creating unhappy marriages – the law merely providing the machinery to end them:

1. The nuclear privatised family puts greater pressure on the marriage relationship (see section 4.4).
2. The breakdown of the established roles for husband and wife creates uncertainty and tension (see section 5.1).
3. Equality of job opportunity creates a greater likelihood of men and women forming alternative liaisons at work.
4. The younger the age of marriage, the greater the statistical likelihood of divorce. In the 1960s there was a trend towards earlier marriage. Although this is now reversed, there were more young people marrying in the late 1970s and early 1980s because there were more young people in the population. (In 1971, 2.6 per cent of males and 10.8 per cent of females between the ages of 16 and 19 were married, compared with 1.4 per cent of males and 6.5 per cent of females in 1980.)
5. Marriages which are forced by pregnancy are more likely to break down – such marriages have increased.

"I have a feeling we've met before. Were we once married?"

6. People are living longer and therefore have longer to get tired of each other! An increasing proportion of divorces takes place between those married for more than twenty years.

Where marriages have broken down, not only is it easier to terminate them legally but there are now fewer social penalties than in the past:

(a) there is a greater social acceptance of marriage breakdown and less social stigma attaches to the divorce;
(b) welfare benefits and a more equable share-out of family possessions decreases the financial penalty of divorce for women, particularly for those with children.

Although divorce is increasing, so also is marriage and re-marriage so that divorce does not appear to be a symptom of the rejection of marriage as an institution.

Family change – Gain or Loss?

We all know by now how high the divorce rate is, in first and second marriage. One in four of all marriages is now predicted to end in divorce. In second marriages, 40 per cent end in divorce. Our falling birth rate is another powerful indicator of the national mood of instability.

For the last century, the birth rate has steadily fallen – and is now slightly below replacement level. This is presumed to be the result of women wanting to stay in the adult world of work, and wanting to return to it as fast as possible after the infancy of their children. Today 62 per cent of wives and mothers work outside the home. But *why* do they want this independence? Naked ambition has perhaps less to do with the declining birth rate than naked fear. At the moment, it isn't *safe* for a woman to have more than one or at most two children. Who can contemplate bringing up more than two children alone with any kind of ease or comfort? Yet the possibility of ending up as a single parent is one that every sensible woman knows she now faces.

In the 1960s we were all newly aware of children damaged by a claustrophobic family upbringing and twisted by their parents' 'frustrated lives'. Now we are able to point to children made ill by the tension and disruption of breaking marriages, and by the stress of growing up with adults who are not their parents and who may regard them with very little warmth.

The losses for men also have to be counted alongside the gains. Men have gained livelier, better educated women as life companions, and a freer sex life. But it is too easy to overlook the difficulties men have in adjusting to the demands of living with today's women. Frequently they can end, through general ineptitude, cut off not only from their wives but also from their children. Marriage break-down over the last generation has often meant discarding the husband and father. When 50 per cent of fathers lose touch with their children one year after divorce, the alienation of men from the modern family can seem to have reached proportions that are as disastrous for them as for the next generation.

The second huge area of hubbub is the 'realignment of roles' inside marriage and without. What is a woman's role, inside marriage or in the world outside? What is a man's role? Over the last fifty years we have drastically changed the way we educate and bring up our daughters. A boy's education and expectations are often very little different today from in the past. Yet we are amazed when the two sexes find it difficult to work out a satisfactory marriage together. At its crudest, we bring up our girls to have a career as well as a marriage, but do we bring up our sons to have a marriage as well as a career? And it is not just a question of *both* learning how to boil an egg. A balance between an inner world of 'feeling' and an outer world of 'doing' is increasingly what we hope both sexes will be able to achieve, but the details are just beginning to be sorted out. Parents are being remarkably slow to digest the obvious, that unless they bring up their sons to be good at marriage, they may not see much of their grandchildren. [Maureen Green, *Marriage* (London: Fontana, 1984).]

The number of petitions for divorce increased from about 400 in 1880 to 172 000 in 1980 but the population also increased substantially. A better guide to the increase in divorce is the number of persons divorcing per thousand married people in the population:

1961	1966	1971	1972	1977	1980
2.1	3.2	9.5	9.5	10.4	12.0

5.4 MARRIAGE BREAKDOWN – ITS SOCIAL AND PERSONAL COST

More than 60 per cent of divorcees have children under the age of 16 and, in 1979, £5 million a week was paid out in supplementary benefits to about 250 000 families unsupported after separation and divorce. These figures illustrate the two main factors that give most cause for concern in estimating the damage caused by marriage breakdown: the effect on children and the cost to public funds.

The cost of marriage breakdown is incalculable in terms of human misery whether or not it ends in divorce. The full financial cost would be difficult to estimate as one would have to add work-days lost, medication, and court costs to the more obvious direct payments. The psychological cost cannot even be estimated. There is some evidence that the trauma associated with marriage breakup or marital disharmony may contribute to delinquency and educational problems. The Welfare State may provide a cushion for the one-parent family, but it is often a very uncomfortable one. The average income of one-parent families is under half of that of two-parent families.

Single parents – the changing nature of the modern family

It is estimated that there are around 730,000 single parents in Britain, involving 1.25 million children. Single parents, whether they are divorced or separated women, unmarried mothers, widows, or lone fathers have much lower incomes on average than two-parent families. Their children are likely to be brought up in relative poverty, and perhaps suffer emotionally. This has been considered a serious enough problem for a government committee report—that of the Finer committee in 1974.

The break-up of families has accelerated in recent years. According to the most recent government survey (*Family Formation*, 1976) the divorce statistics reveal only about half of all broken marriages. Of women in this survey who were married between 1961 and 1965, 11 per cent were separated and 6 per cent divorced ten years later.

What effect this will have on family life, nobody is certain. Most people who get divorced marry again, and before they do so a large number live with someone else, so a high rate of separation and divorce does not necessarily mean an equivalent increase in the numbers of parents trying to survive on their own. But if the family does disintegrate as an independent economic unit, a greater number of people will have to rely on the state.

In historical terms, sociologists have sometimes seen in the development of the family a gradual 'shedding' of its functions, which are handed over to other institutions. Whereas at one time it might have provided all the education, financial support, and welfare an individual was likely to get, these 'functions' have been taken over by schools, social services and so on. Part of this process, it is argued, has been the break-up of the bonds between a wide range of relatives (the extended family) and the whittling down of the family to its core—the nuclear family of parents and children living in isolation.

It is important to remember here that an extended family is not the same thing as a big family. The extended family is made up of a series of nuclear families linked by blood, marriage or adoption. The nuclear family contains only two generations (parents and children), whereas the extended family contains three and sometimes four (grandparents, parents and children) . . .

The argument about exactly what has happened to the family through the last 200 years of industrial upheaval continues to rage. In *The Making of the Modern Family* (1976) Edward Shorter argues that there has been a dramatic change, despite some of the evidence to the contrary. A revolution in sexual behaviour, the nature of romance, the relationship of the family to the wider community, and in ideas about child-rearing have created the modern, conjugal family (as Shorter calls it) hidden away in the privacy of its own comfortable little house.

Shorter's view is that because modern family ties between husband and wife are essentially based on sexual attraction, rather than some pre-arranged property deal, the family is essentially unstable. And because children have little sense of their family past, their parents lack authority. Shorter is not entirely gloomy. This instability, he says, was the price we had to pay for freedom: freedom for people to choose who they wanted to marry, and from the interference of the community in 'private' affairs. [Adapted from *New Society*, 17 January 1980.]

QUESTIONS FROM PAST O LEVEL GCE PAPERS

1. **Either**, (a) Describe and comment on any **three** changes in family life that have taken place in western societies during the past 100 years.

    Or, (b) Distinguish between 'separated conjugal' and 'joint conjugal' roles within the family, and offer a sociological explanation for each.   Welsh Joint Examining Board

2. 'To understand why these different forms of marriage exist it is important to realize that in a society in which, for example, one man marries six women there are probably not five un-married men for every married one. This is partly because a polygynous society usually has a surplus of women, a poly-androus one a surplus of men, and a monogamous society about even number of both sexes. However, the surplus of men and women in polygamous (that is either polygynous or poly-androus) societies is usually not large enough for all men or all women to have more than one partner and the imbalance is sometimes artificially increased; for example in polygynous societies girls are usually married as early as possible while men usually wait until they are thirty or so. Additionally, polygyny is mainly a privilege of the wealthy as a dowry must usually be paid to the father of each of the brides. Most men, even in a polygynous society, have only one wife and only a very small

proportion have more than two, although the pastoral Turkana in Uganda have been recorded as having 28 per cent of men with three or more wives. Polygyny also assists a man to become richer because his wives provide sons to herd cattle or work in his fields, while the wives themselves provide him with a work force. Also, marriage to more than one woman is a means of forming alliances with a number of other families, thus gaining power and influence. (*The Human Web*, G. O'Donnell, 1974)

(a) Explain briefly the meaning of the terms monogamy, polyandry, and polygyny.

(b) Using the information from the extract and from elsewhere explain why marriage patterns vary from society to society.   Associated Examining Board

3. How important have both geographical and social mobility been in the decline of the 'extended' family?
                                        Oxford Local Examining Board

4. 'The Newsons found that only 22 per cent of the parents in their sample were able to arrange an evening out together once a week or more often. Thirty-eight per cent went out occasionally, and 40 per cent had been out together only once or not at all since the birth of their one-year-old.' (Source: *'Leisure'*, SUSAN DICKINSON.)

(a) Present the above information in the form of a table headed: 'The social life of young parents—Newson sample %'   4 marks

(b) Some sociologists have argued that the modern nuclear family is isolated. What evidence have they offered for this?   6 marks

(c) What do they suggest are the effects of this on the various members of the family?   10 marks
                                        Associated Examining Board

5. Describe and account for changes in the divorce rate in Britain during this century.   Oxford Local Examining Board

6. 'On the one hand it is pointed out that the modern family is showing signs of decline in the form of reduced size, an increasing divorce rate, and the support given to individuals by the Welfare State; and on the other we are told that the modern

54

family is becoming more integrated, stable, and child centred.'
Explain these arguments in more detail.

Associated Examining Board

7. *The sexy secret of Lego*

Plastic building bricks are not a particularly sexist toy, one might think. Yet a Danish toy firm that makes them has discovered interesting sales differences which show how even a simple playbrick can reinforce differences between masculine and feminine behaviour.

Overall, the firm of Lego sells its bricks (and various matching building components) three times more often to boys than girls. Even the so-called basic sets, which can be used to make a variety of objects, sell two-thirds more often to boys than girls.

Thus 95 per cent of model cars, planes and train sets are sold to boys, while 85 per cent of dolls furniture sets go to girls. Since the same plastic bricks are used throughout, there can be no difference in the way the child handles or enjoys the toy. The difference is in the picture on the packet—and thus what the child makes.

The most fascinating differences exist in the sets for making various buildings. A family house set sells 30 per cent to girls, as does a hospital. Yet a generalised building set sells only 15 per cent to them, while a fire station building set goes 95 per cent of the time to boys.

All this might be used as evidence that differences are natural between the sexes—but for two facts. Firstly, only 7 per cent of the sets that are sold are bought by the children themselves. Parents and grandparents buy the vast majority. Secondly, at the nursery stage Lego make a larger plastic brick and these sell more equally between the sexes—40 per cent to girls. It is after the age of four, therefore, that parents, particularly mothers, decide that little John will have a train and Janet a dolls furniture set.

(Celia Haddon—*The Sunday Times*—4th September, 1977.

(a) What does the above quotation add to the suggestion that boys and girls are prepared for very different roles in society?

(b) In what other ways are boys and girls prepared for different roles in society?

Associated Examining Board

8. In our society there does not seem to be any definite point in time when young people grow up. Instead there seems to be a fairly extended process during which time there is considerable confusion about the status of young people: they are often expected to fulfil adult roles such as looking after younger children, taking a job, and in general behaving like adults, but do not enjoy all the rights and privileges associated with adult status. At the same time they are not completely able to shake off the remnants associated with child status such as school rules and parental authority. This confusion can last for a long period—perhaps even eight or ten years of gradual change.

The status of the child is quite clearly defined in the western world with clothes, toys, activities, food and even language which act as symbols of the child's status. Similarly, adults enjoy rights, privileges and possessions which identify their status to the rest of society. Even the elderly enjoy an identifiable status.

For those in between childhood and adulthood there is no such clearly defined status—some societies do have a special class of 'young warriors' whilst other societies and groups have ceremonies and initiation rituals to mark the passing of a child into adult status.

It may be that many of the behaviour patterns which young people of today share with their peers can be understood as attempts to establish a clear identity for those in the growing up process and to create another clear status group in society.

(a) Select **one** way from the extract in which other groups or societies give young people a definite status.   (1)

(b) Why does the confusion or uncertainty about young people referred to above not exist with regard to children and adults?   (2)

(c) What is the meaning of **each** of the following sociological terms as used in the extract:

  (i) status;   (2)
  (ii) peer group?   (2)

(d) How and why has the status of the child within the family changed during the last 50 years?   (5)

(e) Young people are sometimes regarded as deviant. How does your understanding of the **labelling** process help to explain this?   (8)

Associated Examining Board

PART III
THE SOCIOLOGY OF
EDUCATION

INFORMAL AND FORMAL EDUCATION

6.1 THE PURPOSE OF EDUCATION

People start to learn from the moment they are born: initially most of this learning takes place in the home (Chapter 3) but later other agencies such as neighbourhood, religion, media and 'peer group' - the term used for people of the same age - all join in this process of informal education.

Because family and friends can no longer teach most people all they need to know in order to earn a living in our increasingly technological and complex society, more formal institutions such as schools, colleges and Universities have developed to prepare people for the world of work. Because relatives are no longer usually in a position to find young people jobs, careers advisers and teachers have replaced them.

Of course, educational establishments do not only prepare people for work - they are also concerned with passing on the norms and values of society. Sometimes the school or college's views of what norms and values are appropriate differ from the views of the home, and young people experience considerable difficulty in coming to terms with this conflict. Schools may well put an emphasis on discipline, team-work, theoretical learning and formal relationships; while the home is unstructured, less disciplined and individualistic. When such a divergence is marked the young people involved may well become alienated from either the school or the home.

There has been an increasing emphasis in recent years on 'social education' in the schools. This development of personal qualities may be seen as further intruding on the function of the family or as a necessary development to meet the needs of a society in which job specific skills may be outdated very quickly. The privatised nuclear family may not provide a sufficiently wide range of relationships; and more leisure or unemployment may increase the need for people to develop the ability to make appropriate relationships with others.

In 1958, Cotgrove pointed out that although the extension of education to all had not proved the disaster that some expected, neither has it led to the equality anticipated by others. 'As certificates and diplomas are more and more the means of entry to the better paid, more secure, higher status jobs, education becomes increasingly important as a basis for occupational achievement and upward social mobility. The emphasis has shifted from socialisation to selection – an essentially aristocratic structure has been modified so that schools which once educated a social élite now educate an intellectual élite.'

6.2 SOCIALISATION

Socialisation is the process of learning by which people of all ages acquire the culture of their society and of the various groups within the society to which they belong. Because we are constantly joining new groups throughout our lives, socialisation never stops. We have to learn the behaviour appropriate to a student, a husband or wife, and eventually of an old age pensioner.

If we were not socialised we would not behave like human beings at all, as is illustrated by the many stories of children found living with animals and behaving in a similar way to them. Some of these were no doubt abandoned in the first place because they were mentally deficient but some apparently were not.

A child is first taught to behave like a child and the 'expectations' of how a child should behave will vary from society to society; as the child grows older they will be expected not to be too babyish or too grown up. The child will learn its 'gender roles' (section 1.2) and the norms and values of its home. If these differ from those of the general society, the scene is set for future conflict.

6.3 SOCIAL CONTROL

In most cases the norms and values of the home are likely to reflect those of the society. The child will therefore be taught to accept the rules of that society by example, punishment and reward. These rules will receive more emphatic reinforcement in the formal education process.

British society is formed by layers of people in differing positions of power. This 'hierarchy' is reflected in nearly all schools with the Head at the top and layers of Deputy Heads, Senior Teachers, Heads of Department, teachers on various scales, caretakers, kitchen ladies and pupils. The pupil learns to behave appropriately within this rigid structure and to obey a

Young Asians in Bradford acquire part of the culture of their society

myriad of rules and regulations, ranging from the very necessary to the (apparently) very silly. It has been suggested that schools have a 'hidden curriculum' preparing pupils for their roles in industry and bureaucracies; being prepared to accept subordination and alienation from decision-making. The structure of the school will be protected by a variety of formal and informal punishments and rewards 'sanctions' - exam passes, a smile, 'lines', detention, and in Britain (although in virtually no other country) beatings. Schools reflect the values current in their society and there is an increasing amount of informality in many British schools.

As well as being one of the agencies of social control in the sense of trying to ensure that pupils and students operate within the guidelines established by the society; educational establishments are also 'custodial' institutions in which children and young people are placed to get them out of the way, both for their own safety and for the security and comfort of others. The increasing complexity and maturity required for many jobs today has resulted in the age of employment being postponed. Equally, taking large numbers of young people out of the job market is an effective means of rationing scarce employment. In this situation some formal education is seen as transparently artificial by some young people, to the extent of increasing the discipline problems that formal education is intended to assist in decreasing.

Discipline and the school

Patterns of discipline

There has been surprisingly little systematic research into the effects of different patterns of discipline. However, the few studies that have been undertaken both point to its importance and emphasise that discipline and punishment should not be seen as synonymous. As already mentioned, Reynolds observed that the combination of good discipline (in terms of rule enforcement), the involvement of pupils in discipline (as shown by the use of a prefect system), and a low use of corporal punishment was most likely to be associated with good attendance. Heal (1978) found that misbehaviour was worst in schools with formal punishment systems: and Clegg and Megson (1968) noted that delinquency rates tended to be highest in schools with a great deal of corporal punishment. They also describe the improvement in one school where a new head reduced the number of rules . . . The use of some sanctions is clearly an essential element in any school organisation, but taking the findings on rewards and punishments together, the results do tend to suggest that the balance between punishments and rewards may be less than helpful in some schools. It may be difficult to design systems of rewards which will maintain their value and appeal to secondary school pupils, and especially to the oldest age groups. Where this had been attempted in the schools we studied, the results appeared to be positive, in contrast to the findings on punishment which suggested low, and generally rather negative relationships. [M. Rutter *et al.*, *Fifteen Thousand Hours: Secondary Schools and their Effects on Children* (London: Open Books, 1979).]

6.4 THE MEDIA AND YOUTH CULTURE

'Rites of passage' exist in most societies to mark the different stages in a person's life. These rites are ceremonies such as baptism and circumcision or marriage which announce that a new person has been accepted into a society, or make it clear what sort of behaviour is expected of them, or towards them by others.

Many societies have an initiation ceremony near the time of puberty, announcing that the person concerned is no longer a child and that they are entitled to the prestige and privileges of an adult member of the society. At the same time the child accepts the responsibilities inherent in adulthood.

Although at about the age of puberty many young Christians are 'confirmed' in their faith and Jewish boys become full members of their religion at their Barmitzvah the increasing gap between puberty and work in modern industrial society has meant that there is a lengthening grey area in which the adolescent is neither fully child nor fully adult. Lacking prestige and privileges, many young people become 'alienated' and set up their own status systems dependent on fashion, music, boy/girl friends and rebelliousness. Often responsibility is also rejected and authority derided – the peak age for crime is between fourteen and twenty years.

Without the responsibilities of adults – rent or mortgage, rates, petrol, children's clothes – many young people have more surplus wealth than do adults to spend as they choose. It is not surprising that commercial organisations have sought to exploit this wealth by providing and advertising an appropriate consumer life-style in entertainment, fashion, cosmetics and 'durable' goods such as 'hi-fi' and motor bikes. This 'exploitation' (not necessarily a word implying wrongdoing) makes the adolescents more visually distinctive than they would otherwise be.

The media depends on sensationalism to sell, thus it is the young rebel rather than the more conventional young person who is newsworthy, setting up a copycat reaction. To an extent 'youth culture' is a creation of the media. However, the influence of the media on youthful behaviour should not be exaggerated. Klapper in *The Effect of Mass Communications* (1960) found that 'media depictions of crime and violence are not prime movers to such conduct. The content seems to reinforce or implement existing and

It is the young rebel rather than the more conventional young person who is newsworthy

otherwise induced behavioural tendencies.' On the other hand a minority of teenagers might be influenced, as J. Halloran in *The Effect of Mass Communication - With Special Reference to Television* (1964) found that frustrated children copied actions seen on television to release their aggression.

A special study *Broadcasting and Youth* (1979) by the Broadcasting Authorities and the Manpower Services Commission found little or no support for the "one-step" theory of communication which suggests that all of those who receive a message will react to it in the same way, but that perhaps 'media messages shape our perception of the world in which we live.'

Television Youth Culture

To explore the media we must also explore the day-to-day lives of those who use them. Academics and the media themselves have shown considerable interest in minority youth groups — skinheads, bootboys, bikeboys, mods, rockers, juvenile prostitutes, junkies, delinquents and football hooligans (and all should be in quotation marks) — but the ordinary sixteen or seventeen year old gains scant attention, which reflects a general attitude to the population at large. Thus. not only do we know little about young adults, but also the images we present to young adults *of themselves* are often anti-social rigid stereotypes.

The scope of this Study does not allow discussion of the parts played by adult anxiety and disenchantment or the role of 'newsworthiness' in the generation and acceptance of unfortunate images of youth, but it would be foolish to ignore the fact that young adults are searching for new, non-childlike identities and that the contribution of certain media on certain occasions to this quest is the distribution of unrealistic images.

A study conducted in the early sixties found that when a family bought their first television set the total amount of time the family spent together was unchanged. Belson, W. A. — *The Impact of Television* (Crosby, Lockwood, 1967). There was one exception to this general finding: bringing television into the home seemed to push the teenagers out. Perhaps it is significant that the term 'teenagers' appears to have originated in the fifties when television began its attack on the time between working and sleeping.

Teenagers, or young adults, devote roughly 9% of their week to watching television. Although this is a substantial period of viewing, it is less than for any other age group. In contrast, at 12—14 years viewing is peaking for working class boys at an average of 24 hours per week. The exact nature of the dip, even the location of the age at which viewing is at a minimum, has never been recorded. Researchers have concentrated on children and adults, ignoring those in between. For example studies of children and media in England and Sweden revealed that television is much less of an escapist medium than many have assumed. Whilst round about 25% of children reported various escapist or mood control uses of television related to the exploration of reality (learning — or being told about — different places and people, what it's like to be grown up and so on). The most frequently endorsed use of television for these children was as a source of conversation. 30% or more 15 year olds nominated television as being best for: 'letting you know how other people lived', 'finding out about things that happen in different places', 'telling you about things you don't learn in school' and 'giving you things to talk about with friends'.

At nine years of age television seems to be the main source of media based satisfaction, but by fifteen young people are out and about and television is displaced by music and contact with friends. In absolute terms, the young adult is watching, on average, almost twenty hours television each week, but it seems likely that much of this watching is low key and time filling. [*Broadcasting and Youth* Gulbenkian Foundation, 1979).]

A distinctive youth culture is in fact difficult to establish. Most young people do not have a distinctive set of values from the adult population. In *The School Leaver* (1961) Venness found that 'young people do seem to be remarkably like us' and in 1976 a National Children's Bureau survey of 14 000 young people born in 1958 found little evidence of a generation gap – 'Britain's future appears to be in the hands of a remarkably conventional generation of young men and women, not markedly different from the parents who worry about them.' In 1965 Musgrove concluded that if conflict exists between generations it comes mainly from the adult side. It is also important to note that class differences between differing groups of teenagers may lead to more divergent behaviour between these groups themselves than among adolescent and adult society generally.

Although many housing estates lack leisure facilities for young people, and many youth clubs are based in educational buildings from which some adolescents are alienated, many thousands belong to conventional organisations; some like the Scouts and Guides emphasising the values of the general community.

Two reports in 1984 reflected earlier studies – *Ask the Family* carried out by the National Council for Voluntary Organisations found that children are better behaved than ever before, that marriage still matters and that the old are still respected. *Young People in the Eighties*, sponsored by the Department of Education and Science, and based on a survey of 600 people aged 14 to 19 found that 67 per cent completely rejected drug taking and 50 per cent considered drinking alcohol a waste of money; most of their time was spent at home or in their friends' homes, listening to music or watching TV and they were 'friendly, responsible, happy and helpful'.

Youth culture

Talcott Parsons, one of the most influential of American sociologists, used the phrase "socialisation process" to describe the value-teaching institutions—the family, the school and the mass media. But the attraction of the youth culture is that if offers the possibility of finding knowledge, entertainment and an identity outside these areas.

Because an energetic involvement in a youth culture often, though not always, entails rejection of parents and teachers (and sometimes involves violence or political rebellion) it has been viewed with alarm by what is called the Establishment. As Stan Cohen, in his study of youth culture, *Folk Devils and Moral Panics* (1972), writes:

'Societies appear to be subject, every now and then, to periods of moral panic. A condition, episode or group of persons emerges to become defined as a threat to society. The moral barricades are manned by editors, bishops, politicians and other right-thinking people.'

According to Cohen, all the various youth sub-cultures, from beatniks to skinheads, 'have occupied a constant position as "folk devils": visible reminders of what we should not be.' Punks and skinheads are, therefore, modern witches, baddies. In the middle ages the witches were burned, in modern times they are pilloried in the press and television. Both witches and youth cultures are, in Cohen's view, scapegoats for supposed moral and social diseases afflicting societies.

In attempting to define the youth culture, sociologists usually make a distinction between the youth sub-cultures which contain genuine rebellious elements and the wider youth culture, which consists mainly of those products marketed by the teenage leisure industry. To buy a Top 20 single, or boutique clothes, to read the romantic fiction in *Loving* magazine or the profiles of football stars in *Shoot*, would not normally be thought of as subversive.

Some sociologists have suggested that the youth culture is largely an invention of a headline-hungry media and that it is essentially no different in pattern from the rest of society. It is, of course, true that the processes at work in the wider society, like social class, are all present in the youth culture. A 16-year-old boy in an inner-city comprehensive will tend to wear different clothes, speak a different language, have different cultural tastes from a 16-year-old public schoolboy. Beatniks and hippies might be seen as a product of the middle class, while punks and skinheads developed their youth cultures in working class neighbourhoods.

Much of the early work on youth culture was done in America in the Chicago school of sociology. One of the first important books on the subject was W. F. Whyte's *Street Corner Society* (1955), which described the activities of a street gang. Another influential study was by Albert Cohen, who wrote *Delinquent Boys: the culture of the gang* in 1955. The book's conclusion was that gangs, for working class boys, were a society in which they could gain prestige, unlike those societies of the 'straight' world—school and work—where they were invariably failures. . .

In Britain, a lot of work on youth culture has been done in the 1970s by the Centre for Contemporary Cultural Studies at Birmingham University. One of their publications, *Resistance Through Rituals* (1976), by Stuart Hall and others, views the style developed by working class youths as a symbolic protest against class in postwar Britain. . .

Others, more cynical, view the fast-changing trends inside the youth cultures as fashion pure and simple, the continuous need for something 'hip' and new created by the mass media and satisfied by the teenage leisure industry's seemingly endless run of gimmick products. [Adapted from *New Society*, 18 October 1979.]

CHANGES IN BRITISH EDUCATION

7.1 HISTORICAL DEVELOPMENT

The first schools in Britain were run by the Church and produced the clerics who doubled as priests and the civil service of the period. Later, the first 'public' and grammar schools appeared, to provide for the needs of the new merchant class.

In the nineteenth century the public schools grew in number as more administrators and officers were needed to serve the needs of the developing British Empire, while 'elementary' schools began to give basic instruction in reading, writing and arithmetic (as well as religion) in order to provide the skilled workers needed by the industrial revolution. By the middle of the nineteenth century Britain was lagging behind the United States and Germany in providing state education. In Germany one child in six went to school; in Britain only one in ten. Despite concern that the lack of an educated work force would hinder Britain's competing with other industrialised nations some politicians were warned that education would give people ideas above their station and encourage revolution. Others took the view that education would teach respect for superiors and the need for hard work. Towards the end of the nineteenth century the need to educate the masses if Britain was to continue to compete became inescapable.

1870 Forster's *Elementary Education Act* set up School Boards to build schools and to encourage attendance.

1876 (Sandon's Act) Parents were given the responsibility of ensuring that children between the ages of 5 and 13 went to school.

1880 (Mundell's Act) Education became compulsory in theory; parents still had to pay a few pence a week in fees.

1891 *Free Education Act*, most elementary education became free.

1902 (Balfour's Act) Local Education Authorities (LEA's) set up to replace School Boards. New grammar schools were built and others received grants in return for providing a proportion of free places, in order to meet the needs of a better educated work force to occupy the increasing number of 'white collar' jobs in commerce and industry.

1906 All secondary schools receiving public money had to offer at least 25 per cent of their places as free scholarships.

1918 School-leaving age raised to 14 (all elementary fees abolished).

1926 (Hadow Report) The Education of the Adolescent; planned a transfer at eleven and two types of secondary education
  (a) grammar – an academic education with a school leaving age of 16+
  (b) secondary modern – a practically based education with a leaving age of 14+.

1938 Spens Report ⎫ Both these reports rejected the idea
1943 Norwood Report ⎭ of 'multilateral' (i.e. 'comprehensive') schools.

Until this date working-class children were unlikely to receive anything but a basic education; only about 10 per cent of children went to grammar school, and most of these paid fees. The kind of education received depended upon an ability to pay rather than ability to learn.

7.2 THE BIPARTITE AND TRIPARTITE SYSTEMS

In 1944 a new Education Act (the 'Butler Act') was introduced by the wartime coalition government. Its main aim was to increase 'equality of opportunity' so that able children would not be prevented from contributing fully to their society because their parents could not afford an appropriate education. Pressure for reform had grown during the 1920s and 1930s, but it may be that it was hastened by those in authority who were surprised to meet so many people in the armed forces of high ability but little formal education and by middle-class people coming into contact for the first time with ill-educated children from the slums.

The 'Butler Act' raised the school-leaving age to 15 (with effect from 1947) and introduced reforms to raise educational and health standards in the schools. It retained religious instruction as the only compulsory subject. Most importantly it provided for a common education to the age of 11 followed by an education suited to the ability and potential of each child.

The type of educational system that developed from the 'Butler Act' was similar to that envisaged by the Hadow Report – practical education for the non-academic in secondary modern schools, academic education in

Table 7.1 school attended: by socio-economic group of father (prior to the major expansion of comprehension education after 1972)

England and Wales Percentages

Socio-economic group of father

| | Middle class | | | Working class | | | |
	Professional	Employers and managers	Intermediate and junior non-manual	Skilled manual	Semi-skilled	Unskilled	Others*
Secondary modern	3	12	11	42	17	5	10
Comprehensive	3	14	18	40	13	5	7
Grammar	7	20	26	33	8	2	4
Direct grant and independent (11–14 year old)	30	45	13	11	—	—	1
Other school	1	7	16	37	19	11	10

NOTE: By 1972 approximately 50 per cent of secondary school children in England and Wales were being educated in comprehensive schools and 50 per cent in selective schools.*

The chart shows that 37 per cent of these were 'middle class' and 56 per cent 'working class' (7 per cent were not classified as either).

Only 26 per cent of these attending secondary modern school were middle class, while 53 per cent of those attending grammar schools came into that category – 88 per cent of those attending independent and direct grant schools were also the children of white collar workers.

* (By 1981 82.5 per cent of secondary school children were being educated in comprehensive schools.)

SOURCE   Based on material from *Social Trends* (London: HMSO).

grammar schools and secondary technical schools for those likely to become skilled craftsmen, although technical schools did not become widespread. Where all three schools existed the scheme was known as 'tripartite'; where there were only secondary modern and grammar, 'bipartite'.

Although both kinds of school were supposed to be of equal status ('parity of esteem') it quickly became apparent that grammar school pupils had better opportunities when leaving school and selection at the age of 11 became a matter of 'passing' or 'failing'; thus the 80 per cent of the nation's children who did not attend grammar school started their secondary education regarding themselves as failures.

7.3 COMPREHENSIVE EDUCATION

A much greater percentage of middle-class children (section 8.3) 'passed' the 11-plus examination than did the children of working-class parents and so the bipartite system was seen to perpetuate and increase class divisions in society; it was 'socially divisive'.

It was argued that larger schools catering for pupils from all backgrounds and of all ability levels would encourage children from all social groups to mix together, thus increasing mutual understanding and in time reducing friction in industry. In these 'comprehensive' schools children would not pass or fail at 11 and thus all would have the opportunity to study to a high academic level if they had the necessary ability.

It was claimed that larger schools would increase opportunities by allowing subject specialists in minority interest subjects to be employed, perhaps a teacher of Russian or Ancient Greek, and that economies of scale would provide a wider range of facilities.

Opponents of comprehensive education felt that academic children would be held back by the academically less able; that children of lesser ability would be unable to rise to positions of responsibility as they had in the secondary modern schools, and might suffer from the anonymity of larger institutions in that those with greater ability would not be spotted and given special tuition to develop their latent potential.

It was also anticipated that comprehensive schools would accept lower standards of dress and objectives and thus create a norm which would reduce standards overall. It was also argued that the placing of pupils in general ability groups – 'streaming', or subject ability groups – 'setting' might heighten social distinctions if the higher sets or streams were mainly occupied by middle class children. In particular there is evidence that a low place in such streaming creates a 'self-fulfilling prophecy', children come to regard themselves as of low ability and cease to try.

The anonymity of larger institutions

A further argument against comprehensive schools was that whereas bright working-class children often travelled out of their environment to attend a grammar school they would now have to attend their neighbourhood comprehensive; if the neighbourhood was a poor one in which academic achievement was derided and most pupils were anti-authority then the academic child would suffer.

In 1950 there were ten comprehensive schools but the number of comprehensive schools increased rapidly during the 1960s and 1970s and in 1965 the Labour Government ordered Local Authorities to prepare plans for a completely comprehensive system of state education. This order was withdrawn by the Conservative Government in 1970 and renewed by the Labour Government of 1974.

In 1971 just over a third of children were being educated in comprehensive schools. Ten years later the proportion had risen to over 80 per per cent, although there were several different types of comprehensive including 'all through'; 'eleven to sixteen'; and 'middle' and 'upper' schools.

With the growth of comprehensive education there has been a considerable increase in the number of co-educational schools, schools that have both male and female pupils. Many of the grammar and modern schools were single sex but most comprehensive schools outside London are mixed.

The supporters of co-education claim that boys and girls should grow up naturally to appreciate each other as people rather than sex objects and that facilities for all subjects should be available to both male and female. Opponents claim that boys may suffer from feelings of inferiority as girls mature earlier and that both are likely to be distracted from their study.

Comprehensive schools and achievement

The introduction of comprehensive schools has been a struggle between power groups at the local and national levels. The early arguments for comprehensive education concentrated as much on what were thought to be the defects of the selective system of grammar and modern schools, as upon the supposed merits of comprehensive schools. Drawing on the surveys of the *Early Leaving*, Crowther and, later, Robbins reports, a large wastage of educational talent had been shown to occur, particularly among working-class children. This wastage has been attributed to the operation of the secondary selection procedure, shown by Douglas, Floud and Halsey and others to contain a social selection element favouring middle-class children, particularly at the borderline level, and to the value system of the grammar school, which Jackson and Marsden, and King have shown to be unacceptable to some working-class pupils. A major ideological justification of the comprehensive system is that it will widen educational opportunities and reduce the class gap in educational attainment.

Julienne Ford attempted to put some of the claims for a comprehensive system to the test. She examined the pro-comprehensive school literature to produce five propositions: that it will produce a greater development of talent, provide a greater degree of social equality of opportunity, raise working-class levels of occupational aspirations, promote social mixing and the conception of society as a flexible hierarchy rather than a rigid dichotomy ('them and us'). ... She interpreted the results to indicate that none of the five propositions was confirmed.

Reservations must be expressed about this claim. It could be argued that these five effects would only be apparent in a national system of exclusively comprehensive schools.

Other research by Douglas, King, and Holly does confirm that existing comprehensive schools do not necessarily raise the occupational and educational ambitions or school involvement of their working-class pupils to middle-class levels. Unlike Ford, Miller found evidence of more social mixing in comprehensives than in other secondary schools, although using a different method of measurement. Pedley presented some evidence that comprehensive schools can provide more educational opportunities, but Davis has argued that the development of exams in modern schools might have allowed the bipartite system to do as well. Neave has shown that even eleven-plus failures can get to university through the comprehensive system. A problem in comparing the academic outputs of schools is that many existing comprehensives are in areas with grammar schools,* and as Monks has shown, have more working-class pupils and less 'bright' pupils than may be expected. [Ronald King, *Education* (London: Longman, 1979) 2nd edn.]

*Less true by the mid-1980s – more than 80 per cent of all state school pupils are now educated in comprehensive schools (my comment, *auth*.).

7.4 THE FUTURE

Although there is some support for a return to selective education it does appear that comprehensives are likely to remain the norm. The major change in schools is likely to be that more comprehensives will become 'eleven to sixteen' as the number of children in sixth forms reduce and it becomes necessary to rationalise the provision by concentrating 'sixth form' provision in sixth form or 'tertiary' colleges. Tertiary colleges are colleges of further education in which all young people in an area are trained and educated whether traditional 'A' level GCE candidates, apprentices or unemployed; many of the arguments used in favour of comprehensive schools are used to support these comprehensive colleges.

The 'New Training Initiative' (NTI) announced in 1982 recognised that for many young people full-time employment at sixteen is a thing of the past, and sought to integrate work experience with education. The NTI developed into the Youth Training Scheme in 1983, and although criticised as a means of providing cheap labour, the YTS does attempt to meet the changing nature of industry by abandoning the teaching of specific skills (which may quickly become outdated) and substituting 'transferable skills' which can be adapted to changing needs.

As industrialisation and mechanisation (section 14.1) decreases the need for labour, the economic function of education in preparing people for work is likely to change, with a greater emphasis on the creative use of leisure. Equally the kind of work available in the future will be increasingly service-orientated so there will need to be more concentration on personal relationships (and sociology!). Skills are likely to be outdated rapidly so there will be a change from teaching job-specific to transferable skills.

If society becomes less hierarchical and authoritarian then these values will permeate the educational institutions. Already many are developing the concept of 'learning contracts' in which students and staff decide together what needs to be learnt.

Fig. 7.1 *is teaching relevant?*

It may be that young people are changing their attitudes much more quickly than their elders. In a recent MORI survey, commissioned by *The Times*, a large percentage of school leavers were critical of what they had received at school, partly because they felt it lacked relevance to the 1980s.

Home and school

Does/did your school spend too little/too much/about the right amount of time teaching

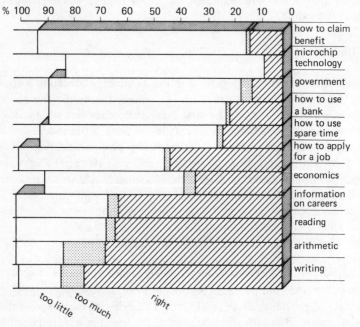

SOURCE *New Society*, 1982.

ABILITY AND ACHIEVEMENT

8.1 HEREDITY AND ENVIRONMENT

In the past it was assumed that some strata of society were superior to others because they inherited intelligence or artistic abilities along with their physical appearance, from their parents. This belief in 'genetic endowment' has been challenged during the last one hundred years and the 'nature *v.* nurture' debate continues.

Many definitions have been given to explain the nature of intelligence. A simple one is the ability to perceive and solve problems – the nature of the problems will, of course, depend on the society in which they exist. In our society intelligence tends to be thought of in terms of an ability to manipulate language and abstract concepts.

A great deal of research has aimed at establishing whether, and to what degree, intelligence is inherited. Conclusions have ranged from that of Watson (1931) who stated 'There is no such thing as an inheritance of capacity, talent, temperament, mental constitution and characteristics', and that of Floud, Halsey and Martin (1956) who argued 'it is well known that intelligence is largely an acquired characteristic', to that of Jensen (1969) and Eysenck (1973) who have maintained that genetic factors are much more important than environmental influences in producing differences in intelligence. Most research concludes that intelligence is in some measure inherited but that environmental factors can be conclusive in its development or otherwise.

In Britain the major argument with regard to heredity and environment revolves round its impact on differences in academic achievement between social classes. Although differences in measured intelligence have been noted, the impact of environment upon a child's educational chances seem of much greater significance.

Environment will include the kind of stimulus a child receives in terms of speech, books, encouragement and example. It will include facilities

Environment includes all the influences that may make an impact on the child

such as housing, privacy and monetary resources; it will include the value system of the home, neighbourhood and local peer group. It will even include nutrition, for there is some evidence that severe malnutrition during the first two years of life effects the development of the brain.

Regression to the mean

> The term 'regression to the mean', in this context, refers to the tendency for children to be nearer to the population mean on a characteristic than are their parents. As a consequence, the children of very dull individuals are likely to be more intelligent than their parents whereas the offspring of highly intelligent persons are likely to be less intelligent than their procreators. [M. Rutter and N. Madge, *Cycles of Disadvantage* (London: Heinemann, 1976).]

8.2 THE CULTURE OF THE SCHOOL

The culture of the school tends to be a middle-class one although schools vary in their education objectives. Some schools will emphasise their 'academic' role and be concerned mainly with achievement; some will concentrate on their 'pastoral' role of developing personal qualities and some will strive mainly to keep a maximum of good order and discipline, their 'custodial' role.

If the culture of the school is predominantly academic or custodial within a community which rejects concepts of betterment and authority then there is likely to be a development of anti-school and delinquent sub-cultures as illustrated by Hargreaves in *Deviance in Classrooms* (1975).

The school is an authoritarian institution (section 6.3) although the degree of authoritarianism will vary. Schoolteachers are middle class by definition. Although as a group they are likely to have a high proportion of first-generation middle-class members, they have reached their position by accepting middle-class values such as 'deferred gratification' (forfeiting immediate satisfaction for future gain) and completing their education at a late age with consequent loss of earnings in their youth.

Bernstein in *A socio-linguistic approach to social learning* identifies the 'elaborated code' (or 'formal language') of middle-class speech patterns, with complex forms, and the 'restricted code' (or 'public language') of many working-class people, which is much simpler in form, using basic words. These language differences do reflect very different cultural backgrounds and present serious problems for youngsters from the lower working class, in particular, as they attempt to learn in school.

Self-fulfilling prophecy

Placing American kindergarten life under the magnifying glass, psychologist Dr R. C. Rist discovered just how far early judgements come to dominate the child's school career. In the kindergarten which he studied the head teacher sat children at one of three dinner tables according to her expectations for their future academic success. Her brightest hopes ate at one table, those she ranked as moderately intelligent at another while the ones she considered almost certain failures had their meals at a third. She picked children for each table on the basis of family background, the way they were dressed and how well they got on with staff. Despite the fact that IQ tests showed there was no real difference between the abilities of children at the three tables these groupings remained virtually unchanged during the next two years. The teacher saw little reason to promote any child from the 'failure' table or to demote any of those at the 'success' table.

As the years passed, however, changes in abilities between the groups became increasingly apparent. Children who had eaten with the success group did well while those who had dined with 'failures' did badly. Was she a highly perceptive teacher or could it be that those initial assessments set the course for the children's future progress through school? On the basis of other evidence the most likely explanation is that the attitudes of the kindergarten staff, conveyed to primary school teachers in the pupils' reports, which would then have gone with them to their secondary schools, established a pattern of prejudgement which played an important role in how each child was perceived. As Dr Rist commented, the head teacher's original predictions 'came to be justified not in terms of teacher expectations, but in apparently "objective" records of previous school working, including by the beginning of the second grade, reading test performance'.

In a study of the effect which a teacher's belief in the pupil's IQ has on attainment, Dr J. Michael Palardy of University of Georgia at Athens, Georgia, discovered that the brighter a child was assumed to be, the better the results the teacher obtained in class. Groups of boys, aged between six and seven, were matched in ability on the basis of intelligence tests. They were then taught reading in separate classes, by teachers with identical qualifications using exactly the same methods. The only difference was that some of the teachers were told their particular group consisted of boys with above average ability who should prove faster and more able readers. There was, of course, not a grain of truth in this statement. But when the boys were tested at the end of the training period the teacher's false belief had been transformed into classroom reality. Those boys falsely credited with better reading ability *could* now read faster and more fluently than those in other groups. . . .

The message from such studies is crystal clear. What teachers believe their students achieve. Classroom ability mirrors the attitudes of those who take the classes and run the schools. [David Lewis, *You Can Teach Your Child Intelligence* (London: Souvenir Press, 1981).]

8.3 THE INFLUENCE OF FAMILY AND CLASS

Bernstein suggests that a major factor in explaining the success of the middle-class child academically is that it uses the same language as its teachers, not in terms of accent but in an ability to grasp the more complicated ideas expressed by teachers in the elaborated code.

Newspeak: It's The Real Thing

By the dawn of 1984 the development of television, and other forms of electronic media, means that mass communication, both verbal and visual, is more pervasive and persuasive than ever before.

This technical potential for control must be set against ideas of how language work, notably those whose theories of the differences in linguistic practice between working class and middle class speakers of English have emphasised how language can define and reinforce the social hierarchy. Bernstein is often interpreted to be talking about accent, especially the accent of the economically dominant

South East, which is the accent spoken by those who attended certain educational institutions, and therefore the accent of national power, prestige and authority. This has also become the accent of broadcasting. In fact, the core of Bernstein's theory is his distinction between a 'restricted code' spoken by some people and an 'elaborated code' spoken by others. 'Restricted code' was supposed to be the use of simple sentences, limited and inexplicit means of referring to things, lack of abstractions and lack of self-reference. Bernstein thought that working class children used this in schools, where 'elaborated code' was expected, and thus did poorly; he also concluded that 'restricted code' led to restricted ability to form concepts.

Orwell's Newspeak looks very like Bernstein's 'restricted code'. It has reduced complexity, few abstractions. But it is also a restricted code peculiar to the ruling class; the proles do not speak it. Its purpose is to provide a medium of expression for the ideology of the ruling elite, and also to make all other modes of thought impossible. [C. Aubrey and P. Chilton (eds) *1984 – Autonomy, Control and Communication* (London: Comedia, 1983).]

Working-class children tend to be slower in learning to read and write than middle-class children because of this language barrier and because intelligence tests are often based on words. This also gives the middle class child an advantage, which decreases when the intelligence test is based on arithmetic.

Many other studies have highlighted the importance of family and class in determining a child's success at school.

In 1962, B. Jackson and D. Marsden published their study of eighty-eight working-class children in Huddersfield who had been educated at grammar school, and found that how a child ultimately performs at school is influenced greatly by home background.

Jackson and Marsden showed that working-class children start school disadvantaged and this disadvantage normally continues. The middle-class advantages often include:

1. A greater concern with education on the part of parents.
2. The speech patterns at home and the availability of books improves the child's vocabulary.
3. The expected behaviour and speech used in school are of the middle-class pattern.
4. The parents have greater expectations of the child.
5. Greater likelihood of travel and educational visits.
6. 'Deferred gratification' – the expectation that work now will lead to better things later.
7. Facilities for quiet private study and perhaps private lessons.

8. More financial resources and therefore a greater likelihood of further and/or higher education.

R. Fletcher in *The Family and Marriage in Britain* emphasises the importance of the 'educative' functions of the family and suggests that the upbringing of children is now undertaken in a far more considerate and careful fashion than in the past – with the child enjoying high status and increasingly treated as an end in him or herself. 'Throughout the entire period of the child's educational experience, the attitudes of the family, and the facilities offered by the family, are of vital importance.'

In 1964, J. Douglas in *The Home and the School* – a longitudinal study of over 5000 children begun in 1946 – investigated a variety of 'variables' and found that:

1. Standards of 'care' were highest in upper middle class and lowest in lower manual working class on all indices. (One must however beware the 'halo' effect of middle-class researchers. For example, there was no investigation into 'the warmth of relationship'.) However these findings were also born out by J. and E. Newson in *Patterns of Infant Care in an Urban Community*.

2. Middle class parents generally take more interest in their child's progress at school and become relatively more interested as the child grows up. This interest and encouragement resulted in improved scores in tests of school performance and mental ability. (First tests at 8, second at 11.) These tests assess *attainment* and *achievement* in mainly *verbal* skills – not *innate ability*. These findings were born out by M. Young and P. McGeeney *Learning Begins at Home*. This stressed the importance of parents and teachers co-operating if children are to get the best out of their education.

3. Children's attitudes and behaviour were influenced by their environment. Teachers were asked to place children at the age of 10 in categories from 'very hard working' to 'lazy'. This assessment related directly to class positions. 'Hard workers – 26 per cent upper middle; 17 per cent lower middle; 11 per cent upper manual and 7 per cent lower manual.

    This was a subjective test, so therefore teachers' own middle-class *norms*, *values* and *attitudes* are likely to influence results, but the children will also be influenced by the high educational aspirations of their family, neighbourhood, friends and the local primary school that they attend. Those children not succeeding were more *disorderly* and *restless* in class.

4. Position in the family influenced ultimate educational attainment. Eldest boys though not showing superiority in tests ultimately did

better than younger brothers and sisters or only children. (Not found in girls.)

5. Linguistic development was influenced by home background. The more children in the family when the child was learning to talk, the lower his score in the 8 year old vocabulary test. This deficiency was not made up later.

6. Middle-class teachers related better to middle-class children because there was a *common ground* and *mutual respect* between teacher and pupil due to similar manners, modes of address, and speech; similar *values* 'hard work', 'achievement' and 'deferred gratification'.

7. The primary school which the child had attended influenced the development of the child. Probably the 'neighbourhood' and the consequent degree of support, encouragement and co-operation from parents accounted for this result.

Douglas concludes that 'perceptive' and 'sympathetic' parents in the early years of a child's life give 'background' and 'meaning' to what is learned.

S. Sharpe in *Just Like a Girl* (1976) emphasises the importance of the family in establishing sex roles particularly in the case of boys.

S. Cotgrove in *Technical Education and Social Change* (now rather dated, published 1958) demonstrated that children from middle-class homes benefit from parental encouragement in several ways but in particular from the guidance which their parents are able to give about careers, interesting courses, or educational alternatives. The cultural background of many children, however, deprives them of this guidance, as their parents have no experience of higher education, no friends with such experience, and often a suspicion that it is of 'no use' to them anyway.

Two Government reports emphasise the importance of home background and parental influence on the educational development of children:

Half Our Future, published in 1963, illustrated the connection between poor environment and poor school performance.

The Plowden Report, *Children and their Primary School*, published in 1967, traced the link between parent's attitudes and school performance:

1. manual workers helped their children less with homework, either from lack of ability, tiredness or disinterest;

2. manual workers were less likely to buy children copies of school books for use at home;

3. two thirds of unskilled workers had five books or less at home (apart from magazines and children's books); this compared with only one in twenty of professional workers having so few books.

This report also reported on the disabilities suffered by children in over-crowded or shared homes and stressed the need to give early help to handicapped children and those with handicapped parents. It also urged 'positive discrimination' to make schools in deprived areas better than those elsewhere.

A move was made in this direction in 1968 when 'social priority area' schools were introduced; teachers in these schools were given a special allowance and the schools some additional finance for equipment. The criteria used to determine which schools were 'social priority' varied but one typical Local Education Authority decided levels of deprivation on the basis of how many children in any school were from large families, one-parent families, immigrant families or in receipt of free school meals, this last factor receiving a double weighting. The special allocations have not been increased in recent years and the effectiveness of the scheme in attracting better staff to the most deprived schools is in doubt.

In 1972 R. Davie, N. Butler and H. Goldstein published *From Birth to Seven* which was the result of a survey carried out for the National Children's Bureau of 17 000 children born during one week of 1958. This report showed consistently lower educational performances by children from working-class homes (a direct correlation between oral ability and social class was found, except that marginally more children from Social class 2 had below average oral ability compared with Social class 3; the biggest divide was between manual and non-manual workers' families).

Children from social class 5 were six times more likely to be poor readers at the age of 7 compared with those from social class 1; and the same children 15 times more likely to be non-readers.

Colin Lacey in *Hightown Grammar* (1970) found that children split into two groups – one accepting the school culture and the other the 'alternative culture' (which might range from supporters of rock music in a public school to a delinquent 'sub-culture' in an urban comprehensive school).

Teachers first assist the groups to develop by ranking the students by a set of criteria based on an academically orientated value system and then repress the 'anti-group' which does not, or cannot, aspire to these norms.

N. Carter in *In to Work* (1966) describes this process of separation: 'The examination groups taking GCE or similar exams have clear targets at which to aim and the work, even if it seems overburdening at times, can be seen to have a purpose. In other groups, however, problems tend to occur through boredom, frustration and, occasionally, aggression. Careers guidance is most difficult in these circumstances. Thus many youngsters, without advice from their parents, tend to drift into jobs knowing very little about the work and less about its prospects.'

The middle-class parents are able to show their children a range of careers, and research shows that they frequently advise their youngsters and discuss career prospects with them either directly or by calling on the assistance of family friends or professional associates. Similarly, the language skills which these youngsters have developed enable them to discuss with others the advantage of differing career structures and they also perform better in interviews with careers teachers, advisers and potential employers.

Various other studies also emphasise the close connection between home, socialisation and academic success.

1. A middle-class child is six times more likely than a working-class child to go to University. The official figures for 1983, collected through UCCA show that 82 per cent of students admitted into Universities are middle class, while only 18 per cent are working class. (M. Rudd, *Higher Education Review*, 1984, disputed the accuracy of these figures as they are based on the applicants' own statement of fathers' occupations, his view was that the true proportion of working-class undergraduates is nearer one third.)

2. About half of what we learn is probably learned before the age of 4.

3. The less formal 'discovery' method of teaching now popular in primary schools probably acts against the working class child who often has not had a home background which encourages the self-motivation required.

4. 'Between eleven and sixteen years, boys become increasingly aware that what they learn at school will influence their future careers and the sort of employment open to them on leaving school. In contrast the girls see themselves entering work which requires little training and which will last only a few years before marriage.' (Douglas, *All Our Future*, Ross and Simpson).

5. Until recently, 16-year-old school-leavers obtained apprenticeships in the following proportions: boys 42 per cent, girls 7 per cent.

6. *Robbins Report* (Report of the Committee on Higher Education 1963) 'The proportion of children reaching full-time higher education is 8 times higher among children whose father left education at 18 or over than among those whose father left school under 16.'

7. 'The less bright in the upper streams tend to make most progress, the most bright in the lower streams will deteriorate most. Streaming is based on 'ability' and the judgment of ability may be influenced by the types of homes the children come from.' (Douglas, *The unconscious biases of selection.*)

8. M. Schofield in discussing the reason for the ineffectiveness of sex education in *The Sexual Behaviour of Young People* (1964) comments 'In fact there is some evidence to suggest that education of all kinds is not the powerful force for social or individual change that we think it is.'

9. G. Peaker studied some of the children seen for the Plowden Report (*Plowden Children Four Years Later* 1971) and estimated that the influence of teaching is only about one third that of home circumstances.

10. A. Little in 1971 ('A Sociological Portrait: Education' in *New Society*) commented that the difference between a good and a bad home is far greater than the difference between good and bad teaching.

It would appear that the problems inherent in the influence of the home environment can effectively nullify any attempt to increase opportunities by changes in school organisation.

Education and equality

Of course, middle class parents may have an advantage. Schools are, on the whole, run by middle class people. So middle class parents are less likely to find the school system intimidating. They know the ropes. They talk the school's language.

Indeed, "talking the school's language" may be of crucial importance. The researches of Basil Bernstein, for example, suggest that the kind of language used in schools may be alien to some working class children and affect their relationship with the school. In America, Labov studied the language of young blacks and found that while their spoken language was extraordinarily rich and sophisticated, they placed scarcely any value on the written language. Through their spoken language, they expressed their own rich culture: a culture which had very little to do with school. Indeed, Labov argues that the reason they did not do well at school was simply because they had no special wish to do well.

This may provide a possible key to the reason West Indians do so poorly in British schools. Professor Alan Little quotes figures for West Indians in London schools, showing that on reading tests they scored far lower than their non-West Indian classmates, lower even than those classmates who came from unskilled manual homes, who traditionally get low scores on such tests.

Little himself (*Education Policies for Multi-Racial Areas*, 1978) thinks teachers may be the cause. He suspects they *expect* West Indian children to do badly and that the children live up to this.

This process, an example of a 'self-fulfilling prophecy', is claimed to work in other areas of education. The current attack on streaming (splitting children into teaching groups of similar tested ability) is based partly on the view that this system damages the changes of the less able and is therefore against the principle of equality of opportunity.

The theory is that children quickly learn what is expected of their stream and conform to the mould. In the top stream, they are expected to be clever and so become clever. In the bottom stream, they are expected to be dunces and so become dunces. The process may then be reinforced by what amounts to streaming the teachers: giving the best teachers and the best facilities to the top stream.

One increasingly popular solution is simply to abolish streaming and teach in groups representing all abilities. This 'mixed ability' approach creates some new problems (it means, for example, much harder work for the teacher). But one fear in particular is often voiced. This is that the system benefits the majority of pupils but sometimes at the expense of the most able.

This was one of the findings of the report, *Mixed Ability Work in Comprehensive School* (1978), put out by the school inspectors. It said that because work tended to be pitched at the level of the average, or below, the most able pupils often either grew bored or 'under-achieved to conform to the level of the majority'.

But then that could be taken as a criticism of poor teaching (why not simply pitch the level higher?) rather than of the mixed-ability system itself—especially as the inspectors say the system worked well for both the average and below, who did better work and had improved self-esteem.

Another attempt to iron out some of the inequalities in education is the idea of 'positive discrimination'. The use of educational priority areas—recommended by the Plowden report, 1967—puts more money into schools in deprived areas. But if American experience is anything to go by, the results may be disappointing (see C. Jencks, *Inequality*, 1972).

Meanwhile, more resources are being put into pre-school education (another Plowden recommendation). Numbers in pre-school training have doubled over the past decade. This, like the raising of the school-leaving age in 1972, and the recent government proposal to pay 16–18 year-olds an allowance if they stay on at school,* reflects a general belief that education can solve social problems. So it is ironic that this all comes at a time when many sociologists are beginning to voice doubts about the use of education, in isolation, as a way of changing society.

A. H. Halsey has said quite bluntly that the usefulness of education as a means of increasing equality of opportunity is now severely in question. 'Schools' he wrote in *Educational Priority* (HMSO, 1972), 'cannot accomplish important social reforms such as the democratisation of opportunity unless social reforms accompany the educational effort.'

So far there is little sign of that happening. (*New Society*, 26 October 1978.)

*The experimental allowance to 16–18-year-olds was not proceeded with; by 1982 spending on pre-school education had been cut back as a result of Government spending cuts. (My comment, *auth*.)

8.4 SEX, RACE AND PEER GROUP

Just as social class influences educational success so does the sex of the child. As the class gap widens as the educational level increases so does the level of achievement between boys and girls.

A study of children born in 1940 and 1941 (HMSO, 1963) showed that 63.8 per cent of boys and only 40.7 per cent of girls continued their education after the statutory leaving age; at 'A' level the gap had widened to 19.1 per cent and 10.6 per cent respectively, and degree studies increased it further to 5.8 per cent and 3.0 per cent.

The raising of the school-leaving age to 16 in 1972 dramatically altered the position at the lower end of the qualification ladder. The number of boys leaving school with at least one 'O' level increased by almost 50 per cent to 201 000; the number of girls by 60 per cent to 212 000; indicating no lack of potential. In fact girls tend to be more successful than boys at primary school and in the first years of secondary education. However the absence of compulsion higher up the ladder has meant that the gap between male and female, though narrower than formerly, still exists. In 1981, 35 per cent of boys and 43 per cent of girls left school with at least one 'O' level; 17 per cent of boys and 16 per cent of girls left with at least one 'A' level and 9.3 per cent of boys and 6.8 per cent of girls went on to degree courses.

Girls are still often socialised to anticipate marriage as their major fulfilment in life. Careers are secondary, and orientated towards traditional 'women's jobs' such as clerical work and nursing which do not demand a level of entry as high as some of the entrants' ability would warrant. It has also been suggested that 'labelling' may also explain gender differences. Teachers tend to expect girls to be more passive and compliant and girls tend to accept this label and think it natural for boys to ask questions, challenge the teacher and demand explanations. Girls have also been socialised to accept an inferior position and be submissive towards males and thus under-achieve.

Many of the disabilities of the native English working class relate also to the members of ethnic minorities, particularly West Indians; but their disadvantage is compounded by colour prejudice and – particularly for the Asian community – language problems. It has also been suggested that culture-biased intelligence tests put many black children in ESN schools who should not be there. (*How the West Indian Child is made Educationally Sub-Normal in the British School System*, B. Coard, 1971).

Fig. 8.1 *the sex gap; the race gap; the class gap*

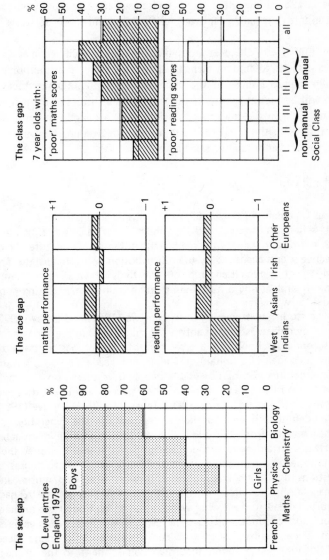

SOURCE   Department of Education and Science (printed in *New Society*, 1984)

Among some black teenagers there is growing alienation to the educational system not only because many fail to achieve within it; but also because they have seen those among them who do succeed fail to get jobs in line with their qualifications. The government-sponsored *Rampton Report* in 1981 showed that black children suffered at school from racism, inappropriate curricula, language difficulties and poor relations with teachers.

The influence of the peer group increases as the child becomes a young adult and seeks to find an identity and status away from the home, and naturally many of those of the same age who will influence the young person will be met at school. If the values and attitudes of the neighbourhood are antagonistic towards education, these are likely to be the values and attitudes of the peer group and an individual young person will find it hard to resist adopting the same approach.

School and youth culture

James Coleman (1961) studied the friendship groups in ten American high schools and concluded that they formed a youth subculture with norms and values at variance with those of adults, often being effectively anti-academic by their distribution of informal status and granting of group friendship on the basis of wearing the latest fashions and having a high dating-rating, rather than getting good grades for work.

The studies of streaming by Hargreaves (1967) and Lacey (1970) have shown the existence of antischool subcultures in the low streams of secondary schools but a great deal of research has contradicted Coleman's idea of a unitary anti-adult, anti-academic youth culture in this country. Studies of young people have shown how strongly conformist many are in terms of their general attitudes and social ambitions (Eppelard Eppel, 1966, Veness, 1962). Musgrove (1964) concluded that if any conflict exists between the generations, it comes mainly from the adult side. Sugarman (1967) investigated fourteen-year-old boys in four London Schools, and measured their commitment to a possible youth culture in terms of responses to questions about smoking, going out with girls, pop music, and teenage fashions. Those with a high commitment to the 'teenage culture' tended to have what were judged to be poorer attitudes to school and conduct, and to have lower levels of academic achievement. These results may seem to confirm some of Coleman's ideas, but Sugarman also found that high commitment to the 'teenage culture' was particularly associated with working-class boys, and so he preferred to explain their poor conduct and achievement in social class terms. He concluded that, 'Youth culture is the culture of the non-mobile working class youth'.

Murdock and Phelps (1972) took Sugarman's analysis further, and in a study of a larger number of teenage school children make a distinction between 'street culture' and 'pop media culture'. The former is particularly associated with working class boys in urban areas, and uses the streets, cafes and other public places for its locale. It emphasises physical toughness, looking after yourself, and sticking with your mates. In contrast, the pop media culture is associated with girls, particularly from middle-class backgrounds. It is home-based and centres on records, magazines, television and radio programmes concerned with pop music. Murdock and Phelps suggest that adherence to either of these two cultures may be associated with rejection of school. In an associated piece of research Murdock and McCron (1973) describe a whole range of identities associated with pop music, ranging from the Top Twenty, followed mainly by younger girls, to progressive rock and underground music listened to by academic, often middle-class older boys. Statements about young people should be viewed with the same caution as any that might be made about 'middle-aged people'; they are as socially diverse and varied as any other age group. [Ronald King, *Education* (London: Longmans, 1977) 2nd edn (slightly adapted).]

QUESTIONS FROM RECENT O LEVEL GCE PAPERS

1. 'Not rebelliousness, but mass consumption and the mass media, have created youth culture.' Discuss.

London Examining Board

2. 'The first five years of a child's life are the most critical in his or her educational development.' Discuss.

Oxford Local Examining Board

3. In a recent sociological study of schools, pupils were asked how they thought teachers saw them and whether teachers put pupils into groups in their minds. This conversation followed:

Pupil: Well, they do. Bright ones over there, dim ones there and medium ones in the middle, things like that.

Sociologist: Where do you see yourself fitting into that?

Pupil: Oh, I'm one of the thick, stupid ones at the bottom.

Pupil: She sort of separates out those who can do it and those who can't do it. If you're stuck with those who can't do it. . .you never get any further.

Pupil: Yes, they're always helping the brainy ones and they're the ones who don't really need help.

Pupil: I mean, I'm pink band, that means I'm not very bright. The teachers tell you that. It's the same in all my lessons. You get split up into groups in the lesson. I'm always with the bottom ones.

Cathy Bird, Deviant Labelling in the School — The Pupils' Perspective, P. Woods (editor) *Pupil Strategies*, 1980.)

(a) Explain how the sort of social interaction described in the passage may influence the pupil's identity and lead to the formation of sub-cultures. [10]

(b) With reference to any *one* sub-cultural group you have studied

(i) describe the cultural style of the group
(ii) explain the social factors which have influenced its development. [10]

Cambridge Local Examining Board

4. 'Differences in socialisation mean little: hereditary differences are what matter.' Discuss   London Examining Board

5. **Either,** (a) Describe in detail **three** ways in which social factors may influence people's educational achievement.

Or, (b) Explain the meaning of 'tripartite' and 'comprehensive' secondary education, and outline the arguments advocating comprehensive secondary schools.

Welsh Joint Examining Board

6. **Either,** (a) Comment on any **three** aspects of the school as a social organisation.

Or, (b) Explain what is meant by *equal educational opportunity* and comment on any two sources of inequality and suggest how these might best be alleviated or overcome.

Welsh Joint Examining Board

7. The attainment of all the pupils in our study was tested at the age of 11 as well as the age of 16 and hence it was possible to examine the scores at 16 of various groups of children who began secondary schooling with the same range of test scores at 11. The results made it clear that the differences in attainment between disadvantaged and ordinary children accumulate during adolescence. The differences that exist when they are 11 increase during the secondary school period. In fact this evidence accords with much of previous research which has shown a

progressively widening gap between children of differing back-grounds.

(From P. Wedge and J. Essen, *Children in Adversity*, 1981.)

(a) What social circumstances are usually regarded as putting certain children at a disadvantage at school?   [8]
(b) How have sociologists explained the progressively widening gap between children of differing backgrounds?   [12]

Cambridge Local Examining Board

THE SOCIAL CLASS OF STUDENTS AT UNIVERSITY

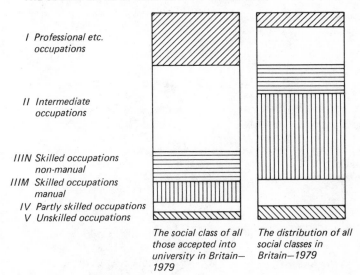

I Professional etc. occupations

II Intermediate occupations

IIIN Skilled occupations non-manual
IIIM Skilled occupations manual
IV Partly skilled occupations
V Unskilled occupations

The social class of all those accepted into university in Britain— 1979

The distribution of all social classes in Britain—1979

(*Adapted from* 'Report' in *New Society,* 18 September 1980)

8.

(a) According to the evidence above, from which social class did the greatest proportion come of those accepted into university in 1979?   (1)
(b) Which social class has a share of university places approxi-mately equal to its proportion in wider society?   (2)
(c) Which of the social classifications used in the chart make up the 'working class'?   (3)
(d) Suggest **three** other ways in which sociologists have shown that the middle class are more 'successful' than the working class in the education system.   (6)
(e) 'Teachers' attitudes can affect the educational performance of pupils.' Discuss.   (8)

PART IV
SOCIAL DIFFERENTIATION

STRATIFICATION

9.1 AGE STRATIFICATION/STATUS

In virtually all societies some people are regarded as more important than others; more worthy of respect or more useful than others either within the society as a whole or in certain situations. This position relative to that of other people in the group is called 'status' and may be based on many factors such as wealth, heredity, possessions, sex, education, skin colour, job, 'social worth' or age. This 'prestige' may also depend on particular abilities regarded as of high worth within the group so that some young people will deliberately spend many hours becoming expert in pop-music so as to earn high status with their peers.

Status may not always be consistent. For example, a person may have high status by reason of occupation but a low status by reason of colour. Nor will everyone necessarily agree with the status ranking. For example, one study (Young and Willmott, *Family and Kinship in East London*) found that about a quarter of those interviewed put skilled manual jobs in a higher status position than routine non-manual.

Status may be 'ascribed', that is, acquired with no effort on our we may have ascribed status as a nobleman or parent. We may also earn our status by acquiring a high ranking job or by earning a reputation for caring for others, in which case our status is 'achieved'.

The most basic way of placing people in layers by their worth ('stratification') is by age. In most societies younger people are not regarded as worthy of as much respect as older people because their knowledge and skill is less. Young people have less responsibility and as a result less power; in some societies the oldest people have most power ('gerontocracies').

In our society the old, as non-producers and often poor, lack power and as a result lose status; this loss of status has increased in recent years as the extended family has lost many of its functions and the old are increasingly isolated.

Status may be based on sex

"In my day we <u>called</u> them ladies and <u>treated</u> them like women."

The young on the other hand often have a greater surplus of income over expenditure on necessities compared with their parents (section 6.4); work skills are no longer usually learned at home; parents are often ignorant of subjects taught at school; the traditional scorn of the old for the ignorant young is often reversed.

9.2 FEUDALISM

Apart from age most societies have some form of general stratification placing certain groups of people in superior and inferior positions, a 'hierarchy', of prestige and power. Most societies can be classified into one of three major types of stratification:
(a) feudal (or 'estate');
(b) caste;
(c) social class.
The three 'estates' were Nobility, Church and Townspeople each with their own status systems; the peasants were sometimes regarded as a fourth estate.

The best known example of the feudal system was in mediaeval Europe where there was a pyramid of interlocking obligations between 'lord' and 'vassal' based upon the grant of a 'fief', which was usually land but could be an office or a means of collecting revenue such as the right to collect a 'toll'. In return for this fief and for protection the vassal accepted certain obligations: to fight for his lord; accept the judgement of the lord's court; and pay his lord certain sums on particular occasions.

Essentially the idea of feudalism was one of 'tenancy'. Everyone was a tenant to a lord higher than themself until one came to the King and he was a tenant of God. As only God was the King's master only God had a right to overthrow him, thus we had the concept of 'the divine right of kings'.

Although feudalism did not always exactly follow the idea of a pyramid structure, for example a Knight might hold land directly from the King rather than from a Baron, it gave each individual a fixed place in a hierarchy which could only be changed by providing an outstanding service to one higher than oneself. Usually marriage took place to others from the same position in the social hierarchy as oneself. Escape from one's social situation was usually only possible by removing oneself from the service contract of rights and duties. Social mobility could however also take place by joining the church, which was open to people of any rank, and churchmen could reach high status positions both in the church itself and as civil servants. However in Western Europe the clergy were celibate and so the social mobility of clerics was for one generation only and did not challenge the established order.

One of the few methods of escaping from the feudal situation was to move to a town, where work could be exchanged for money. It was the growth of towns; increasing circulation of money; political centralisation and professional courts that led to the ending of feudalism in Europe.

9.3 CASTE

A caste system of stratification does not rest as a feudal system does on man-made laws, which can be modified. It is based on a system of religious belief that cannot be changed and it is therefore even more rigid than the feudal system.

The best example of caste is the Hindu caste system of India which has existed for some 3000 years and was only officially abolished in 1947. The restrictions on social mobility imposed by the system are still very much in evidence. Hindus belong to one of four main groups, the Kshatriyas (warriors), Brahmans (priests), Vaishyas (traders and manufacturers), and the Sudras (servants) or they are 'outcasts' doing the most lowly work, or that associated with leather, from the sacred cow. Each group has a rigid status position, and within the main groups are many castes and sub-castes each of which occupies a fixed position in the social structure. The 1901 Census identified 2378 main castes; and 1700 sub-castes within just one of these main castes!

Status does not depend primarily upon wealth. Brahmans are of high caste though bound by poverty, leatherworkers may be rich. The caste system is based on the Hindu doctrine of reincarnation – good behaviour meriting re-birth into a higher caste – and this gives hope of a better future to those who work within the system.

There are strict food laws, and the breaking of these or other caste rules results in ritual pollution and a drop in status. Marriage is 'endogamous', i.e. it must take place within the caste, although within certain limits a woman may move up to her husband's caste on marriage, this being the only form of social mobility permitted.

9.4 SOCIAL CLASS

In both caste and feudal systems it is either impossible or very difficult to rise to a higher social stratum, status is 'ascribed'. If merit is to be rewarded it is difficult for either system to survive.

The economic system of 'capitalism' in which some people are free to sell what is produced for their own profit, while others are legally free to sell their labour where they like made 'feudalism' obsolete. 'Social classes' emerged in which there was no legal or religious barrier to moving up or down the social scale ('vertical social mobility') although there was, and still are, often grave practical difficulties in doing so.

As feudalism died out and social 'classes' became established those families which occupied high prestige positions under the old order often continued to do so, as they had the wealth or 'capital' available to invest in developing their lands, industry or commerce in order to produce a surplus income of 'profit'.

As the industrial revolution developed in the nineteenth century Karl Marx, a German Jew living as a refugee in England, developed a theory of social class in which he saw society as divided between groups of people with a common identity in relation to the means of production – people who owned or did not own the capital to invest, or with which to acquire ownership of the means of production, distribution and exchange.

Marx did not see society merely as groups of people who were poor, rich or somewhere in the middle. A teacher, a shopkeeper, an owner of a small dress factory and a skilled mechanic might earn the same amount of money but would not belong to the same class.

Marx believed that as industry developed, and large numbers of workers were grouped together, they would realize that they had class interests in common. This 'proletariat' would rise up against their exploiters and replace them in a society of equals. Class conflict and class-consciousness are essential parts of Marx's theory of class.

Capital and class

The value of every commodity is measured by the labour required for its production. Labour power exists in the form of the living worker who requires a definite amount of means of subsistence for his existence as well as for the maintenance of his family, which ensures the continuance of labour power also after his death. The labour time necessary for producing these means of subsistence represents, therefore, the value of labour power. The capitalist pays this value weekly and purchases for that the use of one week's labour of the worker.

The capitalist now sets his worker to work. In a certain period of time the worker will have performed as much labour as was represented by his weekly wages. Supposing that the weekly wage of a worker represents three workdays, then if the worker begins on Monday, he has by Wednesday evening *replaced* to the capitalist the *full value of the wage paid*. But does he then stop working? Not at all. The capitalist has bought his *week*'s labour and the worker must go on working also during the last three week days. This *surplus labour* of the worker, over and above the time necessary to replace his wages, is the *source of surplus value*, of profit, of the steadily growing increase of capital. . . The day the capitalist extracts from the worker in the long run only as much labour as he paid him in wages, on that day he will shut down his workshop, since indeed his whole profit would come to nought.

Here we have the solution of all those contradictions. The origin of surplus value (of which the capitalists' profit forms an important part) is now quite clear and natural. The value of the labour power is paid for, but this value is far less than that which the capitalist manages to extract from the labour power, and it is just the difference, the *unpaid labour*, which constitutes the share of the capitalist, or, more accurately, of the capitalist class.

It would, however, be absurd to assume that unpaid labour arose only under present conditions where production is carried on by capitalists on the one hand and wage-workers on the other. On the contrary, the oppressed class at all times has had to perform unpaid labour. During the whole long period when slavery was the prevailing form of the organization of labour, the slaves had to perform much more labour than was returned to them in the form of means of subsistence. The same was the case under the rule of serfdom; here in fact the difference stands out palpably between the time during which the peasant works for his own maintenance and the surplus labour for the lord of the manor, precisely because the latter is carried out separately from the former. The form has now been changed, but the substance remains and as long as 'a part of society possesses the monopoly of the means of production, the labourer, free or not free, must add to the working-time necessary for his own maintenance an extra working-time in order to produce the means of subsistence for the owners of the means of production'. [Karl Marx, *Capital*, vol. I, (abridged).]

Marx died in 1883, and another German Max Weber developed a rather different theory of class in the early twentieth century. By this time it was clear that the class in the middle of the capitalists and proletariat had not disappeared as Marx had anticipated, but had grown in number and importance; while trade unions and Parliament had stopped some of the worst exploitation in industry.

Weber thought that the most important aspect of class was a person's ability to gain access to 'life chances' – that is, goods and services. Although he identified four main classes – manual workers, petty bourgeoise, professionals and property owners – Weber did not think of a polarised society as did Marx, but one where there were many status rankings and power groupings. Usually a person with power also had status but it was not always so.

Today there is still support for Marx's theory, but more generally the word 'class' is used more in the way that Weber used it. The main access to life chances is through occupation, and this has become a major way of dividing people into class (or 'socio-economic') groupings.

The scale used by the government in the census is often called the Registrar-General's scale.

I	Professional occupations
II	Intermediate occupations (including most managerial and senior administrative occupations)
IIIN (or a)	Skilled occupations (non-manual)
IIIM (or b)	Skilled occupations (manual)
IV	Partly skilled occupations
V	Unskilled occupations
	(The armed forces, students, and those whose occupation was inadequately described are listed separately)

Several attempts have been made to produce a more sophisticated scale. One often used is the Hall-Jones scale which splits social class III into three separate classes. This is because more than half the population are in social class III and the division between 'working class' (IIIb and below) and 'middle class' (IIIa and above) is in that group.

Social Class 1 and 2	(The same as the Registrar General Scale)
Social Class 3	Inspectional, supervisory and other non-manual, higher grade
Social Class 4	Inspectional, supervisory and other non-manual, lower grade
Social Class 5	Skilled manual and routine grades of non-manual

Social Class 6   (As Registrar General IV)
Social Class 7   (As Registrar General V)

One criticism of the Hall-Jones scale is that it gives too high a status to white-collar occupations.

In Britain, the 'upper class' of landed gentry is too tiny a group to be recognised by most people as a distinct 'class. and there is no special class of very small scale farmers – 'peasants' – as there is on the Continent.

Official assessment of a person's class position is not always accepted by the person concerned. Many people place themselves in a higher class position than would the Registrar General; such placement is known as 'self-assigned class'. In *Must Labour Lose?* (1961) Abrams and Rose found that 30 per cent of manual workers in their survey considered themselves to be middle class.

CHAPTER 10

WEALTH AND INCOME

10.1 WEALTH AND POWER

Usually a higher class position means that the person concerned is richer either through earnings or investment – this 'wealth' is the accumulation of money or property in its many forms. Wealth buys access to 'life's chances': health care; education; housing; holidays. These life chances may thus influence such factors as expectation of life; infant mortality; height and weight of children; illness or school achievement.

Wealth also buys access to power – positions of authority where there can be a direct influence on the decision-making processes whether as company directors or Members of Parliament. Power is now however much more diffuse than formerly.

Earned income may reflect the fact that a person has reached a position of power, but education rather than personal wealth may have put them there. However, it is much easier for the children of middle-class parents to achieve educationally than it is for children of the working class (section 8.3).

In considering wealth in Britain, it should be noted that the lower one goes on the social scale, the more the wealth that is owned comprises 'consumer durables' such as washing machines or cars, houses, and insurance policies. None of these can normally be sold without replacement and therefore cannot be used to buy access to power. As one goes up the social scale the more the wealth that is owned comprises shareholding, bank deposits and cash which is readily available for use. Such ownership may also be psychologically beneficial to the owners in that they need not be fearful of losing their jobs and therefore feel a much greater freedom to express themselves as they wish.

Although wealth certainly does increase one's chances of access to power it must be remembered that trade unions in Britain are normally controlled today by those with little personal wealth, and yet the trade union movement has tremendous power.

Fig. 10.1 *composition of marketable wealth of individuals*

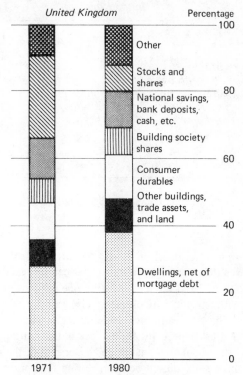

SOURCE *Social Trends 13, 1983* (London HMSO 1982).

10.2 DISTRIBUTION OF WEALTH IN BRITAIN

In *Relative Deprivation and Social Justice* (1962) Runciman stated that 'it can safely be said that only among the non-manual class is there any significant accumulation of wealth' and quoted a 1954 estimate that the top one per cent of British adults owned 43 per cent of total net capital and the top 10 per cent owned 79 per cent. An even higher estimate for inequality of wealth ownership was given in 'The Meaning of Class' (*New Society*, 1964) '5 per cent of the population owned 75 per cent of all personal wealth'.

The major reason for differences in estimations of wealth distribution in Britain is that different surveys take different factors into account; some include insurance policies, housing and consumer goods, some do not. Another problem is that wealth is deliberately concealed to avoid the payment of tax.

Table 10.1 *distribution of wealth in the United Kingdom*

	United Kingdom		Percentages	
			1971	1980
Marketable wealth				
Percentage of wealth owned by:				
Most wealthy	*1 per cent of population*		*31*	*23*
" "	*2* " " " "		*39*	*30*
" "	*5* " " " "		*52*	*43*
" "	*10* " " " "		*65*	*58*
" "	*25* " " " "		*86*	*81*
" "	*50* " " " "		*97*	*94*

SOURCE *Social Trends* 1983 (London HMSO 1982).

The Government publication *Social Trends* lists the distribution of 'marketable wealth', that is, those items that can be readily changed into cash if required. In 1980 the most wealthy one per cent of the population are credited with 25 per cent of the wealth (a drop of 8 per cent from 1971). This decline in wealth ownership during the decade by the top one per cent is counterbalanced by the almost static position of the bottom 50 per cent of the population who shared 6 per cent of the national wealth in 1980, an increase of only 3 per cent during the period (see charts). It is apparent that there is an even greater disparity within the society when one considers what *kind* of wealth. The *less* wealth you have the more likely it is to be in the form of house ownership, consumer durables and insurance policies. The *more* wealth you have the more likely it is to be in the form of shareholding and bank deposits (in other words money that can be used to achieve power).

Income is less unequally shared than wealth. Excluding the lowest paid and others not paying any income tax the bottom 10 per cent of taxpayers received 2.9 per cent of the National Income (3.4 per cent after tax) and the top 10 per cent of taxpayers received 24.8 per cent of the National Income (22.8 per cent after tax) in the 1979–80 fiscal year.

10.3 POVERTY

In the 1870s a rich Liverpool merchant, Charles Booth, objected to a statement made by the Social Democratic Federation that a quarter of the population were living in poverty. He carried out surveys himself to prove the point and was shocked to find that his estimation was even higher.

The old are often poor in modern Britain

Later, Booth expressed his own concern at the lack of any systematic study of poverty: 'More minute, patient intelligent observation has been devoted to the study of earthworms than to the evolution, or rather degradation, of the sunken section of our people. Here and there in the immense field individual workers make notes, and occasionally emit a wail of despair.'

Booth drew up a statistical definition of poverty and as a base defined a 'poverty line' under which it was impossible to live a healthy life, this concept of poverty is known as absolute (or subsistence) poverty. Booth published his findings in *Life and Labour of the People* (1889-91) and *Life and Labour of the People in London* (1891-1903). He went on to assist in the passing of the *Old Age Pensions Act* in 1908.

In 1899 Rowntree developed Booth's work in a survey of poverty in York in which he showed for example that 'infant mortality' – the number of children who died in their first year of life out of every 1000 who had been born alive during that year – was 247 for families under his poverty line and 173 for those above it. Rowntree found that in a quarter of his 'poor' families the major wage-earner was dead, ill, disabled or unemployed. About half of the poor families had an employed head, but their earnings were insufficient to keep the family above the poverty line.

In modern times many money allowances and grants in kind have been introduced to reduce poverty, but those in poverty still tend to be those in the categories listed by Rowntree: the old; the mentally and physically disabled; the ill; single-parent families, and those with large families but low incomes, or who are unemployed.

Supplementary benefits, old age pensions, rent and rate rebates, and family income supplements, for those who have a family and a job but whose earnings fail to reach a certain level, have all helped to reduce poverty. However, benefits still guarantee only a fairly low level of subsistence and because many of those who are poor are also least able to care for themselves, or to manage money, their position is made worse. Also, many do not know the benefits to which they are entitled or are too proud to make a claim.

A 'culture of poverty' often exists among the poor which leads to a passive acceptance of their position allied to a hostility towards authority. Children growing up in a neighbourhood where such attitudes are the norm are likely to leave school early and enter unskilled and often low paid, uncertain employment; marry early, and have larger families than people elsewhere in Britain. In turn their children are likely to grow up equally deprived so that poverty becomes 'cyclical' – it is likely to be unbroken like a circle from generation to generation.

Poverty

However, the Beveridge plan has never been fully implemented as it was intended. Neither family allowances (now called child benefits) nor national insurance benefits have been paid at the level advocated by Beveridge. The result has been that more and more people have to come to depend on supplementary benefits, which are means tested. For instance, government figures show that the number of people claiming supplementary benefit rose from little over a million in 1948 to almost three million by 1977 [3 910 000 by 1983].

The type of people who are poor has also changed in that time. In 1955, retirement pensioners and their dependants made up 61 per cent of people dependent on supplementary benefits. By 1976, that proportion had fallen to 42 per cent.

Today's poverty line is generally reckoned to be the level at which supplementary benefits are payable. According to the government's Family Expenditure Survey, the numbers of people living below the official poverty line rose from nearly $1\frac{1}{2}$ million in 1974 to nearly $2\frac{1}{4}$ million in 1976. The number of people who were in full-time work and earning less than they could get on supplementary benefits rose from 130,000 to 290,000 in the same period. These kind of figures certainly help to put into perspective the newspaper headlines we often see about dole-scroungers.

Who are the poor in Britain today? One major group, obviously, is the low paid. One way of defining low pay is as anything less than two thirds of average earnings. On current rates, this is about £60 a week. Last year there were 1.7 million men and 2.7 million women earning below this level. Very often these people are in such trades as catering, laundries, motor repairs and hairdressing. But the government employs many low-paid people, particularly in the health service, education and public administration.

The low-paid, unskilled worker is estimated to have about eight times more chance of becoming unemployed than the professional worker. This leads to more of the unskilled using up their rights to unemployment benefit (which ends after a period of time) and becoming dependent on supplementary benefit. Last year, almost half the unemployed in Britain were drawing supplementary benefit.

Another big group of poor people is the old. In 1976 870,000 old people were living below supplementary benefit level. This is not only because of inadequate pensions, but because many old people view benefits as charity and are too proud to take them up. Some do not know what their rights are with regard to supplementary benefits. It is very likely that we shall read in the papers in the coming months of old people dying of hypothermia because they have been unable to afford adequate heat or food.

Sickness is another big cause of poverty. The 1976 General Household Survey shows that unskilled people are three times as likely as professional workers to become chronically sick. But these people are also far less likely to be covered by sick pay schemes at work. Disabled and handicapped people also tend to be afflicted by poverty. A survey in 1971 showed that between 35 and 40 per cent of disabled people were on supplementary benefit, that they were often housed inadequately and that their education and employment opportunties were limited. Since then a system of benefits for invalids has been introduced, but there are still about a quarter of a million disabled people on supplementary benefit. Disabled people are also three times more likely to be unemployed.

The poor can also be found among residents of institutions and people who have had to give up work to look after an elderly relative at home. The fastest growing group in poverty, though, is the single-parent family. This does not mean just unmarried mothers, but separated and divorced wives, divorced women, widows and prisoners' wives. Increasingly, it is coming to include single fathers with children, too. The number of single-parent families increased by 32 per cent between 1971 and 1976. [*New Society*, 4 October 1979. (Inserts in brackets have been added).]

Poverty trap

The Welfare State
National welfare benefits supplement low occupational wages or, in some situations, substitute for an earned income. The welfare state

has expanded considerably since the last world war and its general aim has been to help those without alternative support. However, its effectiveness has been questioned (Kincaid, 1973). Abel-Smith (1958) observed that the social services since the war had apparently most benefitted the middle classes and Webb and Sieve (1971) noted that this was still the case over a decade later.

Direct monetary benefits may be either contingent upon circumstance (such as family allowances) or economic status (such as supplementary benefit). The cause of non-take-up is sometimes ignorance of availability or eligibility and sometimes fear of stigma. On the other hand, flat rate benefits will not reduce income inequalities unless they are subject to taxation or clawback.

One criticism that has sometimes been levelled against welfare benefits is that they may have adverse effects upon incentives. The general cry raised is that unemployment benefits will discourage men from work. However, on the whole the evidence is against a major effect of this kind. and the majority of the unemployed appear keen to work. Men who are judged 'workshy' do, in any case, forfeit most of their benefits.

Taxation

Incentives may however be affected by combined effects of benefits and taxation. There is the example of the 'poverty trap' whereby large changes in income status are not reflected in large changes in net take-home pay. This catches the low wage earner hoping to improve his financial position. If he has an income below the statutory requirement level, but is working full-time, he is not entitled to supplementary benefit. His alternative is to gain a larger occupational income. However, if he is able to achieve permanent increases in earnings he may become caught in the trap and make only very slight gains in net income, or possibly even a loss. The trap is that higher wages are accompanied by greater tax demands and the loss of certain means-tested benefits. Piachaud (1971) indicated that a married man with four children could become subject to what amounted to a 130 per cent tax rate on extra earnings below the poverty line. Field and Piachaud (1971) showed that a family man earning an extra £1 gross per week could in fact benefit by only 15p. Income rises might thus have no effect greater than that of combatting inflation. Bradshaw and Wakeman (1972) examined the situation following certain policy changes — including tax threshold moves and the introduction of Family Income Supplements and rent rebates — to assess the hypothetical effects. It appeared that full take-up of benefits would mean a reduction of severe poverty but not an eradication of the poverty trap phenomenon. The low-paid worker would be caught on a plateau at the supplementary benefit level.

Bradshaw and Wakeman (1972) wrote: 'the families that are having to bolster their standard of living by taking up means-tested benefits are trapped in or around poverty. Their situation is hopeless. If they increase their income they may suffer from a deterioration in their living standards. Whether they know the real reason or confuse it with the general effects of rising prices is really immaterial. The important point is that they start in poverty and end in poverty.'

Fatherless families are trapped in a similar way. As described earlier, mothers with dependent children receive supplementary benefit and are not obliged to work. However, if they do wish to have a job they are unable to increase their net income unless they can earn above the supplementary benefit level.

Lower paid workers have increasingly suffered from taxation. More and more people have been drawn into the tax net since the last world war. [M. Rutter and N. Madge, *Cycles of Disadvantage* (London: Heinemann, 1976).]

NOTE In 1979 the Family Expenditure Survey calculated that 30 000 families with children might receive no increase from a £1 rise in earnings; 60 000 might receive less than 25p.

The family and the culture of poverty

The idea of personal life-style as a causal factor in poverty was inherent in Oscar Lewis' (1962) work in Mexico. The concept of 'the culture of poverty' was based on psychological attributes which maintained people in a situation of poverty.

How do the welfare services in Britain deal with poor families who may be deemed to be deviant, or morally reprehensible, or typical of 'the culture of poverty'? Within our services welfare resources have been utilized least by the very poorest and most needy in our society. This fact has been well documented by Kincaid (1973) who described the shadow of Poor Law discriminations in the social security system:

It seems that in spite of enormous advances in living standards, the very poorest consistently fail to utilize the welfare services available; or alternatively this may be due to differential treatment by providers.

Georgie and Joan were a couple in their mid-thirties. They were unmarried, and had four children ranging from five to ten years of age. Joan grew up in the city, she was the fourth of six children and her father was an unskilled workman. Joan spent most of her early life in a council house in an area that has a stigmatized reputation. On leaving school Joan worked in a variety of domestic occupations, but she continued to live at home.

She met Georgie in a pub, and brought him home one night to sleep when he was locked out of his lodgings. Georgie afterwards continued to live with Joan's family, and the couple in the ensuing years had three children. Georgie had come from Liverpool; he was the only child of a labourer. They had lived in a poor area of the inner city, and during his childhood the family were rehoused on an estate at Kirkby, referred to as 'The New Jerusalem' by Barbara Castle (1979) when it was built; it is now a desert of vandalized and deserted dwellings.

Georgie described his first impressions of the area as follows: 'We had never been in the country you see . . . there was a cornfield at the bottom of the road. We all ran through it, you know, creeping through the long grass, hiding from each other and rolling about. I'll always remember it – it was so lovely. We were prosecuted for trespass and fined £2.10 shillings each, I'll always remember it.' This was his first brush with authority.

When Joan was expecting her fourth child, the family were still living at her mother's home. The household consisted of seven children and eight adults; Joan and Georgie and their three children, Joan's sister and her husband and one child, another sister, her husband and three children, her mother and unmarried brother.

The Housing Department at this point evicted the whole household for rent-arrears. The other members of the family found shelter with friends or relatives elsewhere.

Joan and Georgie had nowhere to go, and the birth of the fourth child was imminent. The Social Service Department took the family to a Hostel for the Homeless . . . After five years in the substandard house Georgie contracted pulmonary tuberculosis. He began coughing up blood before he sought medical advice and the disease was finally diagnosed, and he was admitted to hospital for three months.

The house had deteriorated further, and there were two broken windows. The bailiff was calling regularly and threatening the family with eviction if the rent-arrears were not paid off. At this time they were about £60, and Joan often 'lay low' and did not answer the door. One night Joan was late collecting her children from an after-school club, the teacher took the children home, was shocked by the condition of the house, and called the Social Services Department. A subsequent visit from a social worker resulted in the children being taken 'into care' temporarily . . . The Housing Department had agreed at this time to provide another house for the family to give them a chance to begin anew.

However, this was agreed on condition that the present house they occupied was improved. Joan continued to go to work, and acting on advice from the Social Worker she claimed a rent rebate which reduced her rent to 29p per week. However, officials insisted that this rebate could not be back-dated and she was still accountable for her existing debt. There was an unpleasant encounter with the bailiff, who embarrassingly came to interview her at her place of work.

Georgie returned home resentful and angry, and still very weak after his prolonged stay in hospital. The Department of Health and Social Security Officials insisted that he came to the office personally; he was at this time sleeping downstairs as he had difficulty with the stairs.

Georgie took a taxi to the Social Security Office about two miles away. I saw him by chance sitting in the queue. An official was shouting to him from behind the counter: 'You say you have no money, how can you afford a taxi then to get here? You say you have had TB, why are you smoking then?' Georgie sat on the chair a small frail figure, reduced physically from his former confidence and strength, his feet barely touching the floor.

While officials struggled to make Georgie conform, his children grew up in the shadow of poverty, chronic unemployment, ill-health, poor housing and alcohol addiction.

The cycle of deprivation can be traced in this history – Joan began her life in a street with a stigmatized reputation, she moved full-circle down to the bottom of the public housing hierarchy and back to her former position on the housing estate where she grew up. Housing officials took little account of Joan's chronic ill-health or the obvious poverty of the household. The bailiff was not trained, or professionally equipped to deal with tenants' problems, but for an extensive period he was the only official who made any contact with the family. Similarly, the sporadic visitations of social workers exhorting Joan to clean the house and pay the rent were ineffective in counteracting the downward spiral of the family fortunes. Despair and apathy overwhelmed Joan when Georgie went into hospital.

Joan's fear of the bailiff presented her from contacting the Housing Department, she had avoided officials because of her inability to pay the rent. In so doing she had failed to claim the benefits to which she was entitled.

Much of the household furniture and equipment had been bought 'on the club' on credit. Georgie and Joan had four club cards. When they had tried to obtain Hire Purchase from the local shops, they were refused when they revealed their address on a stigamatized housing estate. However, the local 'clubman' who went door-to-door allowed them to have anything but at high interest rates.

Georgie died in 1978 at the age of thirty-six. The fact was that, relatively speaking, Georgie as a semi-skilled workman could have provided for his family. However, his life-style and heavy drinking in particular created health, emotional and financial problems, and an environment of almost Dickensian poverty for his wife and four children. By his own admission he was violent and unstable, and his drinking had caused him to have several minor encounters with the law.

His whole life had been a battle with authority. 'They' were the planners who forcibly moved the family to Kirkby during his boyhood, 'they' were the magistrates that fined him when he rolled in the cornfield. He felt that some external force was always there to be thwarted and battled with whenever it presented itself in the tangible form of the police, the medical profession or welfare officials.

Whatever the reasons which stimulated this fear and anger with authority, it was an aspect of life which caused him to feel bitter and frustrated. He feared going to the doctor, and on several occasions refused medical attention, or quarrelled with the family doctor. His deepest fears were realized in some of his encounters with authority when officials treated him with open contempt publicly; this happened to my knowledge in Department of Health and Social Security and in the Housing Department. Georgie felt deep shame and this turned to anger. His stories of bravado helped to compensate for his own feelings of loss of self-esteem. [Patricia Owens, *The Family, the Culture of Poverty and Welfare Provisions* (Royal Anthropological Institute, 1984) (abridged).]

10.4 RELATIVE POVERTY

The welfare state will normally act as a safety net for the worst cases of poverty so that people are unlikely to die of malnutrition or lack of heat

"That's our problem, Charlie—the more we get, the more we want."

if the welfare authorities are aware of their situation.

Rising living standards generally in society have however led to rising expectations so that when people compare themselves with others in modern Britain they may feel that they are badly off even although their standard of living might have been regarded as acceptable in Charles Booth's day. This 'poverty by comparison' has been termed 'relative deprivation', a theory detailed by Merton in *Social Theory and Social Structure*. Essentially, people tend to compare themselves with others in their 'reference group' to which they think they may fairly be compared because of broadly similar characteristics.

In *Poverty, Inequality and Class Structure* Peter Townsend described those in relative poverty as having 'resources so seriously below those commanded by the average individual or family that they are, in effect, excluded from ordinary living patterns, customs and activities. In the first study of relative poverty in the United Kingdom undertaken in 1960 by Townsend and Abel-Smith (*The Poor and the Poorest*) it was claimed that $7\frac{1}{2}$ million people (14.2 per cent) lived in relative poverty.

Fig. 10.2   *Northern Ireland's multiple disadvantages*

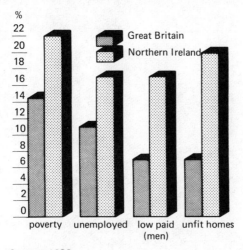

SOURCE   *New Society*, 1982.

In the past, opportunities for comparison were normally limited to the neighbourhood – now they have been opened up by the media. Living standards of small families with a father in regular skilled work have tended to increase quite sharply in recent years. 'Relative poverty' may therefore have increased. It may be true to say that the number of people

116

in *need* is decreasing but the number of people in *want* may inevitably increase.

Some areas of the United Kingdom have considerably more poverty and other disadvantages than other areas. Figure 10.2 compares the most disadvantaged area of the United Kingdom with the rest. Consider how the factors shown might contribute to the civil disturbances in Northern Ireland.

SOCIAL MOBILITY

11.1 THE EXTENT OF SOCIAL MOBILITY IN BRITAIN

There has been a significant change in the proportion of privately owned wealth in the hands of the top one per cent of the population, but the proportionate change diminishes as one climbs down the ladder of wealth ownership (section 10.2).

Table 11.1   *decline in the proportion of marketable wealth 1971–1980*

The most wealthy   5% of the population had a 9% decline in wealth

The most wealthy 10% of the population had a 7% decline in wealth

The most wealthy 25% of the population had a 5% decline in wealth

The most wealthy 50% of the population had a 3% decline in wealth

Attempts to redistribute wealth more evenly have only been partially successful because the very rich are able to protect their positions by employing skilled accountants and lawyers. For example, the Vestey family, whose interests include the Dewhurst butchery firm, have their wealth in the form of a family trust which provides the incomes and housing expenses of its members. In 1980 a political storm erupted over newspaper disclosures that the Dewhurst chain paid only £10 in tax on 1978 profits of £2.3 million.

But social class is not just a matter of wealth. Although this is a key factor, it also has to do with access to high status occupations; educational opportunities; and social acceptance generally, particularly with regard to 'life styles'. Some growing similarity in dress, access to foreign holidays, car ownership and the like has resulted in claims that class differences are declining.

There still remains a remarkable educational elite

There are still great variations in housing – dependent upon income and wealth; access to schools of variable quality; dress itself has all sorts of little nuances that can determine a person's class, and therefore their acceptability to others. The middle-class person endeavouring to 'join in' in a working men's club would have problems; just as would the manual worker at one of the London 'Clubs' like the Athenaeum.

Among the young there appeared to be a brief flirtation with 'classless' life styles in the 1960s ('flower power'). Now there appears to be a move back across the class divide in youth culture (for example in the early 80s there were not many middle-class 'skinheads').

Professor MacRae in an article 'Classlessness' in *New Society* (1972) doubted whether the British class system was even a system. He claimed that equal opportunities in education and the consequent 'rise of the meritocracy' had led to the discarding of class labels. In other words he was saying that Britain was becoming a classless society.

Although few would accept that Britain is a classless society, there are some trends that indicate a slow movement in that direction:

1. Patterns of behaviour do appear to be more uniform generally as a result of exposure to the media, greater mobility and increased earnings by many manual workers.

2. There has been some limited convergence of earning rates for manual and white-collar workers. (Male non-manual workers' pay rose by 233 per cent between 1973 and 1979, male manual workers' by 244 per cent; the comparable figures for women being 260 per cent and 280 per cent).

3. There is apparently no barrier to the children of manual workers moving to non-manual occupations. Vance Packard in *The Status Seekers* (1959) found that one third of the sons of manual workers proceeded to non-manual work, but usually to routine non-manual.

4. There is a greater degree of home ownership among manual and routine clerical workers than in the past.

However, accent and differing behaviour patterns do exist, educational opportunities vary by area of residence, and status judgements are still made on overt signs of class difference. For example school-children listed BBC English and 'affected English' as of high status, and cockney and Birmingham accents as of low status in a 1973 study.

There is evidence that access to high status positions is still considerably easier for those whose parents are themselves in similar occupations. Such judgements are usually based on whether children have been educated in 'public' schools (see Glossary). Less than 7 per cent of the population were being educated in public schools in 1980.

A high proportion of top jobs go to 'Oxbridge' graduates and in 1980 just over 50 per cent of Cambridge undergraduates and just under 50 per cent of Oxford undergraduates had been educated in public schools. This is a higher percentage of state education students than formerly, but may be largely accounted for by the opening up of 'Oxbridge' colleges to girls who are less likely than boys to be educated at a public school.

Ultimate power in any modern state resides with the armed forces, as it is they who must ensure that the law if enforced, should the police prove inadequate. It is not known what would happen in Britain should the interests of the ruling elite be seriously threatened by an elected government, but in many countries such a situation has provoked a military 'coup' (the nearest modern Britain has approached such a situation was the so called 'Mutiny at the Curragh' when Army officers threatened to resign their commissions just before the First World War – see section 25.4). British Army Officers are usually trained at the Royal Military Academy, Sandhurst, and the social origin of our 'officer class' may be indicated by the type of school which they attended (see Table 11.2).

Glass (*Social Mobility in Britain*, 1963) found that 38.8 per cent of 'professional and high administrative' posts were filled by people whose fathers had occupied similar posts; only 1.5 per cent had unskilled fathers. Of unskilled workers 27.4 per cent had unskilled fathers, none had fathers from the top 'professional and high administrative' class.

Table 11.2 *educational background of entrants to Royal Military Academy*

	Public schools*	State schools
1983–4[+]		
Graduates	157	124
Non-graduates	153	95
	310 = 58.6%	219 = 41.4%
Comparative intake 1971–3	48.6%	51.4%

* See glossary for definition of 'public school'.
[+] Not including 54 entrants from 'Welbeck College' as this independent army school recruits from both state and private sector; nor 1 entrant from the Army Apprentices College.)

NOTE There are comparatively few women officer cadets entering Sandhurst and most of these come from the state sector.

SOURCE 1983–4 Ministry of Defence; 1971–3 Royal Military Academy.

Kelsall (*Higher Civil Servants in Britain*) found that among the direct entrants to the administrative class, a larger proportion are privately educated Oxbridge graduates than the number of privately educated children would warrant.

Butler and Kavanagh (*The British General Election of 1983*) found that 70 per cent of Conservative MPs and 14 per cent of Labour MPs had been to public schools (see Table 11.3).

The ruling tribes

Behind all the swings and changes of the last decades was there any meaning left in the old idea of the Establishment, which had cast such a spell over the Macmillan years? Certainly the political leadership now shows little connection with that many-branched family tree of the Devonshires and the Salisburys which spread out to many of the key emplacements of power in the early sixties. Certainly school and university backgrounds have lost some of their significance in parliament. In the Labour party Michael Foot and Tony Benn (however disguised) both come from the old Oxford and public-school tradition; but as the party has moved to the left it has broken most of its links with the patrician or Fabian tradition, and new leaders such as Eric Heffer, Neil Kinnock or Eric Varley have come up from proletarian backgrounds.

The Conservatives have broken with their aristocratic leadership since they chose the Earl of Home, and Margaret Thatcher sees

Table 11.3 *educational background of MPs elected at the General Election*

percentage shown

	Conservative	Labour	Liberal	SDP
Secondary/Elementary	29	61	2	2
Secondary +	19	42	1	—
Secondary and University	71	76	4	2
Public School only	67	—	3	—
Public School and University	211	30	7	2
Total	397	209	17	6
Oxford	103	20	1	2
Cambridge	87	11	3	1
Other University	92	80	7	1
All Universities	282 (71%)	111 (53%)	11 (65%)	4 (67%)
Eton	49	2	—	—
Harrow	11	—	—	—
Winchester	5	1	—	—
Other	213	27	10	2
All Public Schools	278 (70%)	30 (14%)	10 (60%)	2 (33%)

SOURCE D. Butler and D. Kavanagh, *The British General Election of 1983* (adapted).

herself as owing no debts or loyalties to the old guard, and appealing directly to the people. After her reshuffle the Tory cabinet in 1982 was much more in her own mould, with two of her closest supporters—Cecil Parkinson as Tory chairman and Norman Tebbit as Secretary for Employment—both from modest backgrounds. Outside parliament, too, there is now less aristocratic influence; the Governor and the Deputy Governor of the Bank of England both come from outside the 'charmed circle'; the chairman and director-general of the IBA are both outsiders; nearly all chairmen of big corporations, scientists and vice-chancellors come from grammar schools; and none of the leading entrepreneurs have been to university at all.

Yet alongside this new meritocracy there still remains a remarkable educational elite which has maintained its continuity and influence through all the political upheavals. Few people in the early Wilson years would have predicted that in 1982 the chairman of the BBC, the editor of *The Times*, the Foreign Secretary, the heads of both foreign and civil services and half the chairmen of the big four banks would all be Old Etonians, while the Home Secretary, the Chancellor, the director-general of the BBC, a bevy of judges and the other two bank chairmen would come from the rival foundation, Winchester. Such a lasting duopoly must surely have some significance in Britain's anatomy.

Of course it was never likely that two medieval institutions which had survived King Henry VIII, Cromwell, Victorian reformers and two world wars would lightly surrender their influence to Harold Wilson or Anthony Crosland. But far from retreating, they have advanced into new areas of influence; and their success is more marked than in Macmillan's time or (as far as I can trace) than in any earlier time. The Victorian professions were full of self-made men who worked their way up to the top, and several schools prepared the way to power. Macmillan's Britain included outsiders such as William Haley editing *The Times* or Sir Norman Brook running the civil service.

But since then the products of these two ancient schools have reasserted all their old ability to climb the ladders of power, with a continuity which has no parallel in other industrial countries. . . The traditional elites have also retained their own communication system which still gives them a special tribal role in the midst of contemporary Britain. [Anthony Sampson, *The Changing Anatomy of Britain* (Sevenoaks, Hodder & Stoughton, 1982).]

11.2 BARRIERS TO MOBILITY

The most obvious barriers to social mobility are 'lack of opportunity', for example regional differences in employment; and 'motivation', for example a lack of desire to study in order to gain higher qualifications; however these may not be the most important factors.

Many occupations require a particular standard of education for entry and this effectively means that social mobility can only take place between generations. It also means that education is a major avenue of mobility; and a major barrier for those who do not have access to an appropriate education, or who have not been socialised in a way that makes it possible for them to fully benefit from the educational process (section 8.3). Even when all manual workers' children are taken together – those from skilled families as well as those from poorer homes – these were still, in the early 1970s less likely to enter a University than children of 'professional and technical' fathers by a factor of nearly nine times. (*Class in a Capitalist Society* J. Westergaard and H. Resler, 1975.)

Major inequality in the distribution of inherited wealth is the first barrier to mobility in that it gives rise to the direct inheritance of particular positions, for example company directorships; or particular advantages to the children of those who know how the system works and can afford to educate their children appropriately – for example, many doctors are themselves children of doctors. Patronage by relatives is known as 'nepotism'; the term originating from the placing by a fifteenth-century Pope of his illegitimate sons, called 'nephews', in positions of power.

Colour or ethnic origin is also likely to be a major barrier to social mobility for those concerned – 'Black people represent around 4 per cent of the total population. Can any profession boast that anything like that proportion of their colleagues are black?' David Lane (Chairman, Commission for Racial Equality, 1982).

In England, Wales and Scotland there is no evidence that religion is a barrier to mobility but there is some evidence that Catholics are less likely than Protestants to be socially mobile in Northern Ireland.

Perhaps the greatest barrier to mobility is that of attitude, which in turn influences the way the socialisation process prepares children for adult life. 'There is an undoubted sense in which working class values and feeling ... work against the school' Paul Willis, *Learning to Labour*.

Wealth

More is known about family continuities in wealth than in income. Wedgwood (1939) wrote: 'The evidence ... supports the opinion that, in the great majority of cases, the large fortunes of one generation belong to the children of those who possessed the large fortunes of the preceding generation. .... The rich men who have sprung from parents with insignificant resources are almost certainly a minority of their class. The attention which that minority attracts seems to be due to the fact that those who compose it are exceptional phenomena rather than numerous.' Similar conclusions were drawn by Harbury (1962) one generation later in a study modelled on the earlier work of Wedgwood. In both investigations it was found that about two-thirds of sons leaving very large fortunes had fathers in the top 0.25 per cent of wealth-holders.

A further study (Harbury and McMahon, 1973) found that the situation remained virtually unaltered over the next decade; there was no marked change in the role of inheritance in familial wealth between the mid 1950s and the mid 1960s. Over both the time periods inheritance had differential importance for different occupations. For example, in agriculture, forestry and fishing inheritance was important, whereas in metal goods, construction, clothing and engineering industries there was more chance that a wealth-holder was self-made. Marriage apparently played a small role in determining wealth although this issue was not systematically examined.

These studies suggest that, amongst the top wealth-holders, paternal fortunes are inherited by sons in about 60 per cent of families.

A recent Royal Commission (1975) has reviewed the evidence on changes over time in the distribution of income and wealth in Britain. They pointed out the considerable problems of definition and measurement but concluded that, while there had been some decline since 1954 in the share of the income distribution held by the top 5 per cent, there had been little change in the rest of the distribution. The tax system had little effect as the progressive effect of direct taxation was largely offset by the regressive effect of indirect taxation. The evidence on the distribution of wealth was less satisfactory but it was clear that there had been a substantial fall in the share of wealth owned by the richest 1 per cent of the population (from an estimated 69 per cent in 1911–13 to 42 per cent in 1960 and 28 per cent in 1973). However, most of the redistribution occurred within the top 10 per cent so that the increase in share of wealth by the bottom 80 per cent was relatively small. On the other hand, inequalities (although still very substantial) were less marked if State pension entitlements were taken into account.

It can be concluded that the rises in real standards of living over this century have been more dramatic than the reductions of inequality. While there has probably been some contraction at the top end of the distribution of earnings the effects on the overall spread of net income have been quite small. At all times the majority of people have occupied the middle ranges and the minority the extremes. When wealth distributions are considered, however, somewhat different conclusions are necessary. Firstly, patterns of advantage do not parallel those for income, as most wealth is owned by a very small minority of the total population. Unfortunately we have very little information on small wealth holdings and the number of persons who own them. Secondly, although inequalities in wealth have decreased, it is not clear whether there have been noteworthy changes in the distribution of the larger wealth holdings over the last generations. There are contrasting opinions and the issue is not easily resolved. Wealth estimates are based on estate duty or Inland Revenue data and both methods of assessment have their source or error. Finally, the judgement as to whether *much* or *little* change in inequality has occurred is somewhat subjective. [M. Rutter and N. Madge, *Cycles of Disadvantage* (London: Heinemann, 1976) (adapted).]

11.3 AVENUES OF MOBILITY

The major avenue to social mobility in Britain is education leading to an occupation higher up the social scale than that of one's father ('intergenerational mobility').

Provided the ratio of non-manual to manual jobs remained the same some upward mobility was inevitable in that for at least the last hundred years manual workers have had larger families than non-manual. In fact non-manual work has increased as a percentage of all work, thus opening up more opportunities for working-class talent, usually selected by the educational process. For example between 1911 and 1966 the proportion of employers and proprietors in the population halved. The proportion of white-collar workers doubled (from 18.7 per cent to 38.3 per cent). There was a slight increase in salesmen, but three times as many clerical (the biggest single group) and four times as many firemen and inspectors.

'Intra-generational' mobility – starting off one's working life in one social class and then moving to another is less common. Opportunities for mobility within the work situation itself have declined because the expansion of higher education has resulted in many organisations recruiting graduate trainee managers rather than depending upon recruiting on merit from those joining the firm at an earlier age.

Fairly rigid pre-entry conditions have existed for the various grades in the civil service and armed forces since the ending of 'nepotism' in the last century. This emphasis on formal entry qualifications is now also operating to an extent in the police service with graduate entry as well as in industry and commerce.

Generally people marry within their social class but there is some upward social mobility through marriage, particularly in the case of women. In general this tends to be a movement up just one rung of the social ladder but clearly there are notable exceptions.

Windfall gains in terms of inheritance, gambling and the like may result in upward mobility. Such mobility is rare, particularly bearing in mind that most inheritance is within the same social group. Sudden wealth may transfer a person *nominally* into another social class but attitude and life style may leave them culturally isolated. 'Class' does carry with it an implicit assumption of acceptance by a social group of the individuals assigned to it.

Demographic trends and social mobility

Social class is widely recognised as an influential factor when assessing the likelihood of children staying on at school or further education college gaining qualifications suitable for entry into higher education. Social class is defined by reference to the occupation of the head of the household. In projecting the future number of qualified leavers account has been taken not only of the total number of births but also of the numbers in the various social classes and of the social mobility of parents between the birth of their children and when they reach age 18.

Social class at birth Since the mid-1960s the number of births in England and Wales has fallen by about a third whilst the number occurring to families in social classes I (professional) and II (intermediate occupations – administrators, managers) has risen by about a fifth. As a percentage of all births, those occurring to families in social classes I and II remained fairly

constant (about 17%) between 1951 and 1963. Since then the proportion
has risen and reached 30% in 1981.

But information which became available from the Office of Population
Censuses and Surveys (OPCS) at the end of 1983 showed that, contrary
to what had been assumed by some observers, differentials in fertility by
social class had not changed greatly between 1961 and 1981. The observed
changes in numbers of births by social class match the changes in the total
number of women of child-bearing ages in the relevant class. Taking 1961
as 100 the overall rate of births per thousand women aged 15–44 in 1981
was 73. On a similar basis the rate for births to social classes I and II was
also 73 for 1981.

The changes in the proportion of births in each social class reflect the
movements in the occupational structure resulting from a reduction in
employment in the manufacturing sector and a growth in employment in
the service industries. Different social class labels have been assigned to
families because the work the head of the household does has changed
(from manual to non-manual). Between 1960 and 1980 the proportions of
GB employees in employment moved as follows between the three categories into which such employees are divided:

Agriculture
    down 2 percentage points
Production and construction
    down 11 percentage points
Services
    up 13 percentage points

Social mobility between birth and age 18 The social class composition of
the 18 year old population will differ from that of the cohort at birth.
Mortality and migration have a marginal effect but social mobility by a
change in occupation of the head of the household after the birth of the
child is the most significant factor. The 1981 Labour Force Survey has
been used in association with the relevant birth data for each social class to
provide estimates of the social mobility between birth and age 18 of those
born in 1963. It is estimated that nearly half (47%) of those aged 18 in
social class II in 1981 had entered since birth. The proportion of the cohort
in social class I had increased only slightly. There was a substantial net
movement out of the manual classes, some 9.5% of the cohort.

DES Report on Education July 1984 (Department of Education and
Science).

11.4 SOCIAL CHANGE

The degree to which the social structure of Britain is changing is a matter of dispute. In 1961 Zweig (*The Worker in an Affluent Society*) found that the better-paid manual worker was adopting middle-class values and behaviour. This process has been called *'embourgeoisement'*. Goldthorpe, Lockwood, Bechhofer and Platt (*The Affluent Worker* 1969–71) criticised this view and found that although there was some adoption of middle-class life styles, attitudes and values had not altered.

The view that the classes are drawing together – 'convergence' – because of the growth of white-collar jobs and similarities of earnings, rather than one being absorbed into the other is also open to question. Runciman (*Relative Deprivation and Social Justice*) points to the greater security of employment in 'white-collar' jobs and the better working conditions enjoyed by such workers compared with those in blue-collar occupations; together with the fact that manual workers have to work longer hours for the same pay. While overall wage differentials narrow, 'fringe benefits' for white collar workers have increased – private pension schemes, greater holiday entitlement, private schemes and company cars among them.

In terms of wealth ownership even the lower grades of non-manual workers are likely to be better off in the ownership of capital compared with the skilled manual. However, white-collar jobs are becoming increasingly unionised and such workers may begin to identify with manual workers rather than management. This may be in part a consequence of the blocking off of their access to promotion (section 11.3), a consequent reduction in managerial aspirations, hence a loss of identification with management.

It could be said that the growth in the number of working-class children staying on at school implies an acceptance of the middle-class value of 'deferred gratification' (section 8.2). Equally, the growth of credit – particularly credit cards – among the middle class might point to a reduction among them of this middle-class value. Westergaard and Resler have suggested that some white-collar workers are becoming more 'proletarian' (working class) and 'Proletariarisation' is taking place. Others see a degree of 'Convergence' – the social classes becoming similar to each other.

QUESTIONS FROM PAST O-LEVEL GCE PAPERS

1. Discuss the suggestion that the Welfare State has removed poverty from Britain today.   Associated Examining Board

2. What do you understand by the term 'social mobility'? How much social mobility is there in Britain?
                                         Oxford Local Examining Board

128

3. **Either,** (a) Describe the possible effects of any **three** social factors on a person's life chances.

Or, (b) What is meant by 'poverty'? Briefly outline any **three** possible reasons for the existence of poverty in our society.
Welsh Joint Examining Board

4. What do you understand by the concept of the Welfare State? What are the major institutions and services which make up the Welfare State?
Oxford Local Examining Board

5. Poverty as Relative Deprivation

'Poverty is not an absolute state. It is relative deprivation. Society itself is continuously changing and thrusting new obligations on its members. They, in turn, develop new needs. They are rich or poor according to their share of the resources that are available to all. This is true as much of nutritional as monetary or even educational resources.

Our general theory, then, should be that individuals and families whose resources, over time, fall seriously short of the resources commanded by the average individual or family in the community in which they live, whether that community is a local, national or international one, are in poverty.'

(Peter Townsend, from the *British Journal of Sociology*, September 1962.)

(a) How does the above extract help us to understand changing standards of poverty over a period of time and in different places

(b) How can we say that we are experiencing a higher standard of poverty in Britain today than 50 years ago?
Associated Examining Board

6.

Middle classes rise and rise

Chances of going to university are becoming greater for the middle and less for the working class, says a book published this week.

The book, *Social Class Differences in Britain*, by Ivan Reid, throws up stark differences in education according to class. It uses university admissions statistics to show that, despite a growth of nearly 100,000 in the number of entrants to universities between 1970 and 1977, the percentage from social class 1 rose from 30 to 36 per cent while that from class 4 (all manual occupations) sank from 28 to 24 per cent.

Public school pupils have also kept a virtual monopoly of top jobs, his figures show. They comprise 80 per cent of High Court and Appeal judges, 83 per cent of the directors of major insurance companies, 80 per cent of the directors of the clearing banks, 69 per cent of the directors of major industrial firms and 67 per cent of Conservative MPs.

(From *The Times Educational Supplement*, 12 June 1981.)

(a) (i) Why do you think the chances of going to university are greater for the middle class and less for the working class? [4]

(ii) In what ways do Public Schools help to perpetuate an elite in British society? [6]

(b) To what extent do you think that schools *reflect* rather than *overcome* inequalities in society? Discuss your answer with reference to any one study of education that you have come across [10]

Cambridge Local Examining Board

7. What relationships exist between social class and power? Discuss how power is used in a variety of social situations.

London Examining Board

8. Social class is the description applied to social stratification in modern industrial society. It differs from other forms of stratification in that it does not have any official basis, nor is it legally enforced. In fact, definitions of social class in industrial society still vary: the Registrar-General's scale which is frequently used in government statistics is a socio-economic scale based on occupation, whilst Marx's view of social class is very different.

Other forms of stratification, such as caste systems, and the feudal system, tend to be "closed" in that people cannot easily move from one stratum to another. In theory at least, Britain's social class system is 'open' and vertical social mobility is possible.

Some sociologists have suggested that there is extensive mobility between social classes. It has also been suggested that social classes are gradually disappearing from the structure of our society. Others have argued that the differences between the social classes are more difficult to identify.

(a) Give one example from the extract of a closed system of stratification. (1)

(b) What is the difference mentioned in the extract between 'open' and 'closed' societies (systems of stratification)? (2)

(c) What is meant by embourgeoisement? (3)

(d) Briefly describe Marx's view of social classes in industrial societies. (5)

(e) What evidence might sociologists offer for the persistence of social class stratification in modern Britain? (9)

Associated Examining Board

PART V
WORK AND LEISURE

THE MEANING OF WORK

12.1 THE EFFECT OF WORK ON BEHAVIOUR

Work is more than a job. It is a place where we meet other people, make friends, perhaps marry. For many people it is a place where they acquire the status that they carry outside into the general society – a Rover on the drive rather than a Cortina. Others will establish a status recognised by their workmates, as a person of skill or the man who is not afraid of the boss.

The kind of work we do is likely to influence our political views. Women, it is suggested, are more likely to vote Conservative than are men. Partially, at least, because they are more likely to work in the middle-class ambience of an office, with more direct contact with management.

People adopt a role when they take a job; there is a socially shared expectation of how they should behave. 'A judge is supposed to be deliberate and sober, a pilot in a cockpit cool, a book-keeper to be accurate and neat' (E. Goffman *Encounters*, 1972). People adopt their work roles as part of their self-identity and carry them forward into their life outside work. Work is part of the process of socialisation.

The type of work we do is likely to affect our family relationship; perhaps because long absences make our family more strangers than are our workmates or because the nature of our work makes us almost totally disinterested in it, so that we focus our attention on our relationships elsewhere.

In *The Social Psychology of Work* (1974) Argyle lists the main motives for work:

1. economic – obtaining money and fringe benefits;
2. satisfaction – an avenue of achievement and source of personal pride and interest;
3. social – to achieve status, companionship and security.

Alternatively it may be said that the function of work is to provide status, identity and income. Of these three, income may not be the most important, although most people may claim that it is. A survey, *Teenage Attitudes*, of 3925 young people between the ages of 15 and 19 in Ipswich, in 1984, showed that sixty per cent would prefer to be paid the same as the 'dole' and have a job, than to have no job at all. As a mnemonic, or *aide-memoire* it could be said that people work for CISSES:

Contribution
Integration
Status
Satisfaction
Economic Reward
Social contact.

Most people object to what they would call 'charity' - they need to feel that they are making a contribution to their community. Work integrates the young into the adult community and assists them to move from the dependence of childhood. Work provides our status and many people obtain their major feelings of satisfaction and fulfilment from work. Economic motives are the most self-evident reason for work, and without work most people's social contacts - their opportunities to meet people beyond their immediate family and neighbourhood - would be severely limited. If the opportunity to work disappears it is not sufficient to replace it with financial benefits alone.

S. Parker (*The Sociology of Industry*, 1967) divided work into three patterns; 'extension', 'neutrality' and 'opposition'. A person with an interesting job may be absorbed in it and not distinguish readily between 'work' and 'non-work'. A doctor may attend patients at irregular hours and be assisted by his wife; a child care officer may devote much free time to matters connected with work - their work is 'extended' into their other activities.

Some, such as bank employees, work regular hours and there is little relationship between work, family and leisure other than income - the position is 'neutral'. Others, such as miners, whose work is physically or psychologically exacting seek to escape from it as much as possible in their non-work activities - theirs is a position of 'opposition'.

The reason for work

The work ethic

This is an interesting example of *culture lag*—people have been social-ised for a world which no longer exists. This is always a danger at times of rapid technological and social change. A puritanical work ethic was *functional* in a society which needed large numbers of manual workers, but in a society where this kind of work has been taken over by automation and computer control, then such attitudes are *disfunctional*.

In future, it may even become necessary to 'ration' work, whereas, in the past, holidays or free time were rationed. The major difficulty will be to persuade people to re-adjust to a new and very different situation. This will need a change of attitude not only on the part of the unemployed, but also a change of attitude by some politicians who continue to associate the unemployed with scrounging and immorality.

But meanwhile it is quite wrong to equate 'unemployment' with 'leisure'. Leisure implies not only time, but sufficient money and opportunity for enjoyment. Most of the long-term unemployed are both poor and miserable.

The future

It will be necessary to re-think the links between school and work, and school and leisure. We are now rapidly approaching the post-industrial age—what tends to be called the age of the computer and micro-technology revolution. Though much unemployment is temporary, as a result of economic recession, much may be permanent. Many jobs have been lost by the introduction of sophisticated new technology which replaces unskilled and semi-skilled workers. Thus schools will have the task not only of education for leisure, but also adjusting to the kind of learning which will emphasise the teaching of processes, understanding and information retrieval, rather than the accumulation of factual knowledge.

It would certainly be a mistake for schools to yield to the suggestions of those who want more specific job training to take place in schools. Industrial techniques are likely to change so rapidly that to go along that path would simply be to train for obsolete skills.

Long ago, Marx made the point that one of the tragedies of a capitalist society was that work—which should be an enjoyable, social, cooperative activity giving a good deal of satisfaction to human beings, had become exploitation. Men no longer worked *with* each other, but *for* someone else. So, today, only a minority of people really enjoy their work. The majority are more likely to feel *alienation*—for them, work is something they have to do but is not something they really identify with, and therefore it lacks meaning for them.

The majority work in order to be able to live outside work. But many of those kinds of jobs—the alienating jobs—could be swept away by automation and the micro-chip revolution. Not just work in factories, but boring and repetitive work in offices, too. Unemployment is not the inevitable result of such changes—a shorter working week is a real possibility, job sharing is another, and there could be longer periods of education throughout life. All of this means additional leisure time which ought to be catered for by the school. (*New Society*, 11 February 1982.)

12.2 ALIENATION AND JOB SATISFACTION

Marx thought that increasing mechanisation would assist in the final removal of class differences because the worker would become 'alienated from the means of production', realise his identification with others in a similar position as himself, and 'expropriate the expropriators':

In what does this alientation of labour consist? First that the work is external to the worker, that it is not a part of his nature, that consequently he does not fulfil himself in his work but denies himself, has a feeling of misery, not of well being, does not develop freely a physical and mental energy, but is physically exhausted and mentally debased. The worker therefore feels himself at home only during his leisure, whereas at work he feels homeless.

Although the concept of alienation has been challenged, most sociologists see it as an explanation of many problems in industry and of subsequent behaviour in non-work situations.

Typically the worker does not own the tools with which he works, or the capital which is employed in the production process. He is also separated from the product of his work ... a sense of lack of wholeness, a sense of frustration or of loss of humanity. It seems that men's lives and work are controlled by *things* - by money; by 'market forces', by technology. 'Alienation', therefore, is more than just a sense of boredom at work; it also refers to a lack of *power* on the part of the worker. (Peter Worsley, *Introducing Sociology*).

It may be that not only boredom at work but also a feeling that he is unimportant, and without power, encourages the worker to engage in strikes and leads to absenteeism, accidents, lateness and frequent job changes. Weir (*Job Satisfaction*, 1976) illustrates that discontent with boring repetitive work is international: 'In Italy one in seven workers doesn't turn up on a given day. In the Swedish car industry three in ten workers are absent daily in many sections, and a third of the labour force turns over each year. At Chrysler, in Detroit, the turnover rate in 1971 was almost 30 per cent.'

Although it would be nonsense to claim that in some past golden age everyone enjoyed their work, it is probable that job dissatisfaction *did* increase with large scale mechanisation, when machines took over jobs previously performed by hand and thereby reduced the need for individual skills. Equally important is the effect of 'the division of labour' which developed from it. The essential idea of the division of labour is that people perform better if they only have one task to perform. The production process is broken down into a series of tasks and individuals concentrate their activity in only a few of these areas. This principle has led to assembly-line working and has had a number of advantages in addition to the main one of faster, more economical working. Training is simpler and quicker; a worker can be selected and put to do the task he does best all of the time; mentally or physically handicapped people can sometimes do a job whereas they could not master more complicated operations; increasing productivity leads to cheaper goods and an improved standard of living. The disadvantages are mainly social: loss of job satisfaction, boring work may reduce individuality and this may be carried forward into non-work activities as well; monotony may result in fatigue, increasing accidents; direct contact between management and worker decreases, with a consequent lack of communication and possible increase of industrial strife.

The division of labour also lends itself to measurement and in the 1920s 'Speedy' Taylor introduced work study or 'time and motion', earning himself the title of 'the most hated man in America' despite the fact that, after finding the best man for the job and teaching him to do it with maximum efficiency, the intention was to use high wage rates as an incentive to a high rate of production.

However, in the 1920s Mayo's studies of Chicago car-workers already showed that men tended to work better when treated as individuals.

Worker participation

The industrial illness
In any industrialized country today more than half the working population still works in companies with less than fifty employees. But some giant organizations are growing even larger—too large to be comfortable for employees. The individual working in a large modern company too often feels lost in the overall scheme, merely a replaceable cog in the industrial system, with little or no control over his or her own life until retirement . . . I cannot speak directly for the employees at Volvo. I can only observe how I see them behave in different situations. Since 1971, I have been able to see how union leaders conduct themselves as members of the company's board of directors. I have watched as they learned how the board functions and what kind of matters it handles. They now understand that the board is not engaged in activities that imply a conspiracy

against the workers. These employee representatives have thus been able to negate many of the false myths about the board—perhaps one of the best and soundest results of broadening the board representation.

On our Corporate Works Council, I have, since 1971, seen employees discussing Volvo's entire strategy and planning operations. They have done this with an openness which clearly demonstrates the sense of responsibility they feel not only toward those employees they represent, but also toward the company as a whole. Politics and tactics are understandably part of their work. However, if one accepts the motives behind the tactics, one finds a strong desire for cooperation, based on the assumption that the workers have many interests in common with other stakeholders in the company. Furthermore, these people have a clear understanding of the leader's role. They respect leadership, and they understand the need to maintain the decision power within any type of organization, even if they must sometimes query the content and limits of leadership because of political convictions.

In another era, leadership was maintained by disciplinary rules and punishment. A company's management could apply sanctions or even fire people, ruling labor by decrees and notices. 'Spitting prohibited', management could say. That time is long gone, and we can be thankful for the progress. Today we must grow closer to labor, no matter how busy management is . . . It sometimes scares me that what we do in Volvo is presented to others as an innovation, because this demonstrates, after all, how little has been done in work organization. Companies spend almost endless hours trying to provide change, incentive, interest, involvement, and motivation for top executives, yet almost no time is spent in looking at the rest of the work force in the same way. Until now, managers have not found it necessary. We are still in the era that Adam Smith described so many years ago, where 'a worker gives up his ease, his liberty and his happiness when he goes into industry'.

If we can give the worker back his ease, his liberty and his happiness, or at least provide conditions under which he can find them for himself, I believe we will come closer to a healthy, human, 'post-industrial' society. [P. Gyllenhammar, *People at Work* (Reading, Massachusetts: Addison-Wesley, 1977).]

12.3 COAL-MINERS AND FISHERMEN

Coal is Our Life a study of a coal-mining community in Yorkshire by Dennis, Henriques and Slaughter was published in 1956. After more than a quarter of a century it is obviously out of date; however it still gives valid insights into the influence of work on non-work activities, particularly its influence on the family and leisure.

In mining communities, as elsewhere, men and women are now spending more of their leisure time together

Mining is single-sex, dangerous and unpleasant. It requires a considerable amount of team work, and this group cohesion has been carried forward into solidarity in political matters. The average miner expected his home to be the opposite of the pit – warm, comfortable and tidy. The special relationships established at work were also carried forward into leisure. Men tended to drink and gamble together, women were excluded, as they were from the pit. Relationships between husband and wife were often poorly established, the function of the family being restricted in the main to reproduction, and the socialising of the children. The insecurity of mining decreased the incentive to save rather than increasing it. If money were saved it would decrease the miner's benefits in the event of an accident and so the miner sought to enjoy it while he had the opportunity ('short-term hedonism').

Another dangerous and physically demanding occupation is that of the deep sea fishermen. Tunstall's study of the trawlermen of Hull (*The Fishermen*, 1962) illustrated how to most fishermen long term absence from home, linked with shared dangers and discomfort, reduced the importance of the family while emphasising the importance of their mates. Brief shore excursions tended to be spent drinking and gambling with shipmates rather than at home with wife and family.

As with the miners' wives of 'Ashton', the wives of the trawlermen built up their own social relationships with women friends and relatives who would be available to help out when needed. Both groups had a generally low standard of living, the standard being set in early manhood on a low income. Any increase in money merely meant an increase in pleasure.

12.4 LORRY DRIVERS AND ASSEMBLY LINE WORKERS

The Register General's Occupational Classification puts drivers in Social Class 3 (Skilled Worker).

Peter Hollowell's *The Lorry Driver* (1968) divided lorry drivers into three categories and showed how differences in their work situations influenced their non-work attitudes and activities.

Types of lorry driver

Shunter – local delivery driver, often takes over the 'trunkers' lorry and may have to load and off-load (low status).

Trunker – long-distance with set route, often gets home every night or every second night. Does not usually load or off-load (high status).

Tramper – ('rover/roamer') No fixed route. More loading and off-loading. More physically arduous, but more variety and less regularity (medium status).

Shunter: regular hours, therefore able to be part of local community and may know it better than most.
Trunker: although often at home may spend most of his time there asleep.
Tramper: away from home for a week or more at a time.
The three jobs may appear similar but both working and leisure time conditons vary enormously.

Occupation and family life

The lorry driver's occupation meant that his presence in the home was more limited and irregular than in many other occupations. This was greatest at the time when children are growing up as it was at this time that economic necessity often resulted in a move to 'tramping' or 'trunking'; a desire for higher status also contributed to such a change. Particularly therefore in the case of the tramper the wife was likely to take on the role of organising the family, including house repairs.

Many drivers tried to compensate by intensive domestic activities when at home, and time off was likely to be spent in the home. Sexual relations were distorted by absence. Drivers themselves took the view that the tramper should be a single man. Wives however found adaptation to absence more difficult than did the drivers themselves and the opportunity which absence made for extra-marital relations made marriage breakdown more likely. Such breakdown is more probable in most 'mobile occupations' (e.g. Hull fishermen in Tunstall's study accounted for 5 per cent of Hull divorces but only $2\frac{1}{2}$ per cent of the population).

Leisure

Long working hours (56.4 per week private, 50 British Road Services) and absence from home (trampers 4 (nights) average per week, trunkers 3 (days or nights) on average and shunters none) meant that lorry drivers' leisure activities in their own community were severely limited. A considerable minority were also absent at weekends. Unlike the fishermen and coal miners they did not have a geographical base in which their work norms could dominate and influence their non-work activities. Therefore approximately 50 per cent of leisure activities were home centred and slightly less were 'family centred' (e.g. out for runs in car). There was not much participation in organised leisure – some 'club' membership, but all of those were in drinking clubs. 'I sleep, I've no hobbies,' was one lorry driver's account of his leisure. 'Yes, it's a lonely job, but you are independent,' said another. Trunkers had steadier friendships and more personalised conversation as they tended to meet up more.

Working conditions

The drivers had irregular and long hours (trunker the least, tramper the most). Many drivers drove illegally in terms of hours (e.g. 'no one may drive for more than five and half hours without a break of at least half an hour for rest and refreshment'). Rules such as these plus other hazards of driving often resulted in convictions but the drivers were unlikely to complain for fear of losing their job or 'demotion' to worse runs. Convictions could lead to lost licences and therefore lost jobs. (Hence the unofficial 'Drivers' Code' of flashing headlights which, among other things, warns of police.)

Basic pay rates were not high compared with similar jobs but long hours meant that earnings were only slightly below the average for manufacturing industry.

Hollowell noted the lorry driver as a difficult person to organise. London drivers were the most likely to be unionised as London dockers refused to work with any driver not producing a union card. (Unions were therefore weakly placed to deal with abuses.)

Accommodation was usually poor and at the time of the study was becoming more impersonal and more expensive, although accommodation was getting better, food was getting worse. *Headlight*, the drivers' paper, had a bias which was slightly right of centre in politics – which probably reflected their general mood and the emphasis was on individualism rather than the group solidarity of the miner.

The management of private firms was much more popular than the nationalised despite better comradeship, variety, pay and trade union representation in the nationalised sector. ('BRS won't let you use your initiative.') The tramper in both the private and nationalised firms had the most favourable view of management, perhaps because they were least in contact with their work superiors and felt themselves to be their own 'boss'.

Lorry driver compared with worker in textile factory

Hollowell also compared the attitude of lorry drivers to those of a group of textile workers. The lorry drivers expressed more satisfaction than did the textile workers in their jobs. Relations with fellow workers, familiarity with their job and wages were all more important to the textile workers than to the lorry drivers. The major dislike of the lorry drivers was the ordinary road-user. The major dislike of textile workers was monotony and boredom, supervision and management. The main source of inter-personal relationships for lorry drivers were the people they met around the country rather than their fellow lorry drivers. Two-thirds of lorry drivers said they would not consider working in a factory even for more pay (this was particularly true of 'trampers'). A few lorry drivers did find the greater comfort, regularity and domestic routine of the factory worker attractive, but most disliked the idea of factory work for the same reasons as did the textile workers themselves. Particular mention was made by lorry drivers of the satisfaction they experienced from 'responsibility'.

Hollowell expressed his view that the lorry driver was 'alienated', however it may be felt that the lorry driver was not alienated in the *generally* recognised sense because he himself had a feeling of worth, status and responsibility.

Goldthorpe's study of Luton car workers (*The Affluent Worker: Industrial Attitudes and Behaviour*, 1968) found that the skilled men valued their being able to exercise initiative and to express their individuality in the use of their skills. Semi-skilled workers, however, were aware of their lack of control over the production process and *did* feel alienated from it. They accepted their work as a fact of life, they could be satisfied *with* it without being satisfied *in* it. The semi-skilled car workers' attitude has been called 'instrumental' – the acceptance of high pay as a substitute for interesting work. Work merely becomes the instrument by which money is earned to be spent on more interesting activities elsewhere. Workers like these have also been called 'privatised' because their satisfaction is gained in their homes and in their private leisure activities rather than in their workplace.

Leisure

A two-day week; a stimulating job involving decision-making technical skill and social worth; an income sufficient to indulge your wide recreational and educational interests? Sounds exciting? But what would you do with all this free time?

It seems far-fetched in an age of rising unemployment, but with the advent of the micro-chip (the tiny circuit that controls your calculator or watch), most boring and repetitive tasks could be eliminated, and we could all have an interesting job *and* more leisure. The chip, some people argue, could bring work of a different kind, rather than simply fewer jobs.

But at the moment its introduction on to production lines and in office work is proceeding fast and with no central control. This autumn, the white-collar union, ASTMS, launched a pungent campaign drawing attention to the chip, with slogans like 'One chip can replace 800 white collars', and 'Anything you can do, a chip can do better.'

The way we handle this new technology is obviously going to influence considerably our pattern of life. Last year Clive Jenkins, general secretary of ASTMS, called for a programme in Britain to meet what he described as the 'collapse of work', citing forecasts of unemployment running as high as five million in both Britain and West Germany by the late 1980s. Meanwhile, a British woman, Kathleen Smith, recently founded the Work and Leisure Society, which is campaigning for a reduction in the working year to about 1,000 hours from about twice that amount. This, she argues, is the next step forward in civilisation. A few years ago this might have been regarded as cranky, but now it is a serious matter.

If work is becoming less important, the corollary is that leisure is becoming more so. But are we really prepared for what could be a fundamental change in the human condition? Many writers think not, and the vision of future leisure as a great human problem has been summed up recently by one of the most famous science fiction writers. Arthur C. Clarke, author of *2001*:

'In the world of the future, the sort of mindless labour that has occupied 99 per cent of mankind for much more than 99 per cent of its existence, will, of course, be largely taken over by machines. Yet most people are bored to death without work—even work that they don't like. In a workless world, therefore, only the highly educated will be able to flourish, or perhaps even to survive. The rest are likely to destroy themselves and their environment out of sheer frustration. This is no vision of the distant future; it is already happening, most of all in the decaying cities. So perhaps we should not despise TV soap operas if, during the turbulent transition period between our culture and real civilisation, they serve as yet another opium for the masses. This drug, at any rate, is cheap and harmless, serving to kill time for those many people who like it better dead.'

It is useful to see leisure as part of a dual concept alongside work, and the two words can be understood fully only in relation to one another. Unfortunately, unlike certain other easily defined double relationships, like husband and wife or parent and child, there is a large middle ground to the work-leisure relationship. This means that many quite normal and frequent activities such as housework, do-it-yourself, gardening and even eating or sleeping, are difficult to classify completely as one or the other . . .

One important factor in a person's choice of leisure activity is his occupation. In a study in 1963 by Stanley Parker, 200 people in ten occupations were interviewed. Several patterns were found. Bank employees were found to be least involved in their work, tending to see it merely as a means to earning a living. They were not so engrossed in their work that they wanted to take it over into their spare time nor were they so damaged by it that they were hostile to it. Child care officers tended to enjoy their work, and often related it to their leisure. Work and leisure for them were often similar in content, and existed comfortably side by side.

Miners and deep-sea fishermen, on the other hand, had a pattern of opposition between work and leisure. Leisure functioned for them as something totally distinct and separate—something that compensated for dangerous and difficult work. There was what might be described as hostility between work and leisure. . .

Stanley Parker, who has done much modern research into leisure, has said that 'today vestiges of the Protestant work ethic remain, but it has been strongly challenged by a more leisure-based ethic: that work is a means to the end of enjoying oneself in leisure. Earlier, work gave a man his sense of identity. Today, it is claimed, his leisure is more likely to supply it'. The extent to which we in Britain are in such a leisure-centred culture is debatable. [*New Society*, 28 November 1979 (adapted).]

REWARDS AND CONDITIONS

13.1 STATUS

People work for 'CISSES' (section 12.1). The relevant importance that people attach to each is partially a matter of individual judgement and partially a matter of necessity. If people feel that they cannot aspire to a high status position, they may dismiss such an objective and claim that they are only interested in money or job satisfaction.

One motive for work is status

"I'm sorry, J.B., the Company feels that you have failed to live up to the desk."

Work objectives are clearly very mixed. Although financial considerations may appear to be paramount, the objective may be to buy a 'status symbol' – some visible item such as a large car – which will identify them in their neighbours' eyes as belonging to a higher social group.

Some status is not connected with social class position. 'The prestige of the miner in the working class is higher than it has ever been' (*Coal is Our Life*) is a reflection of the miner's position as a successful man of action in industrial disputes rather than an identification of the miner with a higher social class. Individual miners have high status with their fellows as good, reliable workmates.

Within the workplace, status rankings are reinforced by separate toilet, eating and storage facilities. In large bureaucracies, status may be officially recognised by the provision of status symbols such as larger offices and even pieces of carpet of varying sizes.

13.2 HOURS AND CONDITIONS OF WORK

In 1938, as in 1918, the number of hours per week worked by men in manual occupations was 47; in 1983 it was 39.2 (women = 38.2) but the decline in these basic hours has largely been accounted for by overtime working which brought 'actual', as opposed to 'nominal', working hours up to 43.8 in 1983. British men work longer hours than any other in the European Economic Community except those in France and the Irish Republic.

Despite a considerable growth in holiday entitlement for manual workers in the 1970s (see Fig. 13.1) it can hardly be said that there is a problem of too much leisure.

White-collar workers have a much shorter working week than blue-collar employees, largely accounted for by an absence of overtime – 37.1 hours nominal working for men in full-time employment, plus 1.3 hours overtime making an average working week of 38.4 hours (women = 36.5 hours). The apparent 'convergence' of middle and working-class earnings must be viewed in the light of these differing working hours (Chapter 11.3).

Traditionally, manual workers have had less security of employment than non-manual, being 'laid off' more readily in times of recession or when work was seasonal. This meant that it was more difficult for them to obtain extended credit – for house purchase for example. It was also less sensible for them to save, as their savings would have to be used up before they could claim welfare benefits.

The *Employment Protection Act* (1975) and changes in social security regulations have changed the position to some extent; but the pattern of immediate spending has been established and there is still more chance of

Fig. 13.1 *paid holidays: manual employees*

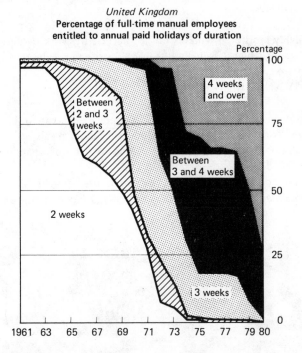

United Kingdom
**Percentage of full-time manual employees
entitled to annual paid holidays of duration**

SOURCE *Social Trends, no 12* (London: HMSO 1982).

non-manual workers saving than there is of manual workers doing so. Such differences are emphasised by the manual worker's weekly 'wage' and the non-manual employee's monthly 'salary'.

The ambience of the office or shop is more likely to encourage the employee to identify with management than is the atmosphere of the shop floor, even although the people in question may have the same earnings. Changes in the work situation for many white-collar workers may result in an end to this situation.

There have been a number of attempts to improve conditions of work:

1. Job rotation schemes which endeavour to increase work satisfaction by training people for several jobs rather than one. Volvo the Swedish car manufacturer replaced their assembly line with teams of workers who carried out all functions jointly. This is a form of the 'cell system' of organisation, also used by Philips' electrical appliance factories.

2. Four-day weeks have been tried successfully as has 'flexitime' where people organise their own working times; both are only suitable in certain situations.

More highly-motivated workers do not necessarily work harder; but there is evidence of reductions in absenteeism, illness and accidents.

13.3 PAY AND FRINGE BENEFITS

Earnings from employment are the main source of income for most people; although 'fringe benefits' may include subsidised meals, company cars, free transport, subsidised mortgages, non-contributory pension schemes

Status symbols such as company cars or houses bought with subsidised mortgages may be 'fringe benefits' – particularly higher up the class ladder

and private medical care. In recent years governments have sought, with partial success, to tax fringe benefits in order to prevent their being used to provide untaxed salary increases. With the exception of subsidised meals and transport, fringe benefits become increasingly prevalent the higher one climbs the class ladder. Table 13.1 shows the average weekly earnings of full-time employees.

Table 13.1 *average weekly earnings of full-time employees*

	Men		Women	
	1970 £	1980 £	1970 £	1980 £
Manual	26.70	111.70	13.40	68.00
Non-manual	35.10	141.30	17.80	82.70

NOTE During this period the earnings of men rose by 315 per cent, and the earnings of women by 380 per cent; increasing the average earnings of females to 65 per cent of that of males, compared with 56 per cent ten years previously.

The criteria used for deciding pay rates are partially a question of what the market will bear in terms of profit; partially a question of rewarding qualifications and scarce skills; partially sheer chance and partially industrial muscle.

13.4 TRADE UNIONS

Well over half the workers in Britain are members of a trade union. In 1980 almost thirteen million people belonged to 438 trade unions. Membership of both manual and non-manual unions have increased rapidly over the past twenty-five years but there are still considerably more blue-collar unionists than white-collar (60 per cent of potential manual and 44 per cent of potential white-collar workers belonged to unions in 1980). Reduced employment in the early eighties had reduced trade union membership to 11 744 000 by 1984.

Unions were originally set up in the middle of the nineteenth century to improve working conditions and pay; they still have these as their main objectives. Many employers are no longer hostile to trade unions, recognising that they stop more 'unofficial' strikes than they start 'official' ones.

The trade unions organised the skilled craftsmen first, restricting entry so that they could bargain from a position of scarcity. Unskilled workers were more difficult to organise and although many unskilled workers, particularly in the public sector (local government workers for example) are now members of unions, a great many others such as those in hotels and catering remain unorganised.

There has been a considerable growth in white-collar unionism during the past twenty-five years, including those in the civil service, health service and teaching. It has been suggested that this is because of an increasing identification with manual workers; open-plan offices like factories; limited promotion because of graduate recruitment; mechanisation and computerisation reducing some clerical skills to operative level; and larger organisations reducing the possibility of face to face contact with upper management (D. Lockwood, *The Black Coated Worker*, 1958). The larger and more impersonal and industrial or office unit is, the greater likelihood there is of it being unionised.

Unions tend to fall into five main groups (Clegg, *Trade Union Officers*, 1961): those representing single industries; general craft unions dealing with several industries; skilled workers' unions; ex-craft unions now admitting semi-skilled workers; and white-collar unions.

The number of unions and the overlapping of union membership within the work place often makes negotiation difficult. In 1978 the Bullock Report advocated that representatives of workers should sit on company boards of directors as they do in many countries including Germany, Sweden and Yugoslavia. Such worker participation should bring a new dimension to industrial negotiations which often appear to be based on conflict. However it should be borne in mind that even in the worst years for industrial disputes the working days lost through strike action have only been about one tenth of those lost because of sickness.

Trade unions and political power

Trades unions seek to represent, and improve the conditions of workers. They grew up to represent mainly manual workers and this is still where their main strength lies, for example, the Transport and General Workers Union, at present with over 2 million members is the biggest union in Britain. Increasingly, non-manual workers are joining trades unions such as the Association of Scientific, Technical and Managerial Staff and the National Association of Local Government Officers. Out of a workforce of about 24 million, approximately 12.4 million are members of trades unions and almost all are members of the 112 unions affiliated to the Trades Union Congress, the co-ordinating body for unions.

Trades unions gain their power from their high membership. An old trades union slogan is 'Unity is strength' and this reflects union attitudes. An individual worker has little power or influence but when he joins a union he and his colleagues can have great power. This visible type of power that unions have tends to be of a negative sort. They can disrupt industry by taking various kinds of action, the most extreme kind of which is the strike. This power to disrupt not only affects the industry concerned, but also tends to affect the public, such effects may be immediate, for example, the bread strike of 1976 or it may have a cumulative effect, for example, the lorry drivers' strike of 1979. But there is a positive side to union power which operates unobtrusively to keep the economic system function-ing. Unions prevent many worker problems reaching a serious level through their routine work; yet such work receives little publicity. Employers recognize, from a practical point of view, the value of continuing consultation with a single committee of workers' repre-sentatives and some favour the closed shop for this reason. Under such an arrangement a worker would not be accepted for employ-ment unless he belonged to a relevant union. The newspaper produc-tion industry operates a closed shop.

As trades unions exist to further their members' aims, one of their main tasks is to try to increase the wages of their members. It is in this field that economic and political forces often collide. Many governments have tried in some way to control incomes in order to control inflation. Unions have, at various stages, been willing to support the government or been wholly antagonistic to such policy. The relative failure of incomes policies has often been used as an illustration of the extent of union power – there has grown a feeling that unions have too much power. Many feel that the unions' power to cripple the country has led to a stage where governments lose if they confront unions. The events leading to the first General Election of February 1974 and the election of 1979 are cited as evidence of this. One of the first acts of the 1979 Conservative Government was to introduce proposals, promised in its manifesto, to tighten controls on unions to stop abuse of union power.

The trades unions have had long and close links with the Labour Party; indeed, some were instrumental in the foundation of the Labour Party. Even now, much of Labour Party finance comes from subscriptions from the unions which are affiliated to the party. [A. Renwick and I. Swinburn, *Basic Political Concepts* (London: Hutchinson, 1980).]

CHAPTER 14

THE CHANGING CONDITIONS OF EMPLOYMENT

14.1 INDUSTRIALISATION, AUTOMATION AND MECHANISATION

Over a hundred years ago Marx saw that the methods used in production influenced all the other processes in society; social, political and intellectual.

Marx was writing at a time when revolutionary changes were taking place in the methods used in industry. People were flocking into the towns to work in factories and mines; machines were replacing many hand crafts, and the division of labour was permitting the development of conveyor-belt industrial processes (section 12.2).

Industrialisation with its concentration of manpower in large centres encouraged the organisation of labour into unions (section 13.4) and mechanisation, with its emphasis on the importance of matter rather than man, led to the alienation of many from their work. The methods of production had created an urban culture, and with it many additional problems of poverty, squalor and crime.

Automation is capable of taking over many industrial and commercial operations by replacing not just physical labour, as mechanisation did, but thought-processes as well. The computer must be programmed by people, but once the program is in operation it can direct machines, alter schedules and correct itself. Automated machines have replaced many repetitive and undemanding work processes, but as computers become more sophisticated, they can be used to replace the more skilled personnel as well. Ultimately the worker merely controls and supervises. Automation reduces the need for a division of labour, because a large work force with each person doing a limited number of tasks is no longer needed.

Just as the Industrial Revolution was a revolution of physical power (steam, electricity, oil power) the micro-chip represents a revolution of brain power. Our society and its decision-makers depend on ever-

Automation and mechanisation has reduced employment for both men and women in industry – routine manual work has been reduced most

Automation replaces both physical labour and thought processes

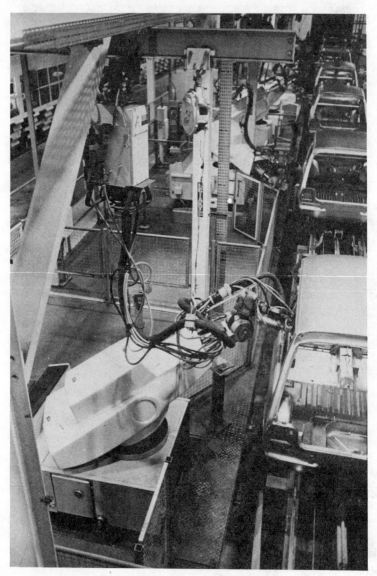

increasing sources of information. Computers represent highly sophisticated calculating machines and memory banks. The silicon chip is a tiny sliver of silicon, smaller than a thumb-nail, upon which over a quarter of a million transistors can be imprinted—possibly a billion by 1990, according to C. D. Renmore (*The Silicon Chip and You*, 1979). The present outburst of gadgets and gimmicks—TV games, calculators and watches—is only the beginning. The new generation of computers can actually be better than their programmers.

Here are some of the technological changes that are on the horizon now:

● Shopping by TV—if you decide to buy from a department store you merely key in your account number and the goods will be delivered to you. *Exchange and Mart*, which advertises everything from cars to jobs, is already being prepared for Prestel, the Post Office's information system.

● People can work from home, communicating through visual display units.

● Self-education will rapidly advance through video-cassettes, while services like Prestel will be able to provide almost any information— a visual encyclopaedia.

● A computer rather than a doctor can make a diagnosis. Experiments have shown that people often tell computers things they would never tell their doctor.

These changes will not only affect the unskilled. As Christopher Evans pointed out in his popular TV series, *The Mighty Micro*, the disseminators of information will be threatened. 'It is interesting, and mildly ironic,' Evans said, 'that the impact of the computer revolution will be greatest in those areas where high levels of skill and training are normally required. Conversely those jobs which are currently assigned a low rating on the economic and social scale, jobs like packing and unpacking, cleaning and simple maintenance, truck driving and door-to-door delivery, even such despised jobs as clearing away dishes, are likely to be immune.' (*New Society*, 28 February 1980.)

14.2 CHANGING OCCUPATIONS AND OCCUPATIONAL STRUCTURE

Automation is neither a good nor a bad thing in itself. It would be possible for the wealth produced by automated factories to be concentrated in a few hands; but this would be counterproductive. For if wealth is not distributed, consumers will not be able to buy the goods produced and the automated factories could not be kept in production.

Alternatively, the process already started can continue with the number of jobs in manufacturing decreasing and the number of jobs in the 'tertiary' sector - such service areas of work as distribution, health, information, and leisure - continuing to increase.

Traditional white-collar jobs will not necessarily become more numerous as they have during the past half century, for many routine clerical functions can easily be automated. In theory the word processor could drastically reduce the number of typists.

Essentially the greatest demand for labour in the future is likely to be in personal services of various kinds. The possibility of expansion in these areas is virtually limitless, given a determination that revenue should be spent on social services; home nursing; the police; education, and leisure-related activities.

The major possible advantage in the computer revolution is that it will reduce alienation by taking over the most tedious, repetitive and soulless processes. The major danger is that society will not respond quickly enough to the change, and produce a balance of work and leisure which permits people to live a purposeful and self-fulfilling life.

Changing occupational structure

At the beginning of the century the occupational division of labour in Britain was such that over three-quarters of the employed and self-employed population were engaged in manual work. Of these, 28.7 per cent were skilled, 34.3 per cent semi-skilled, 9.6 per cent unskilled, and 1.8 per cent were self-employed artisans in 1911. Above these manual workers stood a white collar and professional class, more confidently divided then than now into the upper-middle class and lower-middle class. And above these stood the tiny group of a few thousand—the group which Lord David Cecil termed 'the governing class' of his grandfather's day. By mid-century the proportion of manual workers had fallen below two-thirds and since then it has fallen still further to roughly a half. So the first impression is of a gradual movement away from what might be called a proletarian society: and this transformation has been gathering pace in recent decades.

By 1971 the occupational structure was more differentiated and more balanced. In the middle there were now three main blocks of comparable size, each accounting for one-fifth to one-quarter of the total. There were first the semi-skilled manual workers, second the skilled manual workers, and third the clerical and sales workers. Flanking these three groups were three other small groups, each between 7 per cent and 15 per cent of the total—on the one side the unskilled workers, and on the other the professional and technical workers and the administrative, managerial, and supervisory staff.

These twentieth century shifts of occupational structure, from the shape of a pyramid to that of an electric light bulb, are characteristic of advanced industrial societies in general. Behind them lies economic transformation: from small to large scale; from manufacturing to so-called tertiary sector activity; from personal dealing to bureaucracy; from handling things to manipulating words and numbers; and from private to public organizations.

Some sociologists interpret these trends as involving the development of a middle mass of technical and clerical employees with a consequent decline of class antagonisms, and with the spectre of polarized capitalist society in retreat. But before drawing such inferences about Britain, it is prudent to notice what is perhaps the outstanding feature of occupational change, namely the growth of women's employment outside the home. Male and female involvement in the economy have run different courses over the period we are considering; both sexes were divided between manual and non-manual jobs three-quarters to one-quarter. Subsequently, the female labour force has both grown and shifted substantially into non-manual work, so that by the 1970s three-fifths of the employed women were non-manual while three-fifths of the men were still manual workers. And even the small shift to non-manual jobs among men has mostly taken place since the Second World War. What is more important about it is that the increasing numbers of higher-level professional and managerial positions have largely gone to men, while women have filled the even faster expanding array of lower white-collar jobs. [A. Halsey, *Change in British Society* (Oxford: Oxford University Press, 1981) 2nd edn.]

14.3 UNEMPLOYMENT

In the late 1970s and early 1980s unemployment started to increase rapidly in Britain, particularly among young people. This was partially a result of the new technology, but other factors were also involved:

(a) The decline in family size, increased educational provision and improved career opportunities resulted in a substantial increase in the number of married women working, passing the 50 per cent mark in 1980. Many of these married women 'returners' took work previously occupied by school leavers (e.g. Marks and Spencer).

(b) The baby bulge of the mid-1960s was working its way out of education. Even if there had been the same number of jobs as in the past there would have been insufficient.

(c) A world-wide slump in trading, following the OPEC oil price increases early in the 1970s, was still out of control. A fear of hyper-inflation prevented most countries reinflating their economies in order to boost trade.

(d) Some organisations took advantage of the excuse of the recession to rid themselves of the overmanning which had built up during the boom period, when trade unions could use their muscle to more effect to prevent labour shedding.

(e) Great Britain had fewer young people in full-time post-school education and apprenticeships than any other EEC country; overall 44 per cent of 16 to 18 year olds were available for work or unemployment.

Young people at work

In the UK and throughout the western world a rapidly growing proportion of young people appears to be faced with the almost certain prospect of periods of prolonged unemployment brought about by fundamental changes in the structure of industry and commerce. However, many young people currently in employment find that a lack of initial basic educational skills, together with the lack of access to training facilities at work, means that their ability to adapt to these changes is also very restricted.

Concern is felt, in this country, that unemployment is being disproportionately borne by the younger age groups who, without experience of work, have only recently arrived on a stagnant job market. Moreover, this burden falls most heavily on those who are already disadvantaged in other respects by race or sex prejudice, family background and mental or physical handicap. Much worse, the very success of our educational system in upgrading the qualifications of more young people has made the deficiencies of that 20% who leave school without them so much more prominent. This development has occurred within the last 15 years and it is perhaps surprising that we have not so far considered its consequences, which include making this group more vulnerable to unemployment.

Many people leave school with a feeling of failure or rejection and face the possibility of unemployment and other consequences of rapidly changing economic and social conditons. They are likely to have rejected formal education and any systems of support which appear to share the characteristics of school. . .the array of options at 16+ is growing in number and degree. For example, staying on in full-time education may mean a traditional selective sixth form, a comprehensive sixth form, a sixth form college, a college of further education or a tertiary college. If the choice is to leave school, then the young person may be faced with employment which leads to a career and encourages further education and training, or dead-end work where further education is positively discouraged. Much worse, there is the possibility of being faced with no employment at all.

The wonder perhaps is that so many young people emerge relatively unscathed from the process. But it must be said that in the context of this country's current economic and social problems, particularly in relation to the high levels of youth unemployment, the hazards faced by some young people are greatly increased and

159

"If the economy does pick up there'll be devastating unemployment . . ."

"*Just think—twenty years ago we'd both have been stuck in the kitchen.*"

the numbers still unharmed at the end are likely to be fewer. Moreover, all these aspects of the period of transition should perhaps be set against one general 'disadvantage', that is, that they have been in, and may only now be slowly emerging from a position of subordination.

This notion of subordination should be seen in relation to their parents, to their teachers and, very likely, in the work place too. At home, at school and at work they tend not to be masters of their destinies, nor to be able easily to discover how to proceed along the road to greater independence and self-realisation. They are 'handicapped' by a background of emotional dependence on their family, a lack of experience of the world outside the home and school and, for many, a shortage of money. Room for manoeuvre is often limited and independence frequently has to be struggled for. The world of work offers the chance of this independence. For some it presents the opportunities for a wider range of social contacts; for others, the fulfilment of individual talents or skills; and for all, through the regular provision of an income, the chance to participate in the various elements of today's youth culture. [Adapted from *Broadcasting and Youth* (Gulbenkian Foundation, 1979).]

By 1984 more than 3 million people in Great Britain were unemployed, ranging from about 10 per cent of the working population in the South-East to about 20 per cent in Northern Ireland. The old industrialised areas were the worst affected. Statistics for 1972, 1976 and 1981 are shown in Figure 14.1.

The effects of unemployment

The unemployed girls I met seemed, for the most part, less deeply demoralized than the boys: as they are usually expected to shoulder a share of the housework, they have more to occupy their time than boys; their expectations of life are less heavily geared to career and earning power; and the option is open to them to resolve the problem of inability to afford a night out by going out with boys who are in work. Even for them, unemployment remains a distasteful, distressing experience. Caroline Weymouth, a pretty eighteen-year-old, was still in her dressing-gown at 3 in the afternoon when I called at her parents' home on Nightingale estate.

'I always wanted to be a ground stewardess. Two years before I left school I wrote to all the airlines and they told me to start off in a travel agent's. But the careers teacher told me I hadn't done well enough at school and the only job I could do was shop work. I got a job at British Home Stores, but I chucked it in. Some of the customers who came in treated you like muck. That's why a lot of the

Fig.14.1 *unemployment: by sex and occupation*

Great Britain

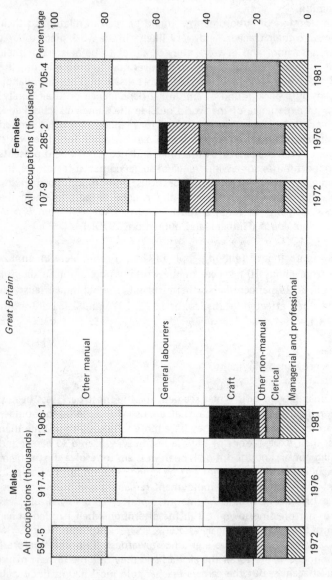

Excluding school leavers and people without an occupation

SOURCE *Social Trends 1983* (London: HMSO, 1982).

girls don't like serving and you see them standing around talking. I am looking now for another job, but I can't afford to go for interviews.'

Unemployment and the high cost of an increasingly commercialized leisure combined to cheat Caroline Weymouth of her carefree years. Much of the risk of crime she fears arises from the clash of these same two factors. Black youth, especially boys, face the roughest job outlook of all. A continuing, concealed discrimination compounds the effect of a low average level of educational attainment, and there is, too, a greater sensitivity to some of the routine humiliations of employment which, when overlaid with a racial dimension, take on more offensive weight. And unemployed black youths live more of their lives on the street, where questioning and confrontation with the police are a perennial hazard.

'Time has no relevance for these boys,' says Stamford Hill project leader Irwin Horsford. 'There is no difference for them between midnight and midday. They just wake up and exist and sleep. They have no purpose and no aim.' The diurnal rhythm shifts forward, out of joint with light and dark. You get up close to lunchtime, go to bed in the early hours of the morning. The capacity for timekeeping decays. Appointments are not kept, and when by a miracle a job does come along, it is often lost because the organism cannot readjust to early rising and clockwork regularity. Thus the unemployed become unemployable. . . Press concern and political initiatives have concentrated on alleviating unemployment among the under-twenties. But the problem of unemployment among twenty-to-twenty-five-year-olds is in many respects more serious. Among manual workers, this is the crucial time of family formation, of heavy expenditure on home-making or house purchase, and, most important, of the rearing of vulnerable and impressionable children whose physical and mental development can be retarded by poor nutrition, whose moral and emotional development can be blighted by conflicts in the home or by family breakdown.

Yet there is no social group that has been worse affected by crisis than families with young children. [Paul Harrison, *Inside the Inner City* (Harmondsworth: Penguin, 1983).]

Unemployment can be reduced by changing the occupational structure of our society (section 14.2); work sharing; abolition or reduction in overtime working; early retirement; extended education; longer holidays; a shorter working week, and new employment in industries yet unthought of that will be created by the micro-chip revolution – just as cars were unthought of before the industrial revolution.

All these solutions have problems of cost or political will and some take a pessimistic view of the future – one in which there is little or no economic growth and the people of the UK are divided into those who number in their households at least one paid worker and those who, because they do not, are largely reliant on whatever unemployment compensation it is decided they should receive.

One of the functions of work is the provision of status (section 12.1). It is probable that in a society of the permanently unemployed, status will be sought in other ways – some damaging to other members of that society.

A major effect of unemployment is that it tends to be socially isolating. At the psychological level there is the shock, shame, loss of confidence and loss of occupational identity. This results in a tendency to withdraw from contact with others. There is also the direct loss of the work place as a source of conversation and social contact. The whole effect is exacerbated by the fact that the economic effects of unemployment enforce curtailing leisure pursuits and social life. Visits to the pub have to be cut down or given up entirely. The car may also have to be given up, so that visits to relatives become rarer, and so on.

For the family man, this means that the family itself becomes the main source of social contact and therefore the major social setting within which the stresses of unemployment are experienced and dealt with. However, when the father of a family ceases to be in full-time work, the balance of the family shifts. He feels he loses not only his occupational but also his sexual identity and comes under pressure to take on a more 'feminine' role: doing the housework, taking the children to school.

A 37-year-old electrician who had lost his job five months before said that 'apart from getting very bored in the morning', he generally did the housework while his wife was out at work and prepared an evening meal for the children. The children still had adequate clothing and food. However, he would not apply for free school dinners for them: 'There's a terrible unemployment situation in Merseyside. I don't think it should have to reflect on the children, that would be begging—it is bad enough that I have to claim, but not to pass it onto the children—I don't agree with it. Children have a wicked nature if they find out. Children take the mickey—I wouldn't like that.'

A 52-year-old man, made redundant four months earlier, said that he and his wife used to go most weekends to shows or clubs, but not now, 'They are out of bounds'. He was always used to being the breadwinner and it was degrading—'The position I held and now having no position at all'.

A 23-year-old man had been out of work for just under a year. He said this was, 'The worst thing that ever happened to me. I can't stand being out of work. You are bad-tempered all the time.'

He said his wife did not have to do anything in the house when he was there—he got fed up sitting there, so he did the cooking and everything to pass the day, not because his wife asked him to – 'I play with the baby all the time.'

Sometimes the stresses of unemployment threaten the marriage itself. A 28-year-old man, married with two children, unemployed for 18 months, when asked what he did with his time replied 'Nothing'. He said he just sat in the house and argued all the time with his wife. His wife had actually been twice to a solicitor about a divorce. He said there was 'nothing to do at home but watch television, night and day'. (John Hill, 'The Psychological Impact of Unemployment', *New Society*, 17 March 1978.)

14.4 WOMEN AND WORK

Before the Industrial Revolution the rural family worked as a unit, although the work roles were segregated with the woman doing the less important jobs – particularly those in and close to the house, such as milking cows (P. Branca, *Women in Europe since 1750*, 1978). As she was likely to be more or less continuously pregnant or caring for babies this might seem reasonable enough. Children were necessary as a labour force and as an insurance policy for the parents' old age. High infant mortality rates required the birth of many so that at least a few would survive.

Enclosures and population growth drove people into the towns. Men went into factories, shipyards or mines, leaving their wives at home so that work became segregated from family life. Women were still bound to the home by children and tradition, and married women were not expected to work outside the home – and less than ten per cent *did* up to the First World War. Even in 1956 the coalminers of *Coal is Our Life* regarded a working wife as a loss of status, the implication being that her man was unable to keep her. Many women worked part-time at home for low wages, and 'outworkers' are still badly paid.

Single women worked in factories, such as linen mills, or went into service. Conditions and pay were poor, and marriage ended their employment. Childbearing would usually cease only a few years before the average age of death, so there was little point in preparing for a career. Because women appeared to be prepared to work for low pay, male unions enforced sanctions against their employment in skilled sectors of industry such as engineering.

Shorthand appeared in 1870, the typewriter was invented in 1873, and the first telephone exchange in Britain was opened in 1876. These inventions provided socially acceptable employment for middle-class women and an avenue of social mobility for the working class; but like nursing – already established as a woman's job – they could be badly paid.

Teaching and the civil service also opened up career prospects for women, but they had to remain unmarried.

The First World War dramatically changed outlooks. Women had to replace the men away at the front, and proved that they could work in munitions factories and drive buses. After the war the unions insisted that old agreements banning women from certain jobs came back into force, but women were given the vote.

The Second World War renewed the demand for women workers, and facilities such as nurseries and school meal services were provided. The post-war boom enabled women to continue in employment and by 1981 56.2 per cent of all women aged between 16 and 60 were at work; the number of married women working rising from 48.8 per cent in 1971 to 56.8 per cent in 1981.

Family limitation facilities and improved education have provided opportunities for many women to plan a career. There are however still inbuilt disadvantages to women in employment; particularly a reluctance to train a woman because of the likelihood that she will marry and leave. Most importantly, women are still socialised to regard only certain jobs as appropriate to them (section 8.4).

Working mothers often experience role-conflict and feel guilty that they are neglecting their children, but there is little evidence that children over three *do* suffer. (Yudkin and Holme, *Working Mothers and their Children*, 1963; Jephcott, Seear and Smith, *Married Women Working*, 1961; Klein, *Britain's Married Women Workers*, 1965).

In spite of claims in the past that the children of working mothers are likely to become delinquent or show psychiatric disorder, there is abundant evidence from numerous studies that this is not so. Children do not suffer from having several mother-figures so long as stable relationships and good care are provided by each. Indeed some studies have shown that children of working mothers may even be *less* likely to become delinquent than children whose mothers stay at home. In these circumstances it seemed that the mother going out to work was a reflection of a generally high standard of family responsibility and care. Two provisos need to be made with respect to these studies. First, there has been little investigation of the effects of mothers starting work while their children are still infants, although such data as are available do not suggest any ill-effects. Second, a situation in which mother-figures keep changing so that the child does not have the opportunity of forming a relationship with any of them may well be harmful. Such unstable arrangements usually occur in association with poor-quality maternal care, so that it has not been possible to examine the effects of each independently.

Much the same can be said about the effects of day nurseries and crèches (as particular forms of care often used when mothers go out to work). Assertions in official reports (WHO Expert Committee on Mental Health, 1951) concerning their permanent ill-effects are quite unjustified. Day care need not necessarily interfere with the normal mother-child attachment (Caldwell, Wright, Honig and Tannenbaum, 1970) and the available evidence gives no reason to suppose that the use of day nurseries has any long-term psychological or physical ill-effects. [Michael Rutter, *Maternal Deprivation Reassessed* (Harmondsworth: Penguin, 1972).]

Equal pay for equal work was supposedly guaranteed from 1975 (by the *Equal Pay Act* 1970) but this is still often circumvented. The Equal Opportunities Commission was established on 29 December 1975 under Section 53 of the *Sex Discrimination Act 1975*. The functions of the Commission are:

(i) to work towards the elimination of discrimination, as defined by the Act;
(ii) to promote equality between men and women generally;
(iii) to keep under review the working of the Act and the Equal Pay Act 1970;
(iv) the commissioning or support of research and educational activities related to equal opportunities for men and women.

In 1982, C. Hakim ('Job Segregation' in *Employment Gazette*, HMSO) claimed that towards the end of the 1970s almost all the progress made in breaking down traditional barriers at work had been reversed as a result of the recession. Women were again a declining proportion of those in skilled and managerial jobs. In 1982 the gap between male and female earnings had begun to widen again.

The role of women

In 1857, an income of £1,000 a year would support a family and at least five servants: an income of £500, a family and three servants. The wages of a 'maid of all work' were then between £6 10s and £10 a year 'with allowances for tea, sugar and beer'. From the mid century on, a large proportion of the rising number of females in the population was taken into domestic employment, which in 1881 accounted for one in seven of the total working population.

Nevertheless, from the 1870s on, domestic servants became harder to get, both because of the growing number of middle-class housewives who wanted them, and because girls who were potential recruits for domestic service began to move into the expanding feminine occupations of sales work, clerical work, and teaching. By 1900, there was a 'servant problem', and the possibility of conflict between the housewife and mother roles for the middle-class woman was widely recognized. It was argued that: 'the middle-class mother must perforce be provided with domestic assistance, not that she might indulge in indolence, but that she might be free to devote all her energies to the proper upbringing of her children.'

The servant shortage made the domestic roles of middle-class and working-class women more and more alike. The combination of the maternal role with the housewife/houseworker role, until then a feature of working-class life only, became the norm. Where the middle-class wife had been idle she now worked, and in this transition lies perhaps one explanation of housework's modern status as non-work. The mid-nineteenth-century role of housewife-supervisor became the twentieth century role of housewife-worker. The working-class woman had long been in this situation, but this fact was concealed beneath her role as productive worker. At the point in history when working-class women began to turn to housewifery as a fulltime occupation in significant numbers, the middle-class woman began to take part in the actual work required by it.

Other changes in the roles of women in the family during the later part of this period followed the same trend towards casting both middle and working-class married women in the modern role of housewife. First and foremost, a revolution was occurring in the role and status of the child in society. General mortality declined from the middle of the nineteenth century, and infant mortality – deaths in the first year of life – fell significantly around the turn of the century. The increasing likelihood that a child would survive into adulthood altered the attitude to children: the individual child came to be seen as irreplaceable. Whilst, in the seventeenth century, childhood ceased at seven or eight, the evolution of the modern school system removed children from the adult world for a much longer time, thus lengthening their period of dependence on adults. In 1833 the first allocation of money for educational purposes was made by the central government; by 1856, the state's expenditure on education had become so large that a Department of Education was set up; in 1870 an Education Act provided compulsory elementary education for all children. Thirty-two years later came an Act which established a state system of secondary education.

The growth of the state educational system proceeded directly from the needs of an industrialized society. The specialization of work roles called for a more literate and knowledgeable population. [A. Oakley, *Housewife* (Harmondsworth: Penguin, 1974).]

Women, education and work

The way that girls see themselves and their abilities determines their range of job opportunities and also combines to temper many of their views on for instance the substance and value of working and having careers, getting married and setting up a home. Their future intentions build on these sorts of foundations, interacting with what they have learnt and feel about 'femininity' and female role. Today all kinds of ideas about women's position are presented and school cannot be accused of putting forward a totally biased picture. Successful women are in evidence and equality is becoming a commonplace word. But it takes more than passive demonstration of this to counter the strength of traditional beliefs which are more acceptably reinforced, and unless girls belong to the minority (mainly middle class) that move upwards into higher education, they tend to fall back on the familiar expectations of feminine roles.

Every girl (or boy) has a unique view of the world and life, and usually shares common goals and values with friends. This is formed out of their 'informal' education: for instance through their own experiences, family, friends, the media, and the teachings of the law and church; and the 'formal' education of school.

Most girls retain a strong hold on many of the traditional ideas about womanhood and this is not surprising. It reflects a depth of internalization of 'femininity', lack of confidence about change, uncritical acceptance of the ways things are, and a lack of viable alternatives, rather than simply the effects of social conditioning. Even where girls recognize and understand their position and its limitations and discriminations, it is hard to conceive of realistic ways to change this. Girls have seldom been allowed much experience outside home and school, and have read relatively little that deals comprehensively with aspects of their own lives. They see many of their relatives and friends doing jobs from which they seem to gain minimal enjoyment. It therefore makes sense to make their priorities love, marriage, husbands, children, jobs and careers, more or less in that order.

Their feelings and views affect areas of decision in their lives already circumscribed by factors like sex and class. They consider and arrange opinions subjectively and objectively, in ways which do not necessarily coincide. These are weighed up with personal needs, self-image and actual school performance to set in motion the motivations that can have irreversible consequences. Girls are aware of the value of academic achievement but see this still as more to do with boys and men, whose relative non-conformity and irresponsibility does not seem to prevent them from gaining the higher positions. It becomes easy for girls to acknowledge the objective worth of scholarship while excusing themselves for not being 'that sort of person'.

Many girls' lives follow a similar pattern – boredom with school, early leaving into a local job that has marginal interest, finding a steady boyfriend, saving up to marry, settling down and having a family. Marriage and home-making appear as a meaningful distraction or welcome release for those with boring jobs or those who have no intention of making work a central part of their lives. Girls' needs and feelings about this form part of an evolving self-identity. This is still malleable and open to change, but the consequences of choices made at this stage are often irreversible. Once technical or academic courses have been rejected it is very hard to pick them up again. Women who have left education a long way behind them while pursuing family roles often realize the vacuum when their children have grown, but their lack of qualifications and training makes only mundane work available. The paucity and narrowness of re-training schemes for women still leaves most with the typical range of lower level employment. [S. Sharpe, *Just Like a Girl* (Harmondsworth: Penguin, 1976) (abridged).]

QUESTIONS FROM PAST O-LEVEL GCE PAPERS

1. WOMEN'S MOTIVES FOR RETURNING TO WORK

'For others the pressure is more subtle: it is not only econo-mic, it comes through isolation, boredom and the lack of status as well. As the Finer report put it, most women now "fit in" child-bearing between leaving school and having a job. Perhaps because this period is now so short it has become the period in life which confers least status. The achievement of giving birth is only briefly recognised. Many young mothers soon lose their own identity, and come to be regarded (by themselves as much as by others) merely as an extension of their children by day and their husbands by night. So the pressure on women today is to go back to work in order to *participate* in society and not simply for economic reasons.'

(New Society, January 1975.)

(a) What arguments support or refute the author's suggestion that the period of child bearing is ". . . short and confers least status"?

(b) What, have sociologists suggested, are the reasons for women going back to work?   Associated Examining Board

2. Explain, with examples, how the occupation which a person follows affects many areas of his life outside work.

Associated Examining Board

3. Comment on the causes and consequences of changes in the proportion of women working in the light of the following table:

Year	Females as % of Labour Force	Married Females as % of Females in Labour Force
1921	29.5	12.9
1931	29.8	15.2
1951	30.8	38.2
1961	32.5	50.2
1971	36.6	63.1

Oxford Local Examining Board

4. How would you distinguish between 'mechanization' and 'automation'? What effects does automation have on job satisfaction?   Oxford Local Examining Board

5. **Either,** (a) Explain what is meant by *division of labour*, and comment on any **four** of its disadvantages.

   Or, (b) Distinguish between 'work' and 'leisure' and discuss any **two** ways in which they are related.   Welsh Joint Examining Board

6. 'Being made redundant and unemployment are always serious problems, but they are more serious for some kinds of worker than for others.' Discuss.   Oxford Local Examining Board

7. **Either,** (a) What is a trade union? Describe and comment on any **three** functions of trade unions.

   Or, (b) Outline and comment on any **three** social consequences of technological change in British society.

                    Welsh Joint Examining Board

8. The table on page 172 reports the results of a piece of research which investigated terms and conditions of employment of three groups of employees. The figures reported in the table represent the percentage of each group who work under each of the selected categories of terms and conditions of employment listed below.

(a) Which occupational group according to the table normally works the shortest hours?   (1)

Terms and Conditions of Employment	% of Factory Workers working under each condition	% of Clerical Workers working under each condition	% of Senior Managers working under each condition
Holidays: 15 days plus	38	74	88
Normal working over 40 hours per week	97	9	22
Pension – employers scheme	67	90	96
Time off with pay for personal reasons	29	83	93
Pay taken off for any lateness	80	8	0
No clocking-on or booking-in	2	48	94

(b) Which group is least closely supervised at work? (1)

(c) Identify the terms and conditions of employment identified in the table which show

  (i) the smallest differences
  (ii) the greatest differences

between the factory workers and the senior managers. (2)

(d) The above table suggests a close similarity in terms and conditions of employment between the clerical workers and the senior managers. Suggest three possible areas of *differences* not listed which may exist between clerical workers and senior managers in their terms and conditions of employment. (3)

(e) In what ways might *the information above* be used to challenge the argument that manual workers are being absorbed into the lower middle class? (5)

(f) (i) What significant changes have occurred in the nature of clerical work this century? (4)
  (ii) How have these affected the position of clerical workers? (4)

Associated Examining Board

PART VI

DEMOGRAPHIC AND SOCIAL

ASPECTS OF POPULATION

POPULATION CHANGE

IN BRITAIN

15.1 HISTORICAL PERSPECTIVE

Demography is the study of human populations, particularly their size, structure and development. The study of demography in a scientific way probably started in 1662 when John Graunt published *Natural Political Observations on the Bills of Mortality* in which he showed a pattern between the proportions of deaths to various causes in London. He also tried to chart what happened to a group of children born at the same time up until their deaths. In the seventeenth and eighteenth century the development of life insurance encouraged the study of health, disease and death. The first major systematic study of population was Malthus's *Essay on Population* (1798) in which he claimed a 'law of population' – 'that the human species, when unchecked, goes on doubling itself every twenty-five year . . . while the means of subsistence, under circumstances the most favourable to human industry, could not possibly be made to increase faster than in an arithmetical ratio . . . man would increase as the numbers 1. 2. 4. 8. 16. 32. 64. 128. 256 and subsistence as 1. 2. 3. 4. 5. 6. 7. 8. 9'. Economic improvements could only be temporary, as the population would reduce itself by war, famine and disease once the optimum point was reached. Some used Malthus's theory to argue against improving the conditions of the poor as this would only mean that more people would survive and bring the cataclysmic collapse of population nearer.

In the nineteenth century the taking of a regular census encouraged interest in the study of population movements, mortality and fertility. The first census was taken in 1801; and there has been a similar survey, including every individual in the country, every ten years since (except the war year of 1941).

The questions asked in the census are not always the same. From 1851 to 1911 people were asked about infirmities, including deafness and blindness; in 1951 and 1961 adults were asked to state the age at which they ceased full-time education; in 1971 educational qualifications were asked for. However, in each census the size of the population has been established and since 1821 (except in 1831) details of people's ages have been obtained.

Since 1837 there has been compulsory registration of births, marriages and deaths. Clearly, the government would not collect such information – at considerable expense – if it was not useful in predicting such matters as how many old people are likely to need care in the future, or how many school places are likely to be required in twelve years.

Demography is an inexact science. In 1972 the projected population of the United Kingdom for the year 2001 was 62.4 million, while the 1979 figures forecast 57.9 million, a difference of 4.5 million could clearly have considerable implications for the provision of services. No demography at all would result in chaos!

In the eleventh century there were probably not many more than one million people in England and Wales. This rose slowly to about 5 million in 1600, about 6 million in 1700, and 8 893 000 in 1801. There was then a 'population explosion' to 22 712 000 in 1871, because the birth rate remained about the same but the death rate generally declined (although not in some industrial centres) as a result of improving hygiene and medical knowledge. More children were surviving to have children themselves, an additional factor being migration from Ireland. Figure 15.1 shows population changes and projections.

Fig. 15.1   *population changes and projections (United Kingdom)*

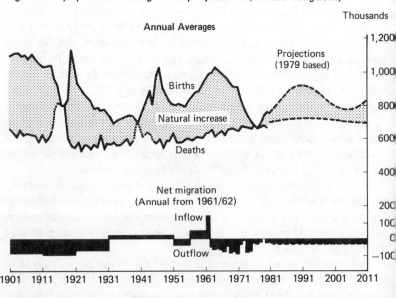

SOURCE   *Social Trends 1983* (London: HMSO, 1982)

15.2 LIFE EXPECTANCY

The expectation of life is the average number of years a person can expect to live at a given age, if the deaths at each age experienced that year occurred in all future years. A man born in 1901 could then have expected to live until 1949 if 1901 death rates remained unchanged between 1901 and 1949. If he survived this 'expectation of life at birth' beyond the average expectancy of 48 years he could at that stage expect to live until 1976, or longer if the death rates continued to decline. In 1978 a boy at birth could have expected to live until 70 and a girl could have expected to live until 76.

Because improving health standards have mainly improved the chances of young people to survive to an older age, the expectation of life for people who *do* survive into old age has not changed much. In 1901, if a man had been fortunate enough to survive until the age of 80 he could expect to survive a further 4.9 years; in 1979 his chances of survival had only increased by another nine months. For comparisons of nineteenth- and twentieth-century populations, see Figure 15.2.

15.3 POST-1870 BIRTH RATE

The 'birth rate' is the number of live births per thousand of the population in a given year. This is sometimes also called the 'crude birth rate' because it can give a misleading impression of fertility, if the number of women of child-bearing age in the population is greater at one point of comparison than at another. The 'fertility rate' is the number of live births in any one year per thousand fertile women in the population, between the ages of 15 and 44. Although used less often, this is a more accurate reflection of the level of child-bearing than the 'birth rate'.

The birth rate started to go down steadily from about 1871. A number of factors were probably involved:

(a) improving standards of health meant that people gradually realised that they did not have to have many children so that a few would survive to look after them in their old age;

(b) the introduction of full-time education made children an economic liability rather than an economic asset as they could not be put to work;

(c) the middle classes started to limit their children in the depression of 1870s when the cost of living rose but their incomes remained the same. The working class gradually followed this example, in order to maintain or improve their standard of living. (J. A. Banks, *Prosperity and Parenthood*, 1954);

Fig. 15.2   *population of Great Britain (in millions)*

POPULATION OF GREAT BRITAIN 1801-1971 (IN MILLIONS)																	
19th Century										**20th Century**							
'01	'11	'21	'31	'41	'57	'61	'71	'81	'91	'01	'11	'21	'31	'41	'51	'61	'71
11	12	14	16	19	21	23	26	30	33	37	41	43	45	no census	49	51	54

SOURCE   OPCS, *People in Britain; Social Studies in the Census* (London: HMSO, 1981)

The 1981 census showed a slight increase to 54 285 422. This population consisted of 26 339 799 males and 27 945 623 females.

(d) birth control became more general following the trial of Charles Bradlaugh and Annie Besant in 1875 for obscenity in circulating a birth-control manual written by an American doctor. The trial publicity boosted sales. Although sentenced to imprisonment, they were released on a technicality.

In 1871 the live births per thousand fertile women (the fertility rate) was 151; in 1881 it had dropped to 146 and by 1891 it was 129. After 1891 the birth rate continued to drop until 1931 when it levelled out, with slight peaks in the late forties and early sixties, followed by a further slight decline. The continued trend after 1891 can be accounted for by:

(a) old age pensions and other welfare benefits making children less necessary to secure one's old age;

(b) improvement in methods of birth control, particularly the introduction of the contraceptive pill;

(c) changing attitudes – including a decline in the effectiveness of religious sanctions on birth control and fashion in family size – as smaller families became the norm;

(d) the legalisation of abortion in 1967;

(e) improvements in educational opportunities and career prospects for girls and women has led to the postponement of families; decisions not to have a family at all and to concentrate on a career, or the earlier completion of family building in order to return to work;

(f) increasing expectations in terms of the standard of living; uncrowded homes, foreign holidays and other material improvements; perhaps also a desire to give fewer children greater opportunities;

(g) the growth of the mobile nuclear family as the main operating unit without the support of the extended family.

The slight increase in the late 1940s can be accounted for by large numbers of men returning from war and delayed families being started; the bulge in the 1960s by the post-war babies growing up and starting families of their own. A slight and temporary decline in the age of mar- riage and, possibly, upward mobility for some encouraged them to adopt the rather larger family pattern of the upper middle class. In addition there was a substantial increase in immigration during this period from areas with a higher fertility rate than Britain – perhaps a third of additional births were as a result of this factor.

In the late 1970s and early 1980s there was a slight increase in the birth rate which may show that there was a postponement of family building in the early 1970s, and we may now be settling to a slightly higher level of family size. Table 15.1 shows birth and fertility rates between 1977 and 1981.

Overall, Britain's population is now static – an increase of 0.5 per cent in the population of England and Wales occurred between the census returns of 1971 and 1981.

Birth projections

The number of births depends on the numbers of women of child- bearing age and the number of live births per woman (the fertility rate). The first of these two factors may be estimated fairly reliably for many years ahead: they will be increasing up to the early 1990s and then diminishing. If the fertility rate were stable the number of births would likewise grow until the early 1990s and then shrink. However, the second factor, the fertility rate, is, unfortunately for our purposes, less predictable and has been at the root of the major fluctuations in births this century.

Setting aside the disturbances of wartime the fertility rate, expressed as the average completed family size, was well over 3.0 per woman in the early 1900s falling to about 1.8 in the 1930s. It subsequently rose again, almost reaching 3.0 in 1964, and then declined to a minimum in 1977 which if continued would have led to an average completed family size of 1.7. By 1980 the rate was up to 1.9 and the annual births total had correspondingly risen by 15 per cent. However, birth registrations were again falling by late 1980 and despite some increase in the second half of 1981 (after allowing for seasonal factors) the total for 1981 was slightly down.

It assumed that fertility rates will tend to increase, reaching a level from the late 1980s onward which would imply an average completed family size of 2.1 per woman, and would, in the long-term, lead to a stable population. Actual births were above the principal projection in 1980 and below it in 1981. The small fall in births in 1981, together with the observed fertility levels of the last few years which have been well below the 2.1 long-term level assumed for the principal projection, provides some grounds for caution before adopting this projection for immediate planning purposes without considering alternatives. (Department of Education and Science, *Report on Education, no. 97*, May 1982.)

15.4 DEATH RATE AND INFANT MORTALITY

The 'death' or 'mortality' rate is the number of deaths per thousand of the population in a given year. The population rose dramatically in the nineteenth century because the death rate declined, although it remained high, while the birth rate remained the same. Although the death rate has continued to decline, the population has not continued to explode because the birth rate has fallen even more. In Britain the birth rate has fallen below 'replacement level', that is, the death rate was higher (at 11.8 in 1975) than the birth rate (11.6 in 1975) and so the population was becoming smaller, if migration was ignored.

Table 15.1 *births and the fertility rate (England)*

	1977	1978	1979	1980	1981 (provisional)
Births (thousands)	537	563	610	618	597
Fertility rate[1]	1.7	1.8	1.9	1.9	1.8

[1] Expressed as the average completed family size.

The major reason for the increase in life expectancy towards the end of the nineteenth century was the drop in the death rate among the young – those who survived into old age often lived as long as the elderly today

The death rate started to fall because of a combination of accident, medical discoveries, legislation and invention. Among these are the success of the brown rat in eliminating the black rat whose fleas caused plague (about 1750); the improvements in farming at the beginning of the eighteenth century which improved the diet of many people; the discovery of vaccination against smallpox by Jenner (1796); the introduction of anaesthesia for operations in 1846; and the *Factory Acts* laying down rules governing the conditions in which children were permitted to work (1802, 1819, 1833, 1844, etc). *Public Health Acts* (1872 and 1875) established sanitary authorities responsible for sewerage, water supply and refuse disposal and thus helped to eliminate cholera and typhoid, while the *Sale of Food and Drugs Act* (1975) and other Acts to improve housing and medical care also contributed to the decline in mortality as did the drop in maternal mortality resulting from excessive childbearing. The death rate was 22.5 between 1861 and 1870; but had dropped to 11.7 between 1961 and 1970.

Infant mortality is the number of live-born children who die before they are one year old out of every thousand live births in the population and is regarded as a good guide to the state of health and health services in a country. In 1980 Britain had a higher infant mortality rate than Sweden, Japan and France but lower than Italy or West Germany.

In 1841, when death rates were first collected in England and Wales, a boy of fifteen could expect to live a further 43.6 years and a girl for 44.1 years; by 1960 he could have expected to live for 55.3 years and a girl for 60.9 years. The expectation of life for males is now fairly static, but that of females continues to improve.

The decrease in infant mortality and the continued slight decline in the death rate generally in the present century has been the result of continued legislation to improve health and hygiene, particularly the introduction of the National Health Service in 1946 and the improvements in antenatal and post-natal care of the mother and child. The infant-killers of the past; diphtheria, whooping cough and measles have either been eliminated or rendered non-fatal. An antitoxin for diphtheria was first produced in 1890 and greatly improved since, so that the 2400 deaths in 1940 had been reduced to nil by 1973. Penicillin brought a spectacular decrease in death from infections after its introduction during the Second World War.

Infant mortality was about 150 throughout the second half of the nineteenth century; dropped to 53 by 1939, to 32 in the late 1940s and was down to 19 by 1965. There has, however, always been a considerable social class variation in the infant mortality rates. In 1972 the figure for Social Class 1 (Professional) was 11.6 and for Social Class 5 (Unskilled) 30.7; by 1980 these figures had reduced to 8.9 and 16.0 respectively.

Social class and fertility

Social class variations in fertility

One aspect of differential fertility suddenly became the subject of violent public controversy in October 1974 as a result of a speech in Birmingham by Sir Keith Joseph. In the course of the speech he drew attention to the fact that disproportionately large number of children were born to parents least able to afford to bring up a family. Some of the mothers were very young, quite unable to cope, had had a poor education, and were unmarried, and in these cases Sir Keith concluded that the whole process operated to the disadvantage of the mothers themselves, of the children (who, in the absence of parental control and guidance, were quite likely to develop into unsatisfactory adults), and of society; if these mothers could be persuaded to practise birth control if would therefore be of benefit all round. Inevitably his speech was seen in some quarters as an attack on the working class as a whole, and as reopening the issue of population quality.

Not long after Sir Keith Joseph's speech the Registrar General published some new figures relating to a 3.3 per cent sample of *legitimate* live births which occurred between 1970 and 1972. These figures showed that within the overall decline of some 8 per cent taking place over this relatively short period, there appeared to have been a social class gradient of a rather unexpected kind, in that legitimate live births in families where the husband's occupation brought him into Social Classes I and II had *increased* by 2 per cent, while for Social Class III there was a 9 per cent *decrease*, and for Social Classes IV and V a 16 per cent *decrease*. Because of possibly substantial sampling errors and other reasons, these figures have to be treated with considerable caution; but they do nevertheless suggest that the traditional social class gradient in fertility may in recent years have begun to change significantly. [R. Kelsall, *Population* (London: Longman, 1975) 3rd edn (adapted).]

THE EFFECTS OF
POPULATION CHANGE

16.1 AN AGEING POPULATION

The fact that the birth rate has declined while more people are living longer means that more old people have to be supported by those of working age. This is sometimes called the 'burden of dependency'.

When Lord Beveridge produced his report (*Social Insurance and Allied Services*, 1942) he suggested that old age pensions should be set at subsistence level in order to prevent the provision for the elderly becoming intolerable to those at work. Effective pressure from increasing numbers of old people, and a reasonable desire that old people should share in the affluence they helped to create, has resulted in substantially higher pensions than originally envisaged and many people share the view that they should be still higher.

Conventionally, a growing army of dependents should result in higher taxes for those at work with a resultant pressure for higher wages leading to inflation, a lack of competitiveness, resulting in unemployment, with fewer people to pay the necessary taxes, therefore higher taxes for those at work, thus completing the vicious circle. However, the computer revolution now makes it possible for more goods to be produced by fewer people, and so the question of provision for the aged becomes a matter of redistributing wealth at source rather than out of income. Changes in work processes may have come just in time (section 14.1).

However, although financial provision may not now be a major problem, there are many social problems associated with an ageing population. The decline of the extended family as an operating unit has resulted in many old people living isolated lives, either independently or surrounded only by their peers in old people's homes. The problems of loneliness and a feeling of worthlessness, allied to relative poverty reduces the quality of life for many of the elderly. Some attempts have been made to harness the knowledge and skills of the elderly for the good of the community – providing

More old people have to be supported by those of working age

surrogate 'grannies' for the children of young housebound mothers for example – but generally the old are regarded as being of little importance in a society increasingly dominated by the young.

16.2 POPULATION MOVEMENT

At the beginning of the nineteenth century only 25 per cent of the population of Great Britain lived in towns. Now the position is reversed, with 75 per cent living in towns, and many of the remainder working in towns, and almost all depending on towns for their shopping, education or entertainment. This process of living in and depending upon towns is called 'urbanisation'.

Although the drift to the towns started in the Middle Ages, it was the industrialisation of the nineteenth century that attracted large numbers from the countryside to the towns and cities of Britain. Now one-third of the population live in seven huge 'conurbations' composed of adjacent towns that have grown and merged together – Greater London; West Midlands (around Birmingham); Merseyside (around Liverpool); West Yorkshire (around Leeds); and Strathclyde (around Glasgow); Greater Manchester; Tyne and Wear (around Newcastle). Britain has the fourth greatest 'population density' (the number of people per square kilometre) in Europe, 229 in 1981. Almost half the population live on 5 per cent of the land area.

The growth of conurbations brought problems of health related to pollution; road congestion and sub-standard housing. Also the less easily quantifiable problems associated with the anonymity of urban living, leading in its extreme form to suicide (P. Sainsbury, *Social Aspects of Suicide in London*, 1955) or more mildly to an increased emphasis on status symbols (section 13.1) which are not needed in the settled rural community where a person's worth is likely to be established by acquaintance.

It would be a mistake to presume that 'sociability' is always lacking in urban centres as there is evidence of 'urban villages' in most big towns where there is a settled community and a network of relationships between people well known to each other. Bethnal Green is 'a village in the middle of London' where 'most people were connected by kinship ties to a network of other families, and through them to a host of friends and acquaintances' (Willmott and Young, *Family and Class in a London Suburb*, 1960).

Crime is very much higher in urban areas. This is partially because there is more about to steal and damage, but it also has to do with a greater readiness to steal or vandalise the property of strangers. It has been demonstrated that the impersonality of the supermarket contributes to the higher rate of shoplifting there, as compared with the corner shop. The anonymity of towns also makes the chances of detection less likely.

Between the wars 'suburbanisation' took place when residential estates grew up round the big towns. People moved to fresh air and gardens but often regretted the lack of a feeling of community and withdrew into their own 'privatised nuclear family' (section 4.4).

To combat the development of conurbations, 'green belts' were established. These are zones where no further development can take place. After the Second World War, a conscious attempt was made to disperse people from the old urban centres to 'new towns' where living conditions were planned to be of a high standard, but where people have often suffered psychologically from the impersonality – particularly the housebound mothers of small children.

Internal migration is mainly a result of economic pressures. There has been a reduction in the population of many of the old industrial centres, particularly in the North of England as traditional industries such as shipbuilding have declined, and from the rural areas of Scotland and Wales as the lure of the metropolitan areas have encouraged many young people to leave. The main areas of population increase have been in the South-East and Norfolk, because of their proximity to London and continental markets, and the South-West, partially because of its popularity as a retirement area.

The effects of urbanisation

A lot of early urban sociology tried to find out what the effects of this 'urbanisation' were. Theories were developed which linked the move from rural to urban with a wide range of other social changes. Much of the work was done at Chicago University, and the ideas of the 'Chicago School' were summed up by Louis Wirth (1897–1952) in a famous essay *Urbanism as a Way of Life* published in 1938.

Wirth draws a sharp contrast between 'urban-industrial' society and 'rural-folk' society. According to Wirth the two societies are very different in their ways of thought, belief, and action. The root of these differences, he suggests, lies in the simple fact that one society (urban) lives in large communities and the other (rural) in small ones.

In a small community, everyone can know everyone else. There is a high degree of 'primary group contact'—that is, contact with familiar people with whom an emotional bond is felt. So there is a sense of belonging, a set of shared ideals, a sense of group solidarity. Social control (making sure people keep to the social and legal rules) can be imposed almost without anyone noticing. The society, in short, is 'integrated'.

But in a large community this does not happen. It is just not possible for everyone to know everyone else. Primary group contacts are replaced by secondary ones: urban dwellers are constantly coming into contact with people who are, more or less, strangers.

Instead of people's relationships being intense, personal and permanent, they are superficial, anonymous, and short-lived. Here there can be no solidarity or shared ideals. Indeed some people begin to suffer from 'anomie'—lack of commonly agreed standards by which to live—to the extent that they disintegrate mentally and go mad or commit suicide. The kind of 'natural' social control (gossip, public opinion and so on) possible in a small community does not work in a large one, so controls have to be much more formal. And since the individual counts for little he has to join in association with others to get his voice heard. This bleak view of urban life was highly influential. But later writers have questioned many of Wirth's ideas. A common criticism is that what he is really describing is not the difference between rural and urban society, but between pre-industrial and industrial society. To put all the changes down simply to the difference in settlement size is too simplistic.

Some immigrants will, it is true, feel lonely and anonymous—though perhaps only for a time. But others will be part of well-defined communities which have kept a strong hold on their native culture and identity. An example is the Cypriot community of North London who have their own churches, shops, schools and social networks—even their own newspaper—and who, to a large extent, have kept their own language.

A 'twilight zone' – this term was first used to describe slum areas scheduled for re-development; as the property was scheduled for demolition it remained unrepaired and deteriorated further. Only those unable to move remained and low property costs attracted the very poorest, with consequent social problems, while deserted property and demolition sites encouraged vandalism. The term is now sometimes extended to cover areas which have similar problems even if re-development is not taking place

The idea that country village life is morally superior lay at the root of many attempts to make urban conditions more rural. 'Model communities' in the 19th century such as Bournville, near Birmingham, built by Cadbury from the profits of cocoa, and Port Sunlight, near Liverpool, built by Lever from the profits of soap, were set up on the theory that better cities would produce better citizens.

This belief—that there were physical solutions to social problems —became part of the thinking of the early town-planning movement. Pioneers like Ebenezer Howard (1850–1928) wanted 'garden cities' —settlements of about 30,000 people, surrounded by a permanent green belt of agricultural land on which it would be forbidden to build.

On the whole the new towns have been a success. The people who live in them have certainly had their physical living conditions improved, and there is some evidence that social problems have been reduced. But new towns are a special case. Typically they have a much higher proportion of skilled workers than do 'old' towns. And in recent years the question has been raised as to whether the money spent on new towns would not have been better spent on helping those in greatest needs—the unskilled left behind in the decaying inner cities. One urban sociologist, R. E. Pahl has this comment on new towns:

'The channelling of resources to skilled manual workers and greenfield sites took away capital and professional expertise from inner city environments and the less-skilled worker.'

Some sociologists single out housing as the central scarce resource. As John Rex and Robert Moore put it in *Race Community and Conflict* (1967): 'There is a class struggle over the use of housing ... *this class struggle is the central process of the city as a social unit*' (italics added).

Rex and Moore looked at Sparkbrook, once a 'respectable' area of Birmingham, but by the early 1960s fast becoming a 'twilight zone', with aging, run-down, overcrowded houses, inhabited by a mixed population of Irish, Pakistani, and West Indian immigrants, together with English down-and-outs and the remnants of the original local community. The authors suggest that social conditions there can best be understood in terms of other, more powerful, groups taking for themselves the lion's share of 'desirable' housing in the city. ('Cities' in *New Society*, 15 February 1979 (abridged).)

16.3 THE BALANCE OF THE SEXES

Women live longer than men and the gap between the 'longevity' of men and that of women continues to widen. There may be biological reasons for this difference in life expectation, but the social ones are the more apparent and may in fact also be a factor in apparently biological causes. For example, more women are currently dying from heart disease and this could be a result of increasing tension as they adopt men's roles in positions of responsibility at work.

Men are more likely to die in accidents, both because their jobs are more likely to be dangerous and because they are more likely to be motorists or motorcyclists. Men smoke more than women and are therefore more likely to die of illnesses associated with smoking such as cancer and heart disease. Until now, men are more likely to have jobs in which tension-related disease is high. In the past men have been more likely to be killed in war but the surplus women resulting from the male slaughter of the First World War are now passing out of the population.

In the past the balance between the life expectancy of men and women has been balanced to some extent by the risk attached to multiple child-birth. However, the great decline in the number of pregnancies the average woman is likely to experience, linked to the decline in the number of women dying as a result of childbirth – 'maternal mortality' – has resulted in a greater proportion of women in the older age categories than formerly. In 1840 the life expectance of a man at birth was 40 and a woman 42, in 1978 it was 70 and 76 respectively.

In most societies there are more women than men because although more boys are born than girls (in Britain about 106 boys for every 100 girls – see Table 16.1), this imbalance has been over-corrected in the past by the greater proportion of boys that died in infancy as a result of the greater delicacy of male infants. However, more boys are now surviving to adulthood. There are two results of this phenomenon: (a) the chances of a woman marrying are now higher than they have ever been, which increases the fertility rate; (b) the prospect of large numbers of males who wish to find a partner but cannot is a phenomenon not previously faced in British society. Will polyandry be the solution? The prospect of parents' being able to decide what sex of child they have is another problem for the future.

Table 16.1 *population of the United kingdom*

	1951	1961	1971	1981
Males	24 118	25 481	26 952	27 050
Females	26 107	27 228	28 562	28 626
Total	50 225	52 709	55 515	55 676

16.4 INNER CITIES

Generally speaking the centre of a city is the core from which it expanded. It therefore often contains the oldest housing stock, which is more likely than that elsewhere to be in a condition of decay. As the housing is undesirable because of its condition, and because of the other disadvantages associated with the area such as noise, pollution and old fashioned school buildings, those who can afford to do so have moved elsewhere.

Recently there has been an outflow of population from some of the biggest cities. London lost 17.5 per cent of its people between the census of 1971 and that of 1981 as people continued the move to the suburbs, or moved further out into dormitory villages, or businesses moved to smaller towns where rents and rates were lower. Twenty-eight new towns have been established, but development has now been stopped as there appears to be a danger that a continued outflow would destroy the infrastructure of the cities and leave an unmanageable proportion of deprived people needing help, as the most energetic and qualified moved elsewhere. Already the centres of many cities – 'inner city areas' – have deteriorated, with an abnormal proportion of problems in terms of deprivation and crime.

Those most likely to live in the inner city areas are the old who cannot afford to move; people who are poor for reasons of unemployment, desertion or disability, sometimes with large families; immigrants who are often unskilled and without capital so that they have to live wherever is cheapest and where they will be accepted; and those who are unskilled, employed but on low wages.

The movement of businesses from city centres because of high rates and other factors has decreased still further the employment opportunities of those who must live in those areas. The deterioration of the inner city environment and rising crime rates make them still less desirable so that increasing numbers of those who are in a position to do so move; the inner city is in a spiral of decline. For more information on the problems of inner cities see the readings in this unit and the specimen 'A' level answer at the end of this book.)

Recently there has been a move in some areas – notably Islington in London – towards 'gentrification'. The increasing costs and inconvenience of travelling to work in the city centre and returning to the suburbs to sleep – 'commuting' – has resulted in some middle-class people seeking homes in the period houses of the inner city and renovating them. This movement has the beneficial effect of creating a vocal pressure group to improve local services and renovate the environment, but the damaging effect of increasing housing shortages for those who cannot afford prices in the improvement areas and perhaps creating a greater feeling of relative deprivation (section 10.4) for the poor neighbours of the middle-class residents.

Inner cities

While there are problems in defining terms such as 'urban', the definition of 'inner' and 'outer' urban areas is particularly difficult and there are many possible definitions.

During 1977 partnerships were established between local and central government to focus on selected parts of the inner areas of the largest cities, where the scale and concentration of problems was felt to be greatest. The inner areas defined by the partnerships provide an agreed definition for those cities. The seven areas concerned are parts of Birmingham, Lambeth, Liverpool, Manchester and Salford, and Newcastle and Gateshead, London's Docklands, and all of Hackney and Islington together.

Britain was the first country in the world to experience mass urbanisation, and by the end of the nineteenth century about three-quarters of the population of England and Wales lived in urban areas, a much higher proportion than in any other country. Not only did urbanisation occur early, it was also extremely rapid, and many of the problems of inner city areas today are related to the way in which cities developed in the nineteenth century . . . The space used for development in the cities in the early nineteenth century was extremely limited since almost everyone had to walk to work. Although the cities offered jobs, they could not provide sufficient houses or social facilities for the people who flooded to the towns from the poor rural areas. Most towns at the beginning of the nineteenth century had only very elementary arrangements, if any, for providing water, clearing refuse and sewage, or treating mass epidemics. These towns were completely overwhelmed by the influx of people, and conditions in large towns were abominable. Life expectancy in Liverpool and Manchester was almost half that in areas such as Surrey, partly because of very high infant mortality rates.

Appreciation of the appalling conditions, brought to a head by the cholera epidemics of the 1830s and 1840s, led in 1844 to the setting up of a Royal Commission on the State of Large Towns and Populous Districts and then to the introduction of the first housing and health reform acts. In the last part of the century the introduction of cheap public transport allowed people to live much further from work, and the boundaries of the cities expanded rapidly. Very high densities were no longer required, and those people who could afford to do so moved to the outskirts of the cities – a trend which has continued ever since. However, the casual nature of employment of many of the working class people, and the need for their wives and children to earn, forced them to remain in the centre.

The core areas of the largest English cities are now losing both population and employment in absolute terms and, in the absence of specific steps being taken to prevent it, may be expected to continue to do so. Some decline in population was necessary to reduce densities but this stage has been passed in most areas.

The average age of dwellings in inner cities is much higher than nationally. Just over a quarter of England's housing was built before 1919; but in the inner areas the proportion ranges between about 40 and 60 per cent, despite the large scale slum clearance programmes which have been implemented.

Not only are the houses old, many still lack basic amenities. Inner Liverpool and Manchester/Salford are particularly affected— over 16 per cent of households lacking at least one basic amenity, most commonly an inside toilet.

As the Inner Area Studies showed, progress with improvement can also be delayed because a significant proportion of inner city residents cannot afford their share of the improvement costs. Furthermore, some of the older residents do not feel improvements are necessary, while absentee landlords of rented properties may not wish to spend money on improvements.

The poor condition of much of the stock is not the only inner area housing problem. More households live in overcrowded conditions, and more share accommodation, than elsewhere. This is in part due to the fact that many of the old properties were built several stories high, to achieve the necessary densities, and these are now multi-occupied, often rented privately, and often overcrowded.

Newer housing is not without problems too. Many of the estates built to rehouse people from slum clearance areas consist of tower blocks of flats or medium-rise deck access blocks, built so as to retain the densities of the earlier period. Many of these estates have become very unpopular, vandalism is often a major problem, the stigma attached to some of the estates may take many years to remove.

Although there are differences between the inner areas, a higher proportion of accommodation in inner areas is rented and less is owner-occupied than nationally. . . The population structures of the inner areas are therefore biased towards the manual working class. Although it is difficult to obtain details of those people who have moved out from the inner areas, all indications are that the trend – begun towards the end of the nineteenth century – for the better-off, more highly skilled, people to move out in the greater numbers has continued. Not only are the better-off people able to afford the increased transport costs to work, but they are also able to afford to buy their own home and are therefore not restricted by the availability of rented housing or the operation of local authority residence requirements.

. . . the unemployment rate of each socio-economic group is higher for inner area residents than for those living elsewhere. Unemployment rates for young people and non-whites are also high in inner areas.

The areas in which the inner area residents can look for employment without incurring high commuting costs have been losing jobs for over a decade, and appear likely to continue to do so. The decline has been most pronounced in the older service industries and the traditional manufacturing industries which caused the major cities to develop so quickly, but which are now declining in the face of technological advance and reduced demand for their products. Just as the original housing all became in need of improvement at the same time, the traditional industries are declining together.

Some service industries have been growing, but not sufficiently to compensate for the decline in employment in the other sectors; and in general they do not provide many jobs for the low skilled manual worker, nor for those with the traditional skills.

The loss of jobs from the inner areas appears to be caused to a greater extent by closure or contraction of firms than by net emigration. This occurs in different ways in different areas; in some cases one major industry such as shipbuilding declines rapidly, in some there is a substantial net loss of small firms, and some are affected by the rationalisation of large multi-plant firms. Inner areas generally seem to have suffered from a lack of new firms.

Many factors have contributed to the low level of creation of new firms in the inner areas, and it is very difficult to determine the relative importance of each. Government planning policies have clearly played their part, but many firms in the newer more mobile industries find that the depressing and deteriorating environment, high land values, scarcity of large sites, lack of appropriately skilled local labour, and the problems of access, congestion, vandalism, and crime are deterrents.

There are considerable demands on the social and health services in inner areas. In any area it is the lowest skilled, low income people who require most assistance from social services, eg child care may be essential for single parent families and ones where the wife must earn to raise the family above the poverty line. Low social groups are most prone to ill-health. Low income elderly households often require special care. High proportions of immigrants can create various problems, eg for educational services because of language and cultural differences.

It should be remembered that the majority of people living in inner cities are not unemployed and do not live in overcrowded houses or lack the use of basic amenities. However they can be affected by dereliction, vandalism, and petty crime; and they may well have difficulty obtaining a mortgage, or find that their address makes it more difficult for them to get new jobs. Thus the concentration of poor housing, unskilled population, and high unemployment can have an indirect effect on even those residents who are not directly affected. [D. Allnutt and A. Geland, 'Inner Cities in England' in *Social Trends no. 10* (London: HMSO, 1979) (abridged).]

A number of reports are referred to in this article including: *Change or Decay*: Final Report of the Liverpool Inner Area Study. (HMSO 1977); *Unequal City*: Final Report of the Birmingham Inner Area Study, (HMSO 1977); *Inner London: Policies for Dispersal and Balance*: Final Report of the Lambeth Inner Area Study (HMSO 1977).

The 'dump' estates in the inner cities

Through its low rents, the inner city ingathers the disadvantaged from a wide area. Through various channels – slum clearance, homelessness, the points system – council housing in turn attracts a large proportion of the disadvantaged. The institution of the estate thus concentrates the social problems of the inner city in an even smaller and more intimate space, where they can interact more destructively. Within the council sector, the allocation game creates pockets of even greater deprivation: the dump estates.

These are the least attractive, worst sited, worst provided with amenities. Usually they are unmodernized estates of pre-war flats, but sometimes more modern estates, more deeply flawed than usual with architectural blunders. They are the inner city's inner city.

Disadvantaged people tend to get very much worse council housing than the norm: older rather than newer; flats rather than houses; higher floors rather than lower. Certain social groups fare badly: the homeless, the unemployed and blacks worst of all, with female single parents and unskilled workers not far behind. The public sector seems unable to allocate desirable and undesirable housing any more fairly than the private. Allocators used to solve part of the hard-to-let problem by offering flats on the worst estates to those who got only a single offer and had no choice: the homeless. The homeless, inevitably, contain a higher proportion of disadvantaged and unstable families, evicted for rent arrears or split up by family disputes. Even among those with a supposedly free choice, there is a subtle self-selection process at work. Rent levels are one element here . . . . Then there is a factor one might call 'staying power': the determination to hold out on the waiting list, turning down the earlier offers until something better turns up, to avoid moving into a dump. Staying power is obviously less among those who are most anxious to escape their present accommodation, because of overcrowding, bad repair, shared amenities or family conflicts. Once again, these people tend to be among the poorest and most unstable families, for whom even a hard-to-let estate may seem preferable to what they have at the moment. Finally there are elements of a culture of silence among society's most unfortunate victims: a tendency to be unaware of rights, to have little confidence in their ability to control their own destiny, and – at the lowest levels – to be so demoralized or so habituated to a squalid environment as to be almost indifferent to their surroundings.

Once an estate acquires more than a certain proportion of disadvantaged tenants – perhaps, say, one-fifth or one-quarter – it can find itself trapped in a descending spiral which may continue until it is demolished or massively rehabilitated. The preponderance of single-parent families and families with conflicts caused by low income or unemployment weakens parental discipline, so vandalism and crime are more prevalent ... The 'better' tenants, with higher incomes, savings or skills, or more persistence over getting a transfer, move out and are replaced by more disadvantaged people. The estate acquires a reputation, usually worse than the reality, which discourages those with any hopes for their own future from even viewing a flat there. It is exactly the same sifting process, in miniature, as that which creates and maintains the inner city as a whole. [Paul Harrison, *Inside the Inner City* (Harmondsworth: Penguin, 1983) (adapted).]

MIGRATION

17.1 EMIGRATION

Emigration from the British Isles started with the colonisation of the New World but became a major movement in the nineteenth century, particularly to America and to the countries now known as the 'Old' Commonwealth; Australia, Canada and New Zealand; and to South Africa. Emigration to these countries was actively encouraged in that it built up a white population of British stock who would maintain the dominance of the existing white settlers and who could be expected to be supportive to the mother country. Emigrants were often poor and sought a new life in countries with labour shortages or ones where whites were likely to be favoured in employment. Some also have seen emigration as providing a greater opportunity of advancement for their children in countries with fewer class barriers to mobility. Emigration to the 'new' Commonwealth countries, mainly in Africa and Asia, tended to be middle-class and the emigrants went as administrators, traders or as owners of enterprises such as plantations or mines.

Emigration has always exceeded immigration (see Figure 15.1) except for the period 1931 to 1951 when there was a net import of some half a million people, many of them refugees from Europe; and from the mid 1950s to 1962, peaking at the end of that period as people sought entry before the first Immigration Act came into force. There was also a slight surplus inflow between 1972 and 1973 when Asians with British passports were expelled from Uganda.

A peak period for emigration was between 1911 and 1921 when almost a million people left Britain but emigration reduced during the mid-1970s as most destination countries experienced recession and unemployment and restricted migrants to those whose skills were required. There was however a substantial increase in emigration in 1980.

17.2 IMMIGRATION

Britain has a long history of absorbing immigrants. French Protestants in the seventeenth century; the Irish in the second half of the present century; Jews from Central Europe at the end of the nineteenth century and the 1930s; 'Iron Curtain' refugees in the 1940s and 1950s.

During the past twenty-five years there have been two major groups of immigrants: West Indians and Asians. West Indians were actively encouraged by London Transport and other undertakings to move to Britain during the 1950s to overcome the shortage of labour resulting from the post-war expansion of the economy. However in the 1970s slightly more West Indians left Britain than entered it. By 1976 there were about 500 000 people of West Indian origin in Britain. West Indian immigration has now virtually ceased.

In the late 1950s a number of Asians were encouraged to enter Britain by former British Army officers who had been in Indian regiments. These saw the surplus population of India and Pakistan (part of which is now Bangladesh) as a source of labour for industries with recruitment problems such as textiles and foundry work. By 1976 there were 800 000 people from the Indian sub-continent in Britain, and it is anticipated that by 1991 there will be approximately twice as many Asians as West Indians in Britain. However, 'primary' immigration from the Asian sub-continent has now virtually ceased – the main source of immigrants being wives and children coming to join those already settled.

The main legislation aimed at restricting immigration is:

1905 The Aliens Act
1962 Commonwealth Immigrants Act
1968 Commonwealth Immigrants Act
1971 Immigrants Act

This legislation has effectively restricted immigration into Britain to those who have a special skill in short supply in Britain; to dependents of people already settled in Britain, and to those who have already acquired citizenship or have a parent or grandparent who was a British citizen.

The only exception to entry restrictions on non-British citizens has been those of the Irish Republic who have a right to unrestricted entry and full political and economic rights while living in Britain. The Irish have traditionally been the major source of immigration to Britain but in recent years there has been a net loss of Irish nationals. (A net inflow of about 10 000 a year between 1961 and 1971 and a net outflow of about 1000 a year since.) Since Britain joined the European Economic Community there has been a right of unrestricted entry to community nationals but the immigration and emigration figures between Britain and the rest of the European Community have remained roughly in balance.

Immigration

If the image of a 'brain drain' has recently given emigration a highly unfavourable connotation in the British public's mind, the rapidly growing immigration of the years up to mid-1962 created an equally unfortunate public impression. For despite the fact that those at least whose schooling had taken place in Britain had been taught what great benefits, material and other, had accrued to this country from *earlier* waves of immigrants, there seemed to be many features of the situation in the late 1950s and early 1960s that were different from previous occasions. For one thing, these were not to any marked degree refugees from political, racial or religious persecution. Nor were they from Europe. They came in larger numbers, from different areas and for different reasons from their predecessors. And though they provided a much needed addition to our over-stretched labour force (and in nursing, in particular, the public gratitude for their help was both genuine and general), their coming came to be associated in the public mind with race riots in Nottingham and Notting Hill—a new and ugly feature of contemporary British life—and there were dark forebodings of what might happen when employment was no longer so full, when overcrowding and health problems became more acute as the flow continued. It was widely believed that assimilation was proving difficult if not impossible in many cases; and that the economic and other difficulties faced by the immigrants were leading them to settle in certain parts of the cities to which they went, with the consequent emergence for the first time of 'coloured quarters' with their attendant social evils and dangers.

As with the emigration case, there was a crying need for authoritative facts and figures, and amongst those who undertook special surveys to fill this need was Mrs Ruth Glass. In her study, *Newcomers*, she obtained information about a large sample of West Indians who had settled in London, between the beginning of 1954 and the end of 1958. Careful analysis of this material, together with published statistics from a wide variety of sources, enabled her to dispel a number of myths. She demonstrated, for example, that the widely held belief that almost all the newcomers were unskilled workers before they came here was unjustified. One in four of the men had, in fact, been non-manual workers, and only one in five had been semi-skilled or unskilled workers or farm labourers. The migrants' job aspirations on arrival here had, of course, often not been fulfilled; downgrading, in status if not in economic terms, had been a common experience. The mistaken belief that almost all Commonwealth immigrants were completely unskilled gained some support even from official pronouncements of the time, despite the cautious wording used. [R. Kelsall, *Population* (London: Longman, 1975) 3rd edn.]

17.3 ETHNIC GROUPS

An ethnic group is a group with a particular 'culture' (section 1.1) a way of behaving and thinking that makes it distinctive, perhaps including religious belief, language, dress and cuisine.

Ethnicity is sometimes confused with 'race'. Essentially race is a classification based on physical differences and usually divides mankind into three major groups: Mongoloid, Caucasoid and Negroid. There is considerable argument among biologists regarding methods of classification, and the concept has little practical value. There is no separate Jewish race or Irish race. There is no evidence of racial differences in intelligence that could not equally be accounted for by environmental factors – intelligence tests given to army recruits in the United States resulted in negroes in each State scoring lower than whites, but the negroes from the Northern States had a higher average score than the whites from the Southern States (A. Barnett, *The Human Species*, 1957).

Ethnicity may include such factors as religious belief, language, dress and food. Celebrating the Chinese New Year in Soho

Immigrants, in a new and often hostile environment, tend to congregate together in areas where housing and appropriate jobs are available; they mix mainly with each other, intermarry and try to maintain the traditions and customs with which they are familiar. Their group solidarity is often reinforced by a common religious belief.

The fact that the first wave of any group of immigrants tend to be young unattached males often leads to stereotyping – to a belief that all members of a group share the characteristics of a few that have been particularly noticed. Their behaviour in terms of drunkenness, fighting and 'chasing girls' is likely to be the same as a similar group of the indigenous population but they are likely to be more highly visible in terms of appearance or behaviour.

The immigrant is likely to be poor, and often unskilled, and will tend to settle in 'inner city' areas (section 16.4) where pressure on services is likely to be already high. The immigrant will be seen as a competitor for scarce resources, although it has been shown that immigrants on average receive less in terms of social service benefits than do native born residents (K. Jones and A. Smith, *The Economic Impact of Commonwealth Immigration*, 1970).

Ethnicity and employment

Immigration from the 'coloured' countries of the Commonwealth is often assumed to have brought a significant new dimension to the pattern of stratification in Britain. The sheer volume of writing and research on the subject since about 1960 suggest the weight which liberal, and sometimes radical, opinion has come to attach to colour discrimination as a divisive force. The effect has been to single out inequality between white majority and black and brown minorities as a distinct and allegedly potent basis of cleavage in British society; to encourage diagnoses, explicit or implicit, that the coloured population is a sub-proletariat, a new dark-skinned under-class beneath the white social order. In fact, there is little sense to such characterisations. They ignore the heterogeneity of circumstances among coloured people, and the concomitant diversity of discrimination in form and impact. They also obscure the overriding common features in the dependent condition of both white and black labour.

Coloured people are not uniformly concentrated at the bottom of the economic order. They are certainly handicapped in the labour market, as they are in a wide range of other respects; but in no way so as to make them, *en bloc*, an 'under-class'. Their occupational distribution is skewed towards the lower rungs of the scale. When only one in twelve of all occupied men in Britain in 1966 had an unskilled manual job, the corresponding proportions were near one in three among men born in Pakistan; over one in five among the Caribbean-born – much the same, it is worth noting, as among men born in the Irish Republic; and about one in nine among the Indian-born. Yet these figures alone square poorly with conventional assumptions: among none of the migrant groups from the 'new Commonwealth' was there anything like a majority of men in unskilled jobs. Even if the semi-skilled are added in – to make, with the unskilled, an aggregate in lower-grade manual work comprising over a quarter of the total male labour force in 1966 – still only the Pakistani-born showed a clear majority confined to jobs of that kind: some two out of every three in their case. For men from the Caribbean countries, the figure was just under half – not very much more, again, than among the Irish-born; and it was one-third in the case of men born in India. Migrants from Pakistan apart, in short, the majority of men from the coloured Commonwealth were in jobs classified as skilled, or in some form of non-manual work. And the pattern of employment among women born in those countries conformed no better to the familiar stereotypes. True, over half the working women with birthplaces in the Caribbean territories had non-skilled manual jobs – mainly semi-skilled, including service work. Yet such jobs in any case accounted for more than a third of the entire female labour force; and for only one in four of women born in India. A large majority of the latter, and around one in every three even of those born in the Caribbean area, had non-manual work. There is some exaggeration of the degree of occupational diversity in these figures: men and women from India and Pakistan include whites born there in the days of imperial dominion. But distortion on this score is limited; and the qualification has practically no application to those born in the Caribbean countries. The plain point is that professional white-collar and skilled manual blacks tend to be left aside in the sterotypes of public debate and research alike. The visibility of colour diminishes the higher the socio-economic position of the coloured, in the eyes of liberal reformers no less than the prejudiced. [J. Westergaard and H. Resler, *Class in a Capitalist Society* (Harmondsworth: Penguin 1975).]

17.4 RACISM

Because members of ethnic groups are often highly visible compared with the host group they can easily become the target for prejudice – a bias (usually hostility) without reasonable reason. Prejudice directed against members of a particular race or a particular ethnic group which results from such group membership is called 'racism'. Racism usually stems from fear – fear of competition for jobs, educational opportunities, housing or mates. Racism is more likely to occur among those who feel most directly threatened, and as many immigrants tend to be in competition most directly with those at the bottom of the social ladder it is usual to find the greatest degree of racial prejudice among the least skilled. Where vested interests are at stake higher up the social scale, as in South Africa, racism is likely to be prevalent among members of the middle class as well. 'English proletarians and Irish proletarians. The ordinary English worker hates the Irishman as a competitor who lowers his standard of life' (Karl Marx).

In the nineteenth century the Irish were the major target for British racism, identifiable by accent and religion. As Jews – escaping pogroms in Central Europe – joined them at the end of the nineteenth century, they too became targets for abuse and discrimination. More recently the even more visible West Indians and Asians have become targets; but gypsies, Chinese, Jews and other groups who can be readily identified as different are also likely to be used as scapegoats and blamed for crime, unemployment, poor educational standards and other failings within society generally.

In order to reduce open 'overt' discrimination, successive governments have introduced legislation:

Race Relations Act 1965 – banned discrimination on the ground of colour, race, ethnic or national origins in 'places of public resort'. Also made incitement to racial hatred illegal.

Race Relations Act 1968 – Widened the concept of illegal discrimination to include goods, facilities and services; employment, housing, and advertising.

Race Relations Bill 1976 – tightened up the law.

Racism however cannot be abolished merely by legislation – it needs to be shown to be illogical and unfair. Fortunately there is a considerable element of tolerance in British society; one survey showed that only 27 per cent of British people were 'prejudiced' or 'prejudice-inclined' (E. Rose, *Colour and Citizenship*, 1969). This is reinforced by the derisory vote received by political parties seeking to exploit prejudice. 'In all the constituencies it fought, the mean National Front vote was 1.4 per cent (in 1979) compared to 3.6 per cent in 1970, 3.3 per cent in 1974 and 3.1 per cent in October 1974. (D. Butler and D. Kavanagh, *The British General Election of 1979*, 1980).

Black children and education

Black children face the same problems ... faced by the indigenous white working class community – by poverty, by overcrowded homes and schools, and by the lack of the influence and knowledge that benefits middle class children at school. This was aggravated by prejudice and discrimination within schools, by the language problems, at first undetected, and by the culture-biased intelligence tests that put many black children in E.S.N. schools. (B. Coard, *How the West Indian Child is made Educationally Sub-Normal in the British School System*, New Beacon Books Ltd., 1971.)

Teaching is dominated by middle class values and language and the progress of schoolchildren is judged by the same standards. This militates against working-class children of any colour. But black children suffered even more from the hierarchical rigidity of the streaming system and, as a result, from the bad behavioural problems inherent in the classes in the bottom streams taught by constantly changing teachers.

West Indian children have a reputation for boisterous and bad behaviour at school, and lack of concentration; these must be considered in the context of the comparative strictness of schools in the West Indies, and of the mode of behaviour often imposed by parents at home. The relatively easy atmosphere in the classroom provides a catalyst for letting off steam or releasing repressed anger or frustration. But these characteristics are also rooted in the social patterns produced by slavery, the unsettled nature of West Indians' historical background and their consequent lack of identity. Knowing this, however, does not make it much easier for them or for the teachers to alter the situation.

Many black parents, particularly mothers, were very distressed to find that their children were being allocated to the worst schools and placed in the lowest forms. In most schools today, as in the Ealing schools, the distribution of black children is such that most are at the bottom and their numbers decrease up towards the higher forms. The assumption of lower ability compared with white children in the same forms has often been implicit in school organization. Militant activity by mothers alleviated this situation in some places, for instance by setting up supplementary schools in black communities in Birmingham, Nottingham, Leeds and London, and by campaigning against racist practices by education authorities (for instance against the 'banding' of black children into special schools in Haringey in 1968), and against particularly bad schools.

(S. Sharpe, *Just Like a Girl*, Harmondsworth: Penguin, 1976)

QUESTIONS FROM PAST O-LEVEL GCE PAPERS

1. 'Population growth is affected by the birth rate, death rate, and net migration.'

(a) Explain the meaning of birth rate, death rate, and net migration.

(b) How and why have birth rates and death rates varied in Britain over the last 150 years?   Associated Examining Board

2.

The Urban/Rural Population England and Wales 1851–1971		
Year	Urban % of Population	Rural % of Population
1851	50.1	49.9
1871	61.8	38.2
1891	72.0	28.0
1901	77.0	23.0
1911	78.1	21.9
1921	79.3	20.7
1931	80.0	20.0
1951	80.8	19.2
1961	80.0	20.0
1971	78.3	21.7

(Source: Census.)

(a) What factors could have produced the changes shown between 1851 and 1951?   4 marks
(b) What explanations might be offered for the recent slight changes in the trend as shown?   4 marks
(c) What is the difference between geographical and social mobility?   4 marks
(d) In what ways do social relationships and behaviour tend to differ in urban and rural situations?   8 marks
    Associated Examining Board

3. How effective have changes in the law been in reducing **either** (a) racial discrimination **or** (b) sex discrimination?
    Oxford Local Examining Board

4. By mid-1970 there were almost 1½ million coloured Commonwealth immigrants and their families in Britain (about 2½% of the population) and about 60 per cent of these had settled in Greater London and the West Midlands ... As long as there is a shortage of housing, jobs and educational opportunity, there is a likelihood of bitterness between those who feel they are being discriminated against for racial

reasons on the one hand, and those who feel they are losing what is 'rightfully theirs' on the other.

From G. O'Donnell, *The Human Web*, 1974

(a) What do you understand by the following sociological terms
social stratification?
ethnicity?
gender?   [6]

(b) (i) In what ways are the disadvantages suffered by many black people in Britain similar to those experienced by some lower class white people?   [8]

(ii) Explain why *conflicts* may develop between these two groups.   [6]

Cambridge Local Examining Board

5. **Either,** (a) Outline the possible causes and consequences of immigration into a country.

Or, (b) Describe any **three** problems of urban growth and discuss any **two** attempts made to cope with such problems during the past 30 years.   Welsh Joint Examining Board

6. Study the following data carefully and then answer the questions.

Country	Population	Birth rate	Death rate	Infant mortality	Expectation of life	
					Male	Female
U.K.	55 millions	18.4	11.5	19.0	68	74
U.S.A.	200 millions	19.4	9.4	24.7	67	74
India	500 millions	38.4	12.9	139.0	42	41
Brazil	80 millions	43.0	11.1	170.0	39	46

(a) Explain briefly the meaning of:
(i) birth rate
(ii) infant mortality
(b) In which country is the population likely to be increasing most rapidly? Explain how you arrive at your answer.
(c) State any **two** possible consequences for an underdeveloped country with a high birth rate.

(d) Suggest a reason for the birth rates and the infant mortality rates being so much higher in India and Brazil than in the U.K. and the U.S.A.

    (i) birth rates

    (ii) infant mortality rates   Welsh Joint Examining Board

NOTE   For this section in the Welsh Board Paper 2 lines are allowed for answers to each of questions (a) (1) and (2), and (d) (1) and (2). 4 lines are allowed for each of the other questions.

7. Describe and account for the changes in the size of the population of Britain since 1900.   Oxford Local Examining Board

8. 'The poor are no longer v.ith us.' Discuss sociologically with reference to town life in modern Britain.

        London Examining Board

PART VII
SOCIAL STABILITY AND
CONTROL

THE NATURE OF SOCIAL
CONTROL

18.1 CONFORMITY

There are many pressures urging the individual to accept particular patterns
of conduct and thought, in order to meet the expectations of others
(section 1.3).

Merton (*Social Structure and Anomie*, 1938) divided people into five
main groups according to their adjustment to the norms of their society.
The first group, the 'Conformists', are those who accepted the goals of their
society, and set about achieving these goals in a most generally acceptable
way.

The 'Innovators' are those who accept the goals of the society but not
the accepted means of achieving them. For example, the desirability of
wealth and all the status symbols that accompany it may be accepted but
the means of acquisition may be fraud or robbery, or gambling which is
now non-criminal but socially dubious.

The 'Retreatists' avoid decisions on, or reject, society's goals or methods
of achieving them and withdraw from society as much as possible, for
example hippies, alcoholics and some hermits.

The 'Ritualists' do not believe in the goals, but go through the socially
approved motions for fear of disapproval. For example, a couple may not
accept the values of our society in relation to marriage, but still do marry
even although they do not regard it as sinful to live together without
marriage.

Merton's fifth group – the 'Rebels' – overtly reject the values of the
society, both goals and means of achievement. For example a young
person may reject the whole notion of private property as an objective
and join a revolutionary group to bring about the collapse of the existing
order. The means he uses will decide his criminality or otherwise.

Conformity is much less interesting to most people than 'deviance', the
breaking of the rules of the society, but it is much more important in that

a society could not survive if most people did not conform to its norms and values. The ways that societies ensure this conformity is therefore of importance.

18.2 DEVIANCE

In *Outsiders* (1963) H. Becker pointed out that 'we must recognise that we cannot know whether a given act will be categorised as deviant until the response of others has occurred. Deviance is not a quality that lies in behaviour itself, but in the interaction between the person who commits the act and those who respond to it.' A nurse injecting morphine into the vein of a patient to relieve pain is not acting in a deviant fashion; a drug addict injecting a friend with the same drug for 'kicks' *is* behaving in a deviant fashion.

Once a person has been 'labelled' a deviant they are likely to be regarded as having a number of characteristics in common with other people in the same category. For example, all homosexuals are likely to be regarded as a danger to small boys even although the available evidence suggests that this is not the case.

Becker also comments, 'labelling places the actor in circumstances which make it harder for him to continue the normal routines of everyday life and thus provokes him to "abnormal" actions (as when a prison record makes it harder to earn a living at a conventional occupation and so disposes its possessor to move into an illegal one).' This view has led prisons and borstals to be regarded as 'finishing schools' for criminals.

This labelling of a person so that the original deviance prevents them operating otherwise as a normal member of the society has been called 'stigmatisation'. 'Most people drift into deviance by specific actions rather than by formed choices of social roles and statuses' (Lemert *Human Deviance*, 1967).

Labelling – moral panic and deviance

Sometimes a theory is forcibly 'shared', either by reason of the rhetorical power of its promoters, or more rarely by exacting physical penalties from those who demur. Outside the imaginations of well-meaning social scientists and novelists that sort of situation is rare. Mostly master and slave *share* a theory. And the reverberations of that shared theory may last for a very long time, long after the institution which was its natural concomitant in day-to-day social practices has gone. A striking example of this is the passive 'loser' social style of many American black people, the style that black militants have tried with some desperation and success to redress. It reflects a conception of themselves inherited from the theory of their nature and place in a slave society, a theory they shared with the slave owners, and from whom they learned it. Depersonalization rituals, including the conditions on the voyage from Africa and the ritual humiliations of their inauguration to the plantation society have been carefully detailed in modern historical studies of the institution. In our case too, pupils and teachers share the theory that the pupils are 'written off'. We do not know how this shared theory came to be acquired.

Moral Panic

To explain the extravagent character of the attributions imposed upon disenchanted and rebellious schoolchildren and rumbustious football fans, we introduce Stan Cohen's concept of 'moral panic'.

Societies appear subject, every now and then, to periods of moral panic. A condition, episode, person or group of persons emerges to become defined as a threat to societal values and interests: its nature is presented in a stylised and stereotypical fashion by the media: the moral barricades are manned by editors, bishops, politicians and other right-thinking people: socially accredited experts pronounce their diagnoses and solutions: ways of coping are evolved or (more often) resorted to: the condition then disappears, submerges or deteriorates and becomes more visible. Sometimes the object of the panic is quite novel and at other times it is something which has been in existence long enough, but suddenly appears in the limelight. Sometimes the panic passes over and is forgotten, except in folklore and collective memory: at other times it has more serious and long-lasting repercussions and might produce such changes as those in legal and social policy or even in the way that society conceives itself (S. Cohen, *Folk Devils and Moral Panics*, 1972).

Since the war, a succession of moral panics have spread through our society, each with its characteristic 'object'. These objects have ranged historically from Teddy Boys through to Mods and Rockers and Skinheads. The most recent are the football hooligans, who for many people, and not least the feature writers of our Sunday newspapers, have come to represent all that is most senseless and destructive in our society. Anyone doubting such a claim should simply scan, as we have done, headlines of the more popular newspapers from about 1968 onwards and note the frequency with which terms such as 'mindless', 'evil', 'thuggery', 'mad', 'violent', 'wanton destruction', etc., crop up in reports concerning football supporters. From reading such reports one might be forgiven for thinking that the football terraces ran deep with blood each Saturday and that fans of Manchester United, like Protestants in parts of rural Spain, really do have horns on their heads.

From a sociological viewpoint, the function of Folk Devils is quite clear. In setting up certain members as visible examples of what is proscribed, by attributing forbidden characteristics to them, they serve as images of disorder and evil. Having created these images, our society is more able to ascribe to the majority of its members – the right-thinking corpus – a comforting sense of order and social propriety... Vandalism, for example, might be thought of as a collection of clearly identifiable acts requiring sanction for the simple reason that they offend against the property, both individual and collective, of members in society. But contrast the the reaction to football fans who run through a town creating damage as they go with the reaction to university students during rag week creating similar damage. The former damage will be viewed as the result of 'destructive hooliganism' and dealt with accordingly, whilst the latter will be seen as arising from an excess of goodnatured high spirits and over-enthusiasm. Although the damaging acts are very similar, football fans are 'deviants' whilst students, for reasons not made explicit, are somewhat excused. We might also note that what constitutes an offence in legal terms also changes over time. Acts such as those involving homosexuality or abortion would, only a few years ago, have been held up as examples of 'hardcore' deviance. And yet those same acts today escape formal sanction. [P. Marsh, E. Russer and R. Harré, *The Rules of Disorder* (London: Routledge & Kegan Paul, 1978) (adapted).]

18.3 SOCIAL CONTROL

The exclusion of a person who is deviant in *one* respect from participating as a full member of the society in *other* respects is one of the ways that social control is exercised. The earlier example of the homosexual might be used to illustrate how fear of being regarded as a perverted child-molester who would be excluded from employment opportunities and other social interaction might encourage someone with homosexual tendencies to sublimate them and either seek socially acceptable heterosexual outlets or enter an occupation where celibacy was the norm.

Such informal social control is the main basis for social stability and operates in the main through approval and disapproval. The social institutions of enforcement 'codes, courts and constables' can only be used in a limited number of cases – the present overcrowding in British prisons is leading to an increasing number of non-custodial sentences, but there is clearly a limit to the capacity of courts, police and probation officers as well as of prisons.

18.4 SANCTIONS

A sanction is a method of enforcing obedience, and although most people will accept the officially 'sanctioned', or approved, behaviour as a result of social conditioning, punishments are also required in most societies to deter at least some of those who are tempted to disregard the accepted norms and values. Equally, rewards such as knighthoods or OBE's serve to emphasise the importance of the norms and value by publicly honouring those who have conspicuously assisted in maintaining them, whether by voluntary work in hospitals, reaching eminence in their professions or assisting a political party. Rewards may also be in the form of direct monetary payments which encourage members of the society to work hard in socially approved ways to attain both practical benefits and higher status.

Punishments are called 'negative sanctions' and those that are the result of laws or laid down in regulations are called 'formal' negative sanctions. A formal negative sanction might include a girl in detention at school for smoking, or a murderer serving a life sentence in prison. An informal negative sanction might include such signs of disapproval as not saying 'good morning' to a neighbour who has offended us, or a man being 'sent to Coventry', so that no one is prepared to speak to him, as a punishment for not going on strike when the rest of his work-mates had voted to do so.

Formal positive sanctions encourage socially approved activities

Rewards are called 'positive sanctions' and may include formal positive sanctions such as an MBE or a good 'O' level GCE pass. An informal positive sanction might include a child being given a sweet for doing a job for his Mum; or being sought after as a reliable friend. Positive sanctions tend to be more effective than negative ones in ensuring social control.

Labelling theory

Apprehension and labelling
The second stage in the process of becoming deviant, and one on which most labellists have concentrated, is that of apprehension. Becker (1963) says:

> One of the most crucial steps in the process of building a stable pattern of deviant behaviour is likely to be experience of being caught and publicly labelled as a deviant . . . being caught and branded as a deviant has important consequences for one's further social participation and self image.

It should be made clear, however, that labellists do not consider the *fact* of being officially registered, or even the ritual ceremonies of status degradation that frequently accompany that official act, to be in themselves sufficient to convert normals into self-identifying deviants. As Lemert (1967) suggests,

> Degradation rituals such as drumming the coward out of the regiment, administering the pauper's oath, diagnosing the contagious illness and finding the accused guilty as charged may dramatize the facts of deviance, but their 'success' is gauged less by their manner of enactment than by their prevailing consequences . . . The ancient ceremonial . . . may strike [the accused] with awe and fear, but if nothing much happens as a consequence, the memory fades or is retrospectively rationalized . . . for stigmatization to establish a total deviant identity, *it must be disseminated throughout society*.

The italics in this quote are deliberate for they prevent a simpleton rendition of labelling theory. Something other than a ritual ceremony has to happen. Being labelled deviant guarantees nothing. From the fact of apprehension and being formally registered as having committed a deviant act, most labelling theorists go on to discuss one serious consequence which might well contribute to further infractious behaviour – incarceration. Matza, however, takes a different route before arriving at incarceration. Most people who are caught are eventually released and not sent to prison. Can we assume that for this majority the process of building a deviant identity is necessarily concluded? 'No,' says Matza; apprehension has given them matters to consider. Not only have they experienced the simple fact of being registered, but during apprehension they have experienced derogation and representation – that is, they have suffered the abuse of people correlating the immorality of the act with their own immorality, and they have been treated in accordance with the status the State, in its bureaucratic routines, allots them – that of a criminal. It is when the State stops the relatively trivial activity of registration and gets down to the serious business of derogation and representation that the subject's conventional identity is shocked. As Matza puts it (1969),

> To be signified a thief does not assure the continuation of such pursuits; but it does add to the meaning of theft in the life of the perpetrator, and it does add to the meaning of that person in the eyes of others ... To be signified a thief is to lose the blissful identity of one who *among other things* happens to have committed a theft. It is a movement, however gradual, toward being a thief ... to be cast a thief ... is to compound and hasten the process of becoming that very thing.

[S. Box, *Deviance, Reality and Society* (New York: Holt, Rinehart & Winston, 1981).]

CHAPTER 19

AGENCIES OF SOCIAL CONTROL

19.1 FAMILY

The most important agency of social control is the family (section 1.2) for although the norms and values we learn in our family as a child can be modified later, all our later social learning will have to force its way through the mesh of this early conditioning. That which is not in accord with our existing value system is likely to be rejected.

The importance of the family as an agent of social control has been referred to by many sociologists. Anne Campbell (*Girl Delinquents*, 1981) found that delinquent children often 'reported a feeling of being rejected by either or both parents. Supervision over the child's activities and discipline was lax and erratic, and parent and child spent little time in recreational activities with one another.'

The family may therefore fail to socialise the child in a socially acceptable way by neglect, or by socialising the child as a member of a delinquent sub-culture. Usually however the family will begin the process of acceptable social learning.

The family will be the agency in which gender roles are learned by providing toys and clothes appropriate to aggressive masculine or submissive feminine roles if those are the roles appropriate to the culture. Parents will provide role models so that sons and daughters will learn by observation what is appropriate behaviour for them as male or female, which may, of course, include drunkenness and violence.

In the family, basic rules such as those relating to ownership of property will be learned as the child is allocated specific personal belongings. Children will learn of their parents' disapproval of certain other people in the community and certain kinds of behaviour; their own behaviour will be sanctioned by rewards and punishments.

We learn our future role in our family

19.2 EDUCATION

When children move into the school situation they have to learn to relate to a more formal, hierarchical structure than in the family (sections 6.3 and 8.2). They begin to learn to conform to a situation similar to that of their future world of work. Rules must often be obeyed without explanation; work is often apparently meaningless and therefore alienating; individuals must be given signs of respect appropriate to their status. Sanctions tend to be more formal. Indiscipline or slackness is discouraged by lines, detentions and the withholding of privileges; 'good' behaviour and hard work is rewarded by exam success and office, such as that of prefect.

However, while the education service encourages most children to adhere to the norms and values of acceptable – and often middle class orientated – culture, some children may be encouraged into deviance by lack of success within the education system.

Hargreaves (*Social Relations in a Secondary School*, 1967) states – 'The low-stream boys are 'failures', they are status deprived both in school and in society; their efforts meet with little success. Their problem of adjustment is solved by a rejection of societal and teacher values, and status is derived from conformity to a reversal of societal and teacher values.' The same link between school failure – followed by boring jobs or unemployment – and crime was seen by D. Downes: 'The streets of our urban slums are slowly filling with young men who have no prospect of finding manhood through work' (*The Delinquent Solution*, 1966).

Schools act within the context of their neighbourhoods and the members of the peer group with whom the child associates are likely to have increasing influence as the child grows older.

19.3 THE PEER GROUP

The peer group controls its members mainly by informal sanctions, principally ridicule and exclusion. The peer group is not necessarily an agency which leads to delinquency. On the contrary, most young people will mirror adult attitudes and values (section 8.4) and will thus tend to reinforce other agencies in encouraging adherence to the mores of the society.

However the majority of criminal offences are committed by both boys and girls between the ages of 14 and 20 (see Figure 19.1) and this is the period during which the influence of the peer group is also the greatest. The vast majority of young people convicted between these ages do not re-offend as older adults.

For those unable to find an avenue of status through the formal system of education, and not yet in a position to gain it through employment and

Fig. 19.1   *youth in trouble*

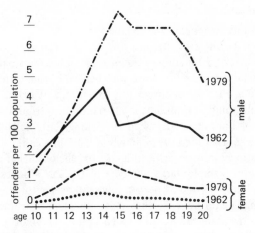

SOURCE   *New Society,* 1984

parenthood, there is a danger that the peer group will provide both status and excitement in ways that disrupt public order. Although the academic failures often find socially acceptable outlets in pursuit of interest and status, such as sport, uniformed organisations, and youth clubs; whether they will become delinquent involves many factors. 'To conclude that the 'basic' causes of crime and delinquency invariably lie in the family is to ignore the extremely complex network of interrelationships between family influences and the simultaneous influences of community values, peer group, neighbourhood behaviour patterns, socio-economic pressures and other relevant factors.' (E. Schur, *Our Criminal Society*, 1969).

The rise in young offenders

In 1979, 164,000 young people (aged between 10 and 16) were cautioned for or found guilty of indictable offences, compared with 98,000 in 1965. Although the definition of an indictable offence did change during this period, there was a steady rise in juvenile crime of about 8.5 per cent a year between 1967 and 1983.

Between 1959 and 1974, the average increase in known offenders for every 100,000 people in the age group was over 10 per cent for girls, 6.4 per cent for boys of 14 to 16, and 3.4 per cent for boys of 10 to 13. But these rises were proportionately no worse than rises in adult crime. The diagram shows that the peak age for girls' committing offences is 14, but the peak age for boys shifted from 14 to 15 in 1972: the year when the school-leaving age was raised to 16. (*New Society*, 1984).

19.4 RELIGION AND THE MEDIA

Two of the other 'relevant factors' in influencing the socialisation of both the child and adult are religion and the media.

Religion can be an effective instrument of social control for some people. The threat of damnation or the promise of heaven are potent negative and positive sanctions for those who believe in them, they have the advantage in that they depend upon the knowledge of wrongdoing being known to an all-seeing God so there is a certainty of retribution or reward. In the words of Pope Pius XII when forbidding Catholics to vote Communist – 'God can see you in the polling booth, Stalin can't.'

In an increasingly secular age the influence of religious belief on morality is debatable. For example, large numbers of Italian Catholics vote Communist, but in the past it has been a powerful agency of social control. Karl Marx summed up his view that religion was an instrument used by ruling elites to maintain the existing social order: 'The mortgage that the peasant has on heavenly possessions guarantees the mortgage that the bourgeois has on peasant possessions' (*The Class Struggles in France 1848 to 1850*).

The media: television, radio, newspapers, magazines and public hoardings, does not operate as the other agencies of social control do by the use of sanctions but can still influence behaviour, although the extent of this influence is debatable (section 6.4). In 1962 the Pilkington Committee reported on the effects of broadcasting: 'Dr Hilde Himmelweit told us that all the evidence so far provided by detailed researches suggested that values were acquired, that a view of life was picked up, by children watching television. Professor Eysenck told us that there were good theoretical grounds for supposing that moral standards could be affected by television and that these grounds were largely supported by experimental and clinical evidence' (*Report of the Committee on Broadcasting, 1960*, 1962). However Himmelweit in *Television and the Child* also emphasised that children are only likely to be influenced by television if the actions suggested are in accordance with the existing values of the child and if it touches on the ideas for which the child is emotionally ready (e.g. torrid sex scenes are unlikely to affect a very young child); she suggested that those most likely to be affected are those who are least critical, in particular the less intelligent thirteen to fourteen year old. J. Halloran in *Television and Delinquency* also emphasised that television was unlikely to stimulate delinquency unless other factors were present, and in *The Effects of Mass Communication* showed that while aggression was likely to be reinforced by TV violence among those with aggressive tendencies, the 'normal' control group were unaffected – a view supported by W. Belson, *TV Violence and the Adolescent Boy*, who concluded that aggressive personalities could be encouraged to real violence by that on television.

The media and female delinquency

The media have two primary functions. The first is to make money, and the second is to put forward a particular, coherent world view or ideology. Sex and violence, as the old cliché goes, sell. These two in combination with females do even better. Not only is the combination titillating, but it is less common than among men – in other words, it does not accord with the stereotypical view of females. . . Female murderers and muggers get a disproportionate amount of attention. On the other hand, most newspapers are far from dedicated to the promotion of the feminist movement, so that such reports are usually censorious. They lead to a particular combination of fascination and moral outrage. In his book *Folk Devils and Moral Panic* S. Cohen (1972) has drawn attention to the way in which certain sectors of society, such as Hell's Angels or soccer hooligans, are singled out for condemnation and censure. Recently, this same process has begun to work against women in crime. The rise in crime figures among females receives more newspaper space than that among men and provokes a much more extreme reaction. If we were to take the labelling of newspapers as our criterion of female delin-quency, we would devote rather little attention to the more mundane and frequent problems of shoplifting and petty theft and would focus instead on precocious sex, prostitution, violence, murder and child-beating. While the role of the media in shaping popular concep-tions of morality is an interesting issue, taken as a criterion it may lead to a very unrepresentative view of female delinquency. [A. Campbell, *Girl Delinquents* (Oxford: Basil Blackwell, 1981) (abridged).]

The media and change

We can now look at findings regarding the more specific effects of one of the mass media which has been studied more thoroughly. This is television, and we shall present some of the conclusions regarding its effects on children, young people, the family and political behaviour. Among the earliest empirical studies concerned with the first aspect were those by Hilde Himmelweit and her team. As concerns displacement effects, i.e. time taken up by viewing, the chief conclusions were that contrary to popular belief children did not watch programmes indiscriminately; the single most import-ant determinant of the amount of viewing done by the child was his intelligence, whilst the social level of the home did not affect this aspect very much. Secondary influencing factors were the child's personality (and how full and active a life he led before television was introduced), as well as parental example. Regarding the effects of programme content, results suggested that a large number of programmes containing violence are likely to make a cumulative impact, particularly on younger children. On the whole, however, Himmelweit maintains that television is 'not as black as it is painted, but neither is it the great harbinger of culture and enlightenment', although children did acquire certain values and an outlook on life consistent with the contents of television programmes. A more general survey by Mark Abrams suggests that the long-term combined effect of television viewing and the increased consumption of the printed mass media, is one of broadening the outlook of the younger generation; making them aware not only of their family circle, neighbourhood and workplace, but also of the wider community and other societies.

As far as family life is concerned, W. A. Belson found that his enquiry did not throw up any evidence which might suggest that television produces radical changes. Thus it slightly reduces home-centred and joint activity, but it also brings the family together. There may in some cases be more substantial reductions in the collective frequency and the range of sociable activities, but after about five years there is a tendency for these to return to the pre-television level. Belson stresses at the same time the importance of other factors and states: 'It is clear that the effects of television on family life and on sociability are highly sensitive to local and seasonal factors. They depend, among other things, upon the viewer's cultural and family backgrounds, and upon the area in which he lives.'

Considering the effects of television on political attitudes in a study at the time of the 1959 general election, Trenaman came to the conclusion that there were certain protective devices at work during election campaigns which screened off electors and at least temporarily suppressed any direct effects, particularly once electors recognized the campaign as propaganda aimed at them. On the whole, group pressures reduced the effects of propaganda and an element of free choice was also at work. A PEP report holds that some views, particularly about politics, religion and social class, are rather resistant to change; but in relation to many new issues, where public attitudes are not yet formed or in cases where people either have conflicting opinions or do not feel strongly about an issue, there is a greater susceptibility to persuasion by the mass media. The report argues that this is bound to have an effect on civic goals and hence on society as a whole. The potency of television is, according to J. D. Halloran, evident in another sense, that is in the influence it brings to bear on the other mass media: 'The radio, cinema, theatre, and magazine are being compelled to change.'

Finally, sociologists have considered the process of attitude formation and change as affected by mass communication. Bryan Wilson, whilst noting that these processes are not yet capable of being accurately measured because of their subtle and gradual nature, suggests that the media are altering our attitudes as concerns crime. They promote values which 'stand in stark contrast to the values entrenched in our existing social institutions—the family, the workplace, the school, the law courts, the church—and in our social relationships'. He claims that the new values are more tolerant of deviant behaviour, and that this results in the mass media 'promoting the erosion of traditional social values and . . . creating confusion, particularly among young people, about standards of behaviour'. Halloran points out that Wilson does not produce sociological evidence to substantiate this indictment of the mass media. But although Halloran's review of research in the area points to a view that 'the mass media are not as powerful as personal and direct experience in changing attitudes', he agrees that 'their potential cannot be played down'. [E. Krausz, *Sociology in Britain: A Surrey of Research* (London: Batsford, 1969) (adapted).]

19.5 THE LAW

Perhaps the most obvious agency of social control is the law. It is also perhaps the least important in that it can only hope to deter possible offenders against the social order, or punish those who do offend, if the majority of people are controlled by other agencies. The law deals not only with 'crime' but also with disputes between individuals or groups, where no crime has been committed. This 'Civil Law' includes such matters as matrimonial disputes and arguments over property ownerships.

Unless a law is acceptable to the majority of people within a society, or at least is not actively opposed by them, it cannot be enforced. In the 1920s and 1930s the prohibition of alcohol in America led to widespread evasion and as a result people who would normally have supported social order connived with gangsters providing alcohol and thus encouraged a general contempt for the law.

The law in the main is based on the 'mores' of the society – the most important rules based upon the prevailing morality. Although the law is usually rather slow to respond to changing attitudes, it must eventually do so or fall into disrepute by being widely disobeyed. Since 1961 the law has changed in a number of important areas. It is no longer illegal to: attempt to take your own life (although it is against the law to aid a suicide); procure an abortion in certain circumstances; have homosexual relations in private provided both partners are over 21: engage in off-course gambling. An example of the 'Civil Law' changing to pay regard to changing relationships within the family is the greater frequency with which the father is given custody of children in matrimonial disputes.

However the law as an agency of last resort does have the most draconian sanctions: fines, imprisonment and in some countries and in certain circumstances – death.

CRIME AND DELINQUENCY

20.1 THE NATURE OF CRIME AND DELINQUENCY

The criminal law will only deal with deviant acts which have been labelled as crimes. 'Deviancy' is deviation from the norm (section 18.2) and is not necessarily criminal. A person may decide to live as a hermit, or they may live saintly lives within a corrupt society and seek to reform it. Such acts are likely to be deviant but not criminal.

A crime is an act which is judged a sufficient challenge to the functioning of the society as to warrant punishment. Such an act is likely to be deviant, but not necessarily so. A dictator may ban certain books but the possession of such books may be regarded as normal by the majority of people. Within a particular group, an act such as petty pilfering from work may be acceptable, although it is a crime.

Although sometimes used to describe all minor criminal acts and behaviour which although not criminal are anti-social or immoral, the term delinquency is usually used of adolescent behaviour in which the young person reacts against adult expectations. He or she does not usually consciously reject adult values, and delinquent behaviour usually ends with the onset of courtship. Delinquency is often an expression of self-assertion – 'not so much a symptom of maladjustment, as of adjustment to a subculture' (J. Mays, *Crime and its Treatment*, 1970).

Delinquent behaviour is often criminal – vandalism, shoplifting, soccer hooliganism – but not necessarily so. 'Troublesome boys go in for crime, whereas troublesome girls merely go with boys' (M. Schofield, *The Sexual Behaviour of Young People*, 1965). Now it is suggested that increasing criminal behaviour among girls is the result, in part, of sexual promiscuity becoming more socially acceptable and therefore an insufficiently emphatic expression of rebellion. What is regarded as delinquent will vary as the norms and values of the society change. Equally, double standards may operate; either between the sexes, as when sexual promiscuity is regarded

Mayday drunkenness by undergraduates may be regarded as youthful high spirits

as being delinquent behaviour in girls but not in boys; or between classes. For example, Mayday drunkenness and damage to property by Oxford undergraduates may be regarded as youthful high spirits; similar behaviour by working-class football supporters will be regarded as holligansim. This class difference in delinquency was noted by T. Morris, 'serious delinquency occurs most frequently among the families of unskilled workers' (*The Criminal Area*, 1957), although he was relating delinquency to inadequate housing, large families and other practical considerations.

Crime too, varies in a similar way; although, because it is officially defined, change follows legislation and may take longer. What is criminal in one society may not be so in another. For example, alcohol is tolerated in Britain but illegal in Saudi Arabia. However there tends to be certain constant principles such as a respect for property, life and sexual rights.

Stereotyping and crime

In two police stations she found that twenty per cent and twenty-seven per cent respectively of those arrested for marginal offences were of no fixed abode. She links this to their vulnerability as 'a small exposed and powerless section of the population' who are therefore particularly at risk to the policeman's interests in making arrests.

As for having sufficient evidence on a specific offence, there is also plenty of scope for legally circumventing that principle. The specific offence may itself be rather unspecific – breach of the peace (whose peace?), loitering with intent or being on premises for unlawful purposes (how does one determine purpose or intent?), possessing goods for which one cannot satisfactorily account (how many people carry receipts and what is satisfactory?), carrying implements that could be used for housebreaking (where does one draw the line?) or as weapons. Even an empty milk bottle has been defined as a dangerous weapon.

So, in vague cases like breach of the peace, the offence exists because the police say they observed someone loitering, drunk, 'bawling, shouting, cursing and swearing', to quote the daily menu for the district courts, or more unusually but nonetheless an observed case, 'jumping on and off the pavement in a disorderly fashion'.

Likewise, one must refer to more than informal stereotyping to explain the arrest of two young boys, a 'known thief' and his companion, who, according to the police evidence, were 'touching cars', according to the boys, 'just pointing at Volvos and things, expensive cars'. Whatever the informal motivation of the police, the legality of their action is indisputable and the stereotyping more than informal.*

A known thief is someone with a previous conviction for dishonesty: previous convictions become therefore not just informal leads for narrowing down suspects on committed crimes but legal grounds for arresting them. A reputed thief is someone who keeps bad company and has no known means of honest livelihood: stereotyping and assuming the worst are thus written into the law. Suspicious circumstances are left to the police to define. [S. Holdaway (ed.) *The British Police* (London: Arnold, 1979).]

* This example is a local act specific to the Scottish city in question but other acts operate on similar stereotypes and fulfil similar functions in other parts of Scotland and England, e.g. the *Vagrancy Act* 1824, or the *Prevention of Crimes Act* 1871.

20.2 CAUSES OF CRIME AND DELINQUENCY

The same kind of argument over heredity and environment as factors in intelligence (section 8.1) has also taken place with regard to crime.

In 1876, an Italian criminologist, Lombroso, examined the skull of an infamous bandit and decided that it had characteristics of an earlier evolutionary type. Lombroso developed a theory that criminals were different from other people and represented a lower stage of evolution (H. Jones, *Crime in a Changing Society*, 1965). Although there is now no support for such a view there is still the possibility of some genetic link with crime. D. Rosenthal found that identical twins shared crime traits at a rate more than double that of non-identical twins (American Association for Advancement of Science Lecture, 1972) and speculation continues over whether this chromosomal link with crime exists.

A biological link with crime is not yet proved, but a correlation between other factors and crime have been identified: socialisation (section 19.1), education (section 19.2) and environment (section 16.4). As early as 1886, G. Tarde (*La Criminalité Comparée*) suggested that criminal behaviour is learned in the family and community. The connection between poverty and crime is long established (T. Morris, 'The Sociology of Crime', *New Society*, 1965) as is that between crime and unemployment (Glaser and Rice, 'Crime, Age and Unemployment', *American Sociological Review*, 24, 1959).

There are a number of fairly obvious explanations for the fact that the British crime rate has increased considerably in recent years although poverty has not, although in this respect the influence of relative poverty must be remembered (section 10.4).

There is a great deal more easily-removable property – such as cars – available to steal. The advertising industry spends millions of pounds persuading us that consumer goods are essential or highly desirable, but does not provide the means of attaining them. This gap between opportunity and objective is likely to be greatest at the bottom of the social ladder. The majority of people found guilty of offences are under thirty; with the largest number between the ages of fourteen and twenty-one – this age group has increased in numbers. The largest single category of offences is that related to the use of motor vehicles – the number of motor vehicles has increased considerably during the past twenty years.

Violence and overcrowding appear to be linked (F. McClintock and N. Avison, *Crime in England and Wales*, 1968). Housing policies have maintained inner city housing densities, for example, by building high rise flats.

Deviance

Despite much research in this area there is a great deal of uncertainty about the incidence of crime and delinquency in modern society as compared with earlier periods. While Leon Radzinowicz sees no sign of a turn in the increasing tide of criminal behaviour of the mid-twentieth century, Barbara Wootton advises caution in the interpretation of crime statistics and maintains that it is now generally recognized that such evidence is unreliable for making long-term comparisons. Again, while there is some evidence to confirm that high-delinquency areas are to be found in the big cities and ports rather than in rural areas, it has been pointed out by Leslie Wilkins that 'areas which have had a bad reputation among those who may be expected to know do not always turn out to be high-delinquency areas when rigorous data are obtained' (Leslie Wilkins, *Social Deviance*, 1964).

On the other hand there is a good deal of agreement regarding sociological explanations of deviance in our society. Many writers stress the changes in the social structure which modern industrial conditions have wrought, and either explicitly or implicitly invoke this as the basic reason for the increase in most criminal behaviour in contemporary society. We summarize below the main points that arise from this view. (1) Lack of cohesion and adequate means of social control due to the impersonalization of social relationships in the highly industrialized city are reflected in weakening kinship ties and community bonds, and lead to a breakdown in culture and the normative system and to a condition of *anomie*. (2) Impersonal social relations resulting in the victim of the crime receding into anonymity, and greater affluence which means more opportunity to commit crime, are factors which encourage criminal behaviour. (3) Thwarted aspirations in some sections of the population, for whom avenues of social mobility are generally closed despite the stress put in contemporary society on achievement-orientation, lead to discontent, rejection of both working-class and middle-class values, and so to rebelliousness, particularly in teenage groups, ending up in deviance (T. R. Fyvel, *The Insecure Offenders*, 1961). [E. Krausz, *Sociology in Britain* (London: Batsford, 1969).]

20.3 CRIME AND STATISTICS

Increasing crime may merely indicate greater opportunity to commit crime; but there are a number of other reasons why criminal statistics should be approached with caution, particularly when trying to compare one historical period or one country with another.

(a) In some areas crime is less likely to be reported because of social mores.

(b) Some crimes are less likely to be reported than others. In America surveys show that only 27 per cent of rape and 31 per cent of burglary cases get reported. All vehicle theft was reported, no doubt for insurance reasons. In a London survey in 1977 it was found that only one third of criminal victimisations are notified to the police. 'From the official rate we cannot tell whether the high proportion of sexual offences in Lincolnshire is because that county is a hotbed of sexual deviation or because such offences are much more likely to be reported in tightknit rural and small town communities' (R. Davidson, *Crime and Environment*, 1981).

(c) Police activity varies. The modern police are highly trained and use sophisticated methods – they may be more likely to detect crime than formerly. Particular forces have campaigns against various forms of crime – in one area marijuana smoking may be tolerated, in another rigorously prosecuted.

(d) Some crimes are more likely to be discovered than others. Crimes against property, mainly committed by those in lower socio-economic class categories, are very likely to be discovered. Tax evasion and fraud, perhaps more likely to be committed by those higher up the social scale, are more difficult to identify.

Why crime statistics are inaccurate

Other research has revealed still further reasons for victims' unwillingness to report a criminal act. For instance, some victims prefer to resort to extra-judicial action rather than submit themselves and the culprit to official judicial procedures, which may be perceived as costly both in economic terms and in the damage to reputations it can cause. Thus, in Martin's (1962) study of English employers' reactions to employee offender, he suggested that on nearly 70 per cent of the occasions on which the employer failed to report the offence to the police he was attempting to keep unpleasantness, both for the firm and the offender, to a minimum. Similarly, Robin (1977) argued that one important reason why American employers refrain from prosecuting their employee offenders is because there is frequently a psychological affinity between the two, and, rather than see an employee publicly humiliated, employers perfer to settle the matter privately. Further, this extra-judicial procedure protects the employer from publicly risking his ability to assess candidates for positions in his firm. Finally, Cameron (1964) discovered that the victims of shoplifting were often reluctant to take official judicial steps because of the uncertainty and difficulty of proving some cases, and because of the cost of releasing employees to serve as witnesses against the suspected shoplifter. In these circumstances, department managers were inclined to release suspects with a warning and a request not to patronize the store again. The ability and willingness of the suspect to pay for the goods was a factor closely associated with this extra-judicial mode of handling offenders.

Fear of embarrassment, or an unwillingness to risk exposing private matters to public gaze, may provide further reasons why some victims of criminal behaviour fail to report an offence. Thus the victims of blackmail usually prefer to keep their dark secret hidden rather than jeopardize their present respectability. Similarly, victims of forcible rape and other indecent sexual offences often prefer to forgo reporting the incident rather than risk their own reputations being brushed by the smutty innuendoes of neighbours, police, doctors, and particularly prosecutors (Toner, 1977). Indeed, it would be no exaggeration to claim that many rape victims avoid reporting it for fear that they will be put 'on trial', so entrenched is institutionalized sexism in our criminal justice system (Clark and Lewis, 1977; Robin, 1977). Another, and final, example provided by some victims of financial swindles, who prefer to remain silent rather than reveal their naivety, stupidity or possible culpable connivance in illegal conduct.

Thus, even in the case of serious criminal offences, such as larceny, burglary, rape, assault, shoplifting, embezzlement and fraud, where a person is perfectly aware of having been victimized, the police frequently remain uninformed and the offence goes unrecorded.

In addition to the aware victim, three other victims can be conceptualized; the person who remains unaware of being victimized (unless some other persons reveal it to him or her); the abstract victim on whose behalf licensed agents keep a watchful lookout without necessarily reminding him/her of their guardianship. and victims who refuse to recognize the label. In each case, the ability or willingness of the victim to report the offence to the police is seriously impaired, thus considerably reducing the accuracy of the volume and pattern of crimes known to the police.

An example of the *unaware victim* is the person who has been involved at the losing end of a confidence trick but who remains ignorant. This appears to be a frequent outcome of such criminal behaviour, for the art of the confidence trickster is to leave the victim either unaware or confused to the point of not realizing what has happened. Similarly, company owners and managers often remain ignorant of embezzlement and other commercial frauds, and store owners remain unaware of shoplifting or employee theft, particularly where stock shrinkage could just as easily result from poor accounting procedures or inadequate recording practices. Clearly, where the victim remains unaware, or where he can interpret what has happened by giving it a non-criminal explanation, the police are not informed and the official statistics are deficient.

Another type of victim exists where no one in particular is a victim, but we all are in general. In the case of tax evasion, for instance, it is possible to argue that there exists an *abstract victim*. Thus, everyone who pays tax, or is the recipient of direct or indirect government spending, is a victim in the sense that 'honest payment by everyone liable to income tax would enable the government to decrease the general tax burden by 40 per cent' (Gibney, 1960).

[S. Box, *Deviance, Reality and Society* (New York: Holt, Rinehart & Winston, 1981).]

20.4 CLASS AND GENDER IN RELATION TO CRIME

Class and gender as factors in crime have been referred to previously. The reasons why lower socio-economic income groups are more likely to feature in cases of reported crime are:

1. Laws are framed by middle-class people and reflect middle-class values. For example, working-class people may be imprisoned for relatively small debts while company bankrupts appear to escape punishment. Social security frauds are more likely to result in punishment than false Income Tax returns.
2. The children of unskilled and semi-skilled workers have less opportunities to obtain status-enhancing employment.
3. The areas in which lower status groups live are more likely to be overcrowded and have a delinquent sub-culture. Equally, these inner city areas have opportunities for cime in the form of vehicles and accessible commercial and domestic property, together with anonymity which makes detection difficult.
4. Lower class groups have little property, but the values of our society emphasizes the importance of wealth. The urge to acquire what is desired illegitimately is bound to be greatest among those who possess least of it, and who have fewest legitimate avenues of acquisition.

Both men and women are subjected to these same pressures; but men are six times more likely than women to be convicted of a criminal offence. It may be that growing equality will narrow the gap, and there is already some evidence of this. There is a biological argument that women are less aggressive, assertive and competitive than males, though this is disputed. Environmental factors may include:

(a) The socialisation process which encourages girls to adopt a submissive role. Males need to act out our society's definition of masculinity, which includes recklessness and toughness. In some environments, legally available means of acting this role may be restricted so illegal ones are sought. The socially approved feminine roles relating to passivity and domesticity are more readily available in a legal form.
(b) There have been more restrictions placed on females regarding absence from home late at night or being in situations – such as clubs and pubs – where violent situations may develop.
(c) There have been more readily available opportunities for unskilled females to earn money in ways which, while not socially approved, are not illegal. For example, prostitution.

Theories on the cause of delinquency

After Freud the writings of Bowlby (1953) took first place in connection with delinquency. He stressed that the relationship between
the child and the mother in the first five years of life was crucial to
healthy psychological development. Children deprived of mother
love were thought to develop a host of psychological disorders,
ranging from subnormality, through schizophrenia and neurosis to
delinquency. The appeal of Bowlby's work in connection with girls
was strong, since it viewed the delinquent as a helpless victim of
circumstances rather than as an individual with free will or a 'bad
streak'. Glueck and Glueck (1934) claimed that 90 per cent of
women from a Massachusetts reformatory had broken or poorly
supervised home lives, and many post-war studies measured the
prevalence of maternal deprivation in incarcerated girls, giving
figures that ranged from 27 per cent (Richardson, 1969), through
33 per cent (O'Kelly, 1955), to 43 per cent (Cowie et al., 1968). Yet
none of these studies used a control group against which to compare
its figures, and the only study to do so (Riege, 1972) found no significant differences between delinquent and non-delinquent girls.
However, an Australian study by Koller (1971) reported that 62 per
cent of training-school girls had experienced parental loss or deprivation, compared with 13 per cent of the control group.

It became obvious that such a theory notably failed to explain
the peculiarly adolescent nature of delinquency. If it results from
such an early disturbance, why is it not manifest until puberty? And
if it has an enduring effect on personality, why does delinquency
usually end in the later teens? Attention turned instead towards the
current child-rearing practices of delinquents' parents. Studies by
Nye (1958), Riege (1972) and Morris (1964) found that the factors
held to be important in male delinquents' homes were equally true
of the homes of delinquent females. The frequency of separation
and divorce among parents varied widely depending on the definition of delinquency and of the intact family. In general, the incidence
of marital break-up was higher in delinquent than non-delinquent
populations, and this was particularly true of girls. For both sexes
quarrelling and discordance were found in the home (with the exception of Riege's startling finding that the parents of non-delinquents
quarrelled more frequently in front of their children than did the
parents of delinquents). Often the child reported a feeling of being
rejected by either or both parents. Supervision over the child's activities and discipline was lax and erratic, and parent and child spent
little time in recreational activities with one another. It would
appear that the precipitating factors within the family for delinquency in females are not substantially different from those for
males. As girls spend more time out of the home and on the streets,

the possibility of their becoming involved in delinquent subcultures increases, particularly in urban, working-class areas. This would seem to focus attention on the peer group rather than the family. While great attention has been paid to this factor in studies of boys, such analysis of girl delinquents is almost completely lacking. We know virtually nothing of their life beyond the family and this reflects the prevailing belief that the behaviour of females can be explained exclusively by recourse to their biology, psyche and home life. [A. Campbell, *Girl Delinquents* (Oxford: Blackwell, 1981) (abridged).]

QUESTIONS FROM PAST O-LEVEL GCE PAPERS

1.

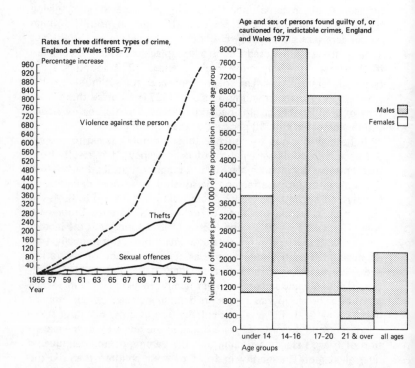

(From Robert Roshier, *Crime and Punishment*, 1980)

(a) What explanations have sociologists put forward for the patterns of crime revealed by the above graphs? [10]

(b) What factors may cause the 'official statistics' (on which these graphs were based) to be inaccurate? [10]

Cambridge Local Examining Board

2. 'What is considered 'odd', 'different' or even 'deviant' behaviour varies within society. Mountaineers, parachutists and soldiers are not considered deviant by the majority of people — and yet they have chosen to behave in a very dangerous, even suicidal way. They are usually praised for their behaviour. But surely, no sane person wants to risk his/her life?

Most of us think of ourselves as 'normal' human beings, yet some of us are regarded as abnormal by other people. For behaviour to be labelled 'abnormal', it has to be judged as going against accepted norms. But what are these 'accepted norms'? And does everyone agree with them? Many people who would judge themselves as perfectly 'normal' are called 'mad', 'crazy', 'unbalanced' by others.

It is not easy then to draw a clear line between 'normal' and 'abnormal' behaviour. People use different standards by which to judge behaviour.'

Adapted from Y. Beecham, J. Fiehn and J. Gates, *Deviance — themes in Sociology*, 1982.

(a) According to the authors it is difficult to draw a clear line between 'normal' and 'abnormal' behaviour. Why do you think this is? [2]

(b) Why is some behaviour which is not against the law sometime regarded as 'deviant'? [6]

(c) It is often the case that what is considered 'abnormal' behaviour in one society is not considered abnormal behaviour in another society. With reference to any *one* society or culture, which is different from your own, explain how this situation might arise. [12]

Cambridge Local Examining Board

3. Suggest ways in which any two of the following influence behaviour in society (examples may be chosen from one or more societies).
  (a) Law and custom.
  (b) Religion.
  (c) Mass media.

Associated Examining Board

4. How would you explain social class differences in rates of juvenile delinquency?

Oxford Local Examining Board

5. 'The woman, delicate and timid, requires protection . . . The man as a protector is directed by nature to govern; the woman conscious of inferiority, is disposed to obey.' (*Encyclopaedia Britannica*, 4th Edition 1800–1810.)

(a) What formal and informal changes have taken place in our society to change this view over the last 100 years?

12 marks

(b) How does society continue to reinforce the kind of attitude shown above?   8 marks

Associated Examining Board

6. Do increases in criminal statistics always mean increased social disorder?   Associated Examining Board

7. Examine the suggestion that relations between the police force and the public in Britain have worsened in recent years.

Oxford Local Examining Board

8. 'The mass media are sometimes accused of promoting violence and unacceptable social behaviour amongst the young, but some claim that the media promote social understanding and tolerance.' What support is there for the above opinions?

Associated Examining Board

PART VIII

SOCIAL CHANGE

REASONS FOR SOCIAL CHANGE

21.1 STAGNATION v. DEVELOPMENT

Societies change for many different reasons. There may be physical conditions such as drought, flooding or crop failure which necessitate a change in production and living patterns, or migration. For example the potato famine of 1846 resulted in a mass exodus of rural Irish peasantry to the urban areas of America and Britain. This clearly influenced the society which they had left, and the society that received them. As with most migration, those that left were often the most active and ambitious, with the result that many rural Irish communities stagnated. In the United States the destruction of the buffalo herds by white settlers and soldiers between 1865 and 1875 ruined the economic base of Indian civilisation.

The same factors which encourage social cohesion are also those which may encourage social stagnation. Socialisation encourages a degree of conformity (section 18.1), and if the family and educational system is too rigid in its enforcement of norms then it will be difficult for new ideas to form and so result in development.

The degree to which societies come into contact with others will also influence the degree of change, both in terms of ideas and technical innovation. Some traditional societies have not changed much for thousands of years. others, like our own, are in an accelerating spiral of change which started to move rapidly with the industrial revolution. We in turn have brought proportionately even more rapid change to other countries through colonialism. But although some aspects of British life have changed dramatically some have not.

21.2 CULTURAL FACTORS

The beliefs, language, rules and folkways – the 'culture' of a society (section 1.1) cannot be dissociated from the process of production (Chapter 12 and section 22.4) but it is also linked to communication with the cultures of others.

242

Lunch at the Sikh temple in Bradford. Immigrants have often brought additional interest and colour to the streets of the UK

The most obvious contact with other cultures is through immigration and in the past the assimilation of peoples belonging to differing ethnic groups have contributed to the culture we now have (Chapter 17). It is difficult to be certain of the long-term effect on British culture of the recent wave of emigration from the New Commonwealth, although the impact of Chinese and Asian cuisine on our national eating habits has been remarkable, as has the influence of West Indians in the field of entertainment.

The ease of air travel has brought a new dimension to the lives of many people whose parents would have known little of behaviour outside their immediate neighbourhood. The increase in wine consumption is a surface reflection of what may well be deeper changes in perspective.

Perhaps most importantly of all television has brought comparative living standards into everyone's home; in some cases increasing relative deprivation (section 10.4), in others widening cultural horizons and contributing to a change in attitudes.

21.3 POLITICAL FACTORS

The last battle on British soil was in 1746 at Culloden and the fact that Britain has not in modern times suffered invasion or occupation has had an influence on such cultural factors as tolerance and liberty.

The stabilising effect of external security and democratic government at home has also perhaps had an impact upon retaining aspects of British society which many might feel less desirable, such as inequality (section 10.2).

This stability might appear to some as 'stagnation'. A German writing in 1922 commented, 'English national life contrasted with the rich variations of the Continent, presents a picture of drab uniformity, fatally congenial to the creation of a featureless and spineless urban population' (W. Dibelius, *England*, 1930).

If change comes from conflict, then the comparative absence of conflict in British society would explain the 'stability' or 'stagnation' – according to one's point of view – in such institutions as the British class system, or the dominance of middle-class professionals in all the major political parties. Marx argued that social change could not occur unless the structure of society was transformed.

The nearest approach to political confrontation on class lines in Britain was the General Strike of 1926 yet the year before, the Conservative Prime Minister, Stanley Baldwin, successfully opposed a private member's bill brought in by his own backbenchers to prevent political contributions to the Labour Party from trade union dues.

Despite the fact that there is a working class majority in the electorate, the Labour Party – which claims to be the party of the working class – has only held office for twenty of the sixty-six years between 1918 and 1984. Political institutions in Britain have therefore tended towards encouraging stability rather than change.

21.4 ECONOMIC FACTORS

The major changes in British society have been the result of economic rather than political factors; although one of the reasons for the change in the position of women – the First World War – could be seen as a political factor rather than an economic one.

Most of these economic factors have been dealt with earlier and they include:

(a)   Changes in methods of production consequent upon the industrial revolution leading to the establishment of large factory units, and resulting in both increasing urbanisation and the development of organised labour in trade unions, which have in their turn been responsible for social change.

(b)   A need for a more educated workforce, leading to compulsory education and contributing subsequently to such factors as smaller families.

(c)   Greater access to education for both men and women; linked to smaller family size helped to establish the nuclear family as the main operating unit, with consequent effect on the roles of husband and wife.

(d)   Changes in production methods have recently led to increasing leisure for some and increased unemployment for others.

CHAPTER 22

PROCESSES OF SOCIAL CHANGE

22.1 RURAL LIFESTYLES

In Britain in 1801 about three quarters of the population lived in rural areas, by 1901 one quarter did. This process of 'urbanisation' has continued during the present century and it is only since the 1970s that the process appears to have halted, and to a limited extent reversed. This reversal is statistical rather than meaningful in terms of behaviour because the new country-dweller is likely to 'commute' into a town for work; and rural dwellers generally are much more dependent on towns for shopping, leisure facilities and education than they formerly were.

It is generally agreed that some fundamental changes took place in living patterns as a result of the movement from town to country (section 16.2). The extended rural family in the nineteenth century was a unit of production and there was a need for close co-operation with relations. It has been suggested that the rural worker is less likely to be alienated from his work than the town dweller because he sees the object of his labour in the end product.

The rural dweller is less likely to be concerned with status symbols, as the 'face to face' relationships of the village mean that everyone knows what a particular person's job and social position is.

Behaviour in rural societies may be more spontaneous because there is less room for choice. There may be a greater feeling of group solidarity; less crime because people are less likely to steal or damage the property of people known to them, and because there is a greater risk of detection.

In face-to-face communities each individual is related to every other individual in his total network in several different ways. In an extreme case a man's father is also his teacher, his religious leader, and his employer. A shopkeeper in the village is also a relative of many of his customers and a chapel deacon, and so on. 'If the shopkeeper has also to behave appropriately in situations involving shopkeeper/shopkeeper's nephew/deacon/

member of congregation we may say that his social life has a complexity which his urban counterparts lack. He has perhaps a smaller choice of roles than he would have in the town, and he has to play them all to the same audience (R. Frankenberg, *Communities in Britain, Social Life in Town and Country*, 1966). Frankenberg also points to the likelihood of friction between kin in rural areas and to fights between 'the lads' of neighbouring villages. Rural lifestyles are not all peace and tranquillity as compared with those of towns.

Tönnies (1887) used the term *Gemeinschaft*, meaning community, to describe rural lifestyles with their stress on family and community and greater mutual involvement and caring. The term *Gesellschaft*, meaning association, he used to describe urban life with associations formed for practical purposes and less of the informal 'nosey' contacts of the village. Relationships in the village tend to be integrated – in the towns they are likely to be isolated.

Roles in urban and rural communities

In truly rural society the network may be close-knit; everybody knows and interacts with everyone else. In urban society individuals may have few friends in common. In a study of urban families, Elizabeth Bott put forward a hypothesis that the nature of a family's network in these terms was related to the division of labour between husband and wife within the home. She distinguished three kinds of family organization. The first she called complementary, where husband and wife have different activities but fit together to form a whole, as in farming communities. The second she calls independent, where husband and wife act without reference to each other. The third she describes as joint organization, when husband and wife work closely together or their activities are covered by either one alternating. . . Theoretically, at least, at the extreme rural end of the continuum, everyone in society has an equal opportunity to interact with everyone else. Even in rural Ireland, however, the nature of women's work has already cut them off from full interaction. . . I would expect that workers would tend to *embrace* their role in rural society and to *reject* it in urban. In other words, *all* the working class who remain in rural areas are locally oriented. Status and class do not coincide exactly in any society. Nor are they the only categories which align individuals and divide them. In rural society the lines of division for different purposes are less likely to coincide.

The relative ease of social mobility between status groups, characteristic of urban society, does not necessarily weaken class solidarity and conflict. T. H. Marshall has pointed out a change from the ideology of 'that education to which your status entitles you' to 'that status to which your education entitles you'. This, however, is an educational train which has to be caught early or not at all. As he writes:

'The ticket obtained on leaving school or college is for a life journey. The man with a third class ticket who later feels entitled to claim a seat in a first class carriage will not be admitted even if he is prepared to pay the difference. That would not be fair to the others' (Marshall, *Citizenship and Social Class*, 1950).

Of course, not all urban areas are like the classical description of Watling – 'not much more than a huge hotel without a roof; the constant turnover of its population is the greatest single handicap to its developing into a community' . . . In some areas, like Bethnal Green, there is a settled population which has endured over several generations. Here individuals become incorporated into a community through their children and grandchildren and the affinal links that they create.

I am suggesting that in rural societies conflict is more omnipresent and more likely to be disruptive if it breaks into open dispute. At the same time, the nature of such society enables, if it does not demand, the channeling and institutionalizing of conflict in such a way that the occasion of dispute becomes the occasion of coherence. The contrast can be expressed in the terms that in rural communities there are divisions but no fundamental cleavages; there are rebellions but not revolutions. The end-point of such rebellions is an immediate reassertion of the values and unity of the group. [R. Frankenberg, *Communities in Britain* (Harmondsworth; Penguin, 1966) (abridged).]

22.2 URBAN LIFESTYLES

Tönnies (1858-1918) also stressed the impersonality and isolation of city life; while Durkheim stressed the sense of normlessness – 'anomie' – of urban lifestyles and suggested many of the problems of urban dwelling could be traced to this lack of set standards by which conduct could be judged.

The problems associated with urban lifestyles (sections 16.2 and 16.4) may be summarised as:

(a) Social isolation; loneliness among crowds. In its extreme form this may lead to suicide.
(b) More crime and violence because of a reduced common identity; fewer shared standards; more crowding; more opportunities; less certainty of detection.
(c) Greater competition for status symbols, more stress.

The contrast between urban and rural life is both physical and psychological

(d)   More pollution, more noise.
(e)   Relationships tend to be superficial – a 'network of associations'. They also tend to be 'segmented', that is, established for particular reasons and not developed.
(f)   There is less 'inter-generational' authority. 'In the shifting populations of large cities, young people are less ready to accord respect to their elders. "Grandad" becomes a term of contempt.' (A. Halsey, *Change in British Society*, 1981.)

In towns people also tend to be less 'homogeneous', they tend to be different from each other. There is thus greater potential for conflict, but also greater potential for social change and more variety and stimulation.

The 'privatised' family of the urban area (section 3.4) with its lack of assistance from kin and greater potential for conflict because its energies are directed inwards upon itself, also has the potential for deeper relationships because of the mutual interdependence of its members. It must however be clearly borne in mind that when 'urban' and 'rural' lifestyles are referred to in a modern context broad generalisations are being made.

Urbanisation and urban villages

Farmers collected together in settlements of over 20,000 inhabitants in West Africa or villages surrounded by the physical expansion of an Indian city can hardly be termed urbanized in a sociological sense. Similarly, certain aspects of 'social disorganization', which are said to follow rapid urbanization—that is rapid immigration to an urban area—are presumably also found in rural areas into which there is rapid immigration for harvests, tree-felling, short-term mining activity and so on. Clearly under these circumstances there will be an unbalanced age and sex structure producing a strong likelihood of the conventional symptoms of 'disorganization' such as prostitution and drunkenness. On the other hand, specific studies of parts of the central areas of cities, such as Delhi, Cairo, East London, Lagos, Medan, and Mexico City, suggest that *urban villages* exist in which there is a high level of social cohesion, based on interwoven kinship networks, and a high level of primary contact with *familiar* people ['A Perspective of Urban Sociology' in R. Pahl (ed.) *Readings in Urban Sociology* (Harmondsworth: Penguin 1968).]

There is ample evidence of long established town communities sharing many of the features mentioned for rural lifestyles. The increasing dominance of urban culture – economic, educational and recreational; together with the growing movement of essentially urban populations to rural areas and the influence of the media has resulted in some of the features mentioned as pertaining to urban lifestyles being adopted in rural areas.

Housing 'choice' compulsion

New estates are not, so to speak, built *in vacuo*; their siting has two probable features. Firstly, they are likely to be at a distance from the people's original homes. Thus Greenleigh is twenty miles from Bethnal Green; South Oxhey is seventeen miles, and Watling is some way out of London. The Sheffield estate is exceptional in being only a mile from the centre of the city. This suburbanization has social effects in terms of a journey to work which costs money and time. It may complete the segregation of living from working and working from playing. In the case of Greenleigh it may effect also reversal of sex roles in the kinship organization similar to the one already noted as marking a difference between Llanfihangel and County Clare on the one hand and Glynceiriog on the other.

The second feature in relation to siting is that often there were privately tenanted or owned houses and a long established community near the estate site. In all the studies there is a history of conflict between the new and the old which goes far to determine the social patterns of the new. The old inhabitants did not choose to have a council estate and indeed often fought bitterly against its being built. If it is true that the old inhabitants suffer from compulsion, so do the new tenants.

By and large, council tenants did not choose where they would live. By slum clearance or through the shortage of housing, they were forced to live wherever there was a council house available for which they were eligible. Circumstances compel them to live in a certain place and with particular neighbours. The kind of house they live in is thrust upon them without consultation; they may be forbidden to keep pets or compelled to have a dustbin, or a garden, or no garden. It is true that the village dweller did not choose his village nor the parishioner of Llanfihangel his parish, but compulsion by birth is different from compulsion by letter from the council when your pattern of living is already set. It is also true, however, that once you have one council house, it is sometimes possible to change it for another and thus exercise an element of choice of neighbours and of site. Nevertheless, most council tenants have to make some social adjustment to neighbour and neighbourhood as the price for house, kitchen, and bath.

Since rents are relatively high and most council house tenants are manual workers on daily or weekly engagements, there is a sense in which, despite their council house, they are fundamentally and patently insecure. This was very evident in the twenties and thirties and emerges clearly from the Watling study. An indication at the present day is the difficulty which manual workers experience if they should try and get Building Society Mortgages to buy their own house.[†] [R. Frankenburg, *Communities in Britain (A Social Life in Town and Country)* (Harmondsworth: Penguin, 1966).]

[†] Is this still true today? (*auth.*))

22.3 THE MEDIA AND CHANGE

The media (section 6.4), particularly television, clearly has influence, or millions of pounds would not be spent on media advertising. However, the degree of influence that the media has on changing our values and behaviour is disputed. C. Wright Mills in *The Power Elite* (1956) claimed that the media were 'a major cause of the transformation of America into a mass society' while D. McQuail (*Towards a Sociology of Mass Communication*, 1969) claimed, 'There is almost no evidence of the production of apathy or passivity by the mass media, nor of effects harmful to sociability and family life or likely to stimulate crime and violence.'

Television is the main leisure pursuit of all age groups in Britain, with the five to fifteen age group watching most – some 25 hours per week in 1981. As Himmelweit (*Television and the Child*, 1958) found that the children most likely to be affected by television are those who are least critical – in particular the less intelligent thirteen to fourteen year olds – it must be presumed that television has some influence on tastes and opinions.

However there is evidence that people in general tend to watch and read features that agree with their own views, or to interpret news and views through a mesh of previously received ideas. There is likely to be no sudden change in attitudes as a result of exposure to the media. However there is what has been called the 'drip effect'; constant repetition tends to familiarise us with the idea that certain types of behaviour, perhaps violent or promiscuous, are normal.

However it is also suggested that the media, like other institutions in Britain, are essentially conservative and are unlikely therefore to challenge accepted norms and values to any marked extent.

The media and social class

Almost since its inception the BBC (with the best of intentions) has been expressing a predominantly middle-class view of life presented in a 'cultured' accent, but public-opinion polls have shown that the working class still regard the BBC as representing 'them' (i.e. the Establishment), the accent has not spread, and although it is true that the Britain of today has become more middle-class in such matters as buying and spending, the basic working-class attitudes to all that pertains to work, livelihood, and social and cultural values have remained little altered. On the other hand, many working-class influences have begun to penetrate literature, the stage, radio, and television, and a great many of the best-known novelists and playwrights are proletarian in origin in spite of the fact that the mass media have remained predominantly in the hands of the upper and middle classes.

The fundamental issue of the mass media in the Western democracies lies in quite another direction from the generally accepted one: it is not that they are a means whereby the foreign ideals and beliefs of a small élite are being imposed upon the masses, but rather that, so far, there has existed a vicious circle, whereby – through a kind of feedback system – what the masses get is but the reflection of their own vociferous needs and demands. In the sphere of opinions and attitudes the élites are not the controllers of the people but their victims. That is the meaning of opinion surveys, Gallup polls, motivational research, and all the other methods of finding out what the masses 'really' think. They are designed to find out what the people want so that both the élites and their productions may be modelled into their likeness. The would-be brainwashers of the Western democracies are being brainwashed, whereas it might well be argued that it is only in the Communist 'people's democracies' that they are performing their proper function. The picture presented by some members of the Pilkington Committee and by such writers as Raymond Williams or F. R. Leavis and Denys Thompson of a once sturdy and self-reliant peasantry living in an 'organic' society with their genuine folk-arts, or of industrial workers who at a later period had a warm and cosy working-class culture worthy of preservation, both now perverted by a mean, money-grubbing, and ignorant élite which has 'brainwashed' them into accepting Western films when what they 'really' want is Shakespeare and John Bunyan, is ludicrous when translated into the terms of modern realities. It is not that there may not be a tiny nucleus of truth in this picture of bygone days, but that the picture is a highly idealized one and the changes which have occurred in popular culture were the result of inevitable technological developments, not a plot designed by a malignant minority trying to pervert the taste of decent people. In fact, as we have seen elsewhere, although it would be as foolish to idealize the motives of those who control our radio and television as it is to idealize the 'organic society' of the past with its ignorance, prejudice, and superstitions, there is every reason to believe that what the people get in the way of culture is usually a good deal better than what they demand.

There is something far wrong with a group in which some members are so bored with their jobs that they use the media solely as a stupefying drug, and those who are in this state of mind are just as likely to be narcotized by Beethoven and the news as by 'pop' music and thrillers. Similarly, those children who are drawn into delinquency are the result of an unsatisfactory home life and an environment within which delinquency is a possible and even socially-accepted way out for frustrated youth. The supposition that they are perverted by the mass media alone is a gross oversimplification of a serious and complex problem. There are, or have been, horror comics and films which should not be shown to children, but to suggest that children have been turned into delinquents in this way is to put the cart before the horse, since it is those who continue to be attracted by such books and films who are showing the symptoms of potential delinquency. Horror stories are, indeed, a natural component of growing up, but few modern tales could be as horrific, offensive (e.g. in their anti-semitism), or terrifying as those of the Grimm brothers on which many of us were reared, and we have tried to show that similar horrific fantasies occur in all children whether or not they are exposed to stories, films, or plays about them. One suspects that when matters of taste are being discussed the question of class prejudice is not entirely excluded. It is 'right' for the middle or upper classes to engage in such time-wasting (and, as some might think, foolish) activities as watching cricket and tennis, playing bridge and chess, or reading detective stories and thrillers, but when the working-class man watches league football in the middle of the week he is 'loafing', while his family, occupying themselves with bingo, darts, or watching quiz programmes on the 'telly', are being perverted by 'vapid and puerile activities'. The fact is that frequently those who profess most concern and admiration for the ordinary man are, at heart, the people who most despise him. [J. Brown, *Techniques of Persuasion* (Harmondsworth: Penguin, 1963) (abridged).]

Author's note Bear in mind that this passage was written over twenty years ago – how true are the points made today?

22.4 INTERNATIONAL INFLUENCE

International influence on social change in Britain is difficult to quantify. There is the obvious impact of immigration (section 21.2) and the mass media makes cultural comparisons possible – between Britain and America for example.

Multi-national corporations in their products and advertising tend to project similar images in a variety of countries which may, in the long term contribute to growing similarities between the countries concerned.

Ease of international travel has certainly contributed towards the growth of drug-taking in Britain and has also been blamed for some of the growth in pornography.

Student exchanges and grant-aided study overseas has made possible a greater exchange of ideas between the future leaders of a variety of cultures.

It is tempting to assume that the opening up of ideas between differing cultures will lead to greater tolerance but there is little sign of this. Without doubt a certain amount of terrorism has been imported and exported!

CHAPTER 23

RELIGION

23.1 RELIGION AND MORALITY

Morality will vary between societies, and the pattern of behaviour which results from this concept of what is right or wrong is called a 'more' by sociologists, and is of great importance in maintaining social order.

Religions are traditionally the justification for a particular morality in society and it is not surprising therefore that they tend to take a leading role in helping to ensure that the appropriate mores are observed (section 19.4). In attempting to maintain the existing morality of a society – for example by opposing abortion, birth control or divorce, they are often seen as essentially conservative institutions standing in the way of social progress. Some people see religion and morality as inseparable and blame the apparent decline in established religion for what they also see as declining moral values.

The degree to which religious observance does influence morality is debatable. One study found that drunkenness and juvenile delinquency were less common among Jews than among other members of the community (E. Krausz, *Leeds Jewry*, 1964); but this could be a result of church membership creating norms which will isolate the offending individual from the group rather than the sign of moral conviction.

In the early years of this century, Charles Booth made a survey of religion in London. He found that only the Irish immigrants were greatly influenced by organised religion and they were 'great beggars, as well as heavy drinkers'.

23.2 THE CHURCHES IN MODERN BRITAIN

Participation in formal religion has certainly declined in modern Britain, although it should not be presumed that in the past the majority of people were keen churchgoers.

The only religious census ever undertaken, in 1851, showed that about forty per cent of the population attended church each week. Rowntree and Lavers' longitudinal study of religion in York showed a regular church attendance of 35.5 per cent in 1901, 17.7 per cent in 1935 and 13.0 per cent in 1948; a national estimate in 1974 was 12 per cent. In 1861 there was one Anglican clergyman for every 960 people, by 1961 there was one for every 4000.

Church attendance is of course only one measurement of church activity; while probation officers, social workers and teachers have taken over some of the roles previously performed by the clergy.

Most people do still claim to belong to a religion; in 1964 a television survey showed that 94 per cent of people claimed to do so, although only 20 per cent of them went to church.

In 1984 *Prospects for the Eighties* (Vol. 2. Marc. Europe) reported that although Protestant churches lost 30 000 members annually between 1975 and 1979, while in the same period Roman Catholic churches lost 27 000 members annually, there was still one full-time Christian priest/vicar/minister for every 1000 adults in the United Kingdom (which is twice the number of GPs). Although 1000 Christian churches closed down overall during the 1970s, 51 000 churches remained (which is twice the number of post offices).

In 1965 a National Opinion Poll asked the question, 'What is your religion?' and got the following answers:

Religion	%
Church of England	63.4
Nonconformist	10.5
Roman Catholic	10.1
Presbyterian and Church of Scotland	8.9
Jewish	1.3
Atheist/agnostic	1.1
Other religion	3.0
No religion	1.8

This should be compared with the figures issued by the Churches themselves (see Table 23.1). In 1979 the Bible Society carried out a nationwide survey of Church membership and found that 18 per cent of the adult population in England belonged to a Christian church. Regional variations were from 35 per cent in Merseyside to 9 per cent in Humberside. Of this membership only 11 per cent actually attended a church. This survey reflected previous findings that proportionately more of the under-fifteens and over-forty-fives attend church. The under-fifteens represented 26 per cent of total church attenders but only 21 per cent of the population. Fifty-five per cent of church attenders are female.

Table 23.1   *changes within the churches in the United Kingdom*

	Adult members		Ministers	
	1970	*1980*	*1970*	*1980*
Episcopal (e.g. Church of England)	2 558 000	2 159 000	17 456	14 686
Roman Catholic	2 524 000	2 342 000	8 164	7 681
Presbyterian (e.g. United Reformed Church and Church of Scotland)	1 896 000	1 580 000	5 657	5 230
Baptist and Methodist	967 000	788 000	6 965	6 448
Other 'Trinitarian' (e.g. Pentecostal, Holiness, W. Indian, Salvation Army)	490 000	542 000	9 031	10 762
Moslems	250 000	600 000	–	1 540
Jews	113 000	111 000	400	416
Sikhs	75 000	150 000	–	–
Orthodox	72 000	106 000	80	131
Mormons	70 000	91 000	3 500	7 331
Jehovah's Witnesses	62 000	84 000	–	8 109
Spiritualists	45 000	52 000	207	290

Geoffrey Gorer found that social class made little difference to the number claiming a religion; ranging from the working class with 72 per cent, to the lower middle class with 81 per cent (*Sex and Marriage in England Today*, 1971).

Most people attend a church sometime (in 1969 Geoffrey Gorer found that some 90 per cent did) even if only for weddings and funerals. In 1901 66 per cent of marriages in England and Wales were performed in the Anglican Church and 15.8 per cent in registry offices. By 1976 the Anglican proportion was 29 per cent and the registry office 50 per cent. (The Roman Catholic percentage of church weddings increased from 4.1 per cent of all marriages to 9.4 per cent.)

However there is still a considerable number of people who prefer to be married in, and buried from, a church; and many charities are church-based. This 'secular function' of religion may increase as religions are seen to provide a focal point for community activities in urban areas with

Fig. 23.1 *some of the Harris Research Centre's findings in a survey of British attitudes in 1984*

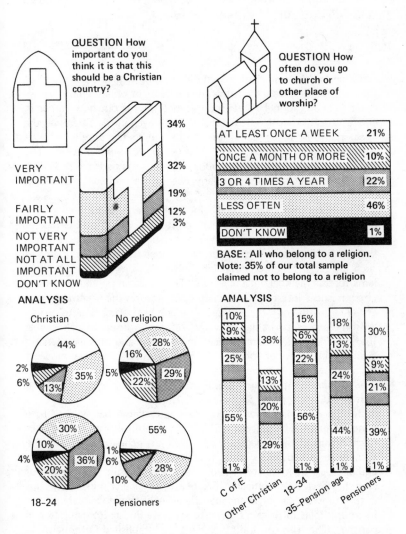

QUESTION How important do you think it is that this should be a Christian country?

34%
32%
19%
12%
3%

VERY IMPORTANT
FAIRLY IMPORTANT
NOT VERY IMPORTANT
NOT AT ALL IMPORTANT
DON'T KNOW

QUESTION How often do you go to church or other place of worship?

AT LEAST ONCE A WEEK	21%
ONCE A MONTH OR MORE	10%
3 OR 4 TIMES A YEAR	22%
LESS OFTEN	46%
DON'T KNOW	1%

BASE: All who belong to a religion.
Note: 35% of our total sample claimed not to belong to a religion

ANALYSIS

Christian

44%
2%
6% 13% 35%

No religion

28%
16%
5% 22% 29%

18-24

30%
10%
4% 20% 36%

Pensioners

55%
1%
6% 28%
10%

ANALYSIS

C of E
10%
9%
25%
55%
1%

Other Christian
38%
13%
20%
29%

18-34
15%
6%
22%
56%
1%

35-Pension age
18%
13%
24%
44%
1%

Pensioners
30%
9%
21%
39%
1%

(*Britons Observed*. Conducted for the *Observer* by the Harris Research Centre 1984.)

highly mobile 'privatised' families; who can pick up social connections quickly from a denominational base as they move around the country. This phenomena has already developed in the United States - 'Not to be - that is not to identify oneself and be identified as - either a Protestant, a Catholic, or a Jew is somehow not to be an American. Religion is "a way of sociability or belonging"... It is thus frequently a religiousness without serious commitment, without inner conviction' (W. Herberg, *Protestant - Catholic - Jew*, 1960).

Religion

Looking for the results of the studies dealing with the sociology of religion, we find that the integrative aspects of religion have mainly been stressed. John Highet, for instance, points out how earlier in this century in Scotland the local church, even in the cities, was the focal point of many activities in addition to the purely religious activities. (John Highet, *The Churches in Scotland Today*.) The study by Conor Ward in Liverpool highlights the parish as providing closely knit social units for many within the limited geographical areas.

The integrative effects of religion within partly segregated groups also come to the fore in a number of studies. Whilst on the face of it the very existence of such groups suggests divisiveness when society is taken as a whole, the fact is that religion usually acts in such groups as a factor of social control. It irons out certain problems for the members of the groups. Thus one can see that in certain circumstances internal group integration ensures the necessary inter-group adjustments for society as a whole. According to Bryan Wilson, sects act as small 'deviant' reference groups which enable the individual to gain more favourable status and prestige than are available in the wider society. The sect provides 'the reassurance of a stable, affective society.... Its ideological orientation and its group cohesion provide a context of emotional security' (B. R. Wilson (ed.) *Patterns of Sectarianism*, 1967).

In the case of minority groups, too, religion has worked as a cohesive force. The present writer has pointed out that among Jews membership of the synagogue, and even just occasional worship and activity in it, provides a major avenue of identification with Judaism and the Jewish minority. Within the Christian fold membership of churches or sects specifically linked with particular minority groups is an important factor in the identification of the individual with his in-group. Poles in Britain belong to separate Polish Roman Catholic parishes. The Irish, on the other hand, re-established Catholicism in Britain, and 'the Roman Catholic Church has played an important part in preserving Irish interests among the immigrants'. It has also been pointed out that West Indians have brought with them special

Pentecostal sects to which they belong and which provide them, in this strange setting, with 'a buffer against the society at large'.

David Martin points out that for Christians in Britain there are numerous options which represent different combinations and developments produced by a long period of Christian germination and general historical events. 'Sociologists have developed a shorthand for reducing the infinite variety of these options to three basic "types" which between them include an enormous range of possibilities.' The three models are 'church', 'denomination' and 'sect'. Martin's analysis points up the predominant characteristics exhibited by these type constructs. The 'church' claims social inclusiveness, identifies with the State, has a sacred hierarchy and insists on a comprehensive dogmatic scheme with the accent on past events. The 'denomination' is usually not a social majority, explicitly separates itself from the State but does not reject the wider society. . . . The 'sect' is typically a small exclusive dispossessed minority, which radically rejects society and its institutions [E. Krausz, *Sociology in Britain: A Survey of Research* (London: Batsford, 1969).]

23.3 CHURCH AND STATE

Both Church and State are seen as upholding the same norms and values; and often as maintaining the existing social order, including the rights and privileges of particular sections of the society.

People wish to be convinced that they have a right to what they have, 'Good fortune thus want to be "legitimate" fortune' (Max Weber). This often implies that the less fortunate also deserve their positions, as in the Hindu caste system; that they are in some way inferior. They may of course be promised better things in an after life, and this may help them to accept their earthly suffering. 'Religious distress is at the same time the expression of real distress and the protest against real distress. Religion is the sign of the oppressed creature, the heart of a heartless world, just as it is the spirit of a spiritless situation. It is the opium of the people' (K. Marx and F. Engels, *On Religion*). Marx, of course, thought that once the real enemy was identified the criticism of heaven would turn into the criticism of the earth.

Because of the apparent identity of interest between the objectives of Church and State – the maintenance of the social order – the Church usually comes to reinforce the State. The King may even come to be seen as a god, as was the Inca of Peru, the Pharaoh of Egypt and until 1947 the Emperor of Japan.

In mediaeval Europe the Church and State were united. Bishops of the Catholic Church – and after the Reformation the Church of England – sat in the House of Lords. Cardinals were often Chancellors; education was in the hands of clerics; priests were also leaders of their local community. Even in eighteenth century England the younger son of the local squire was often the local vicar, the 'living' for which was supplied by the family.

In modern Britain the 'Established Church' is the Church of England and its leader, the Archbishop of Canterbury, is still a moral leader. His views are still reported with respect in the media. However political power has gone. Bishops still sit in the House of Lords, but that House has now lost most of its power. Secular institutions have taken over education and most of the social functions of the Church. The Church remains nevertheless part of 'The Establishment'.

It would be wrong however to assume that Church and State are inevitably united. Norman Cohen (*The Pursuit of the Millennium*, 1957) describes how, in Europe during the Middle Ages, the poor were periodically swept by an intense belief that the World was about to be miraculously transformed, and developed strange cults. The same has happened in modern times in the Melanesian Islands where 'cargo cults' promise the return of the aeroplanes that brought sudden wealth during the Second World War.

More soberly, the Methodist Church was an important factor in the rise of reforming Liberalism at the end of the nineteenth century, the development of the trade unions, and of the Labour Party. Modern Catholic priests in South America – preaching what has been called 'liberation theology' – have taken a leading role in condemning poverty and the ruling totalitarian regimes.

23.4 SECULARISATION

Secularisation is the process in which religious beliefs and sanctions become less important as guides to behaviour and decisions: 'the process whereby religious thinking, practice and institutions lose social significance' (B. Wilson, *Religion in a Secular Society*, 1966). Functions previously carried out by clergy, such as providing advice to families, looking after the sick, education and providing community entertainment, are carried out by a host of governmental and voluntary agencies.

Comte (1798–1857) claimed that man no longer needed to have a supernatural explanation for the human condition now that social development could be analysed and understood.

It has been suggested that secularisation is the result of two main developments: the growth of Protestantism which invited man not to accept traditional explanations; and industrialisation/urbanisation which removed individuals from traditional communities and made them require rational solutions to the social problems thereby created.

"For heaven's sake, write it down! You'll only forget."

Opinions vary as to the degree of secularisation in modern British society. This difference of opinion is largely based on differing views of what religion is. If one takes the view that an essential characteristic of religion is church membership and worship, then the decline in these factors can be seen as evidence of secularisation. If religious belief is taken as the major criteria then measurement becomes very difficult. We cannot be certain whether people attended church in the past mainly because of social pressure and because of the social functions which the church performed, rather than from a belief in its teachings; equally, people today may have strong religious beliefs which they prefer to express in private rather than by church attendance.

The proliferation of religious sects in Britain is seen by some as a sign that the traditional churches are in a stage of collapse, and as further evidence of the spread of secularisation – in that there are no clear religious values to be seen as community values and religion has therefore lost its role of reinforcing social solidarity (B. Wilson, *Religious Sects*, 1970). Others see the increasing membership of organisations such as Jehovah's

Witnesses, Mormons and Hari Krishna as signs of a growing interest in religion and a rejection of the materialism of secular society.

QUESTIONS FROM PAST O-LEVEL GCE PAPERS

1. 'Britain is now a secular society.' Explain and comment upon this statement. Welsh Joint Examining Board

2. Sociologists are interested in whether the mass media shape or reflect the views of their audience. Discuss the sociological evidence as to the effects of mass media in any *two* of the following areas:
    (a) Youth culture.
    (b) Consumer behaviour.
    (c) Behaviour of young children.
    (d) Religious behaviour. Associated Examining Board

3. Attendance at Church of England services has fallen steadily over many years. Does this mean that the relationship between Church and State is no longer important?

Associated Examining Board

4. 'Socialisation attempts to ensure conformity—acceptance of the cultural patterns of the society in which one lives.' How does social change occur? Associated Examining Board

5. Using sociological evidence, assess the influence of the mass media on attitude formation. London Examining Board

6. How does each of the following contribute to social control in modern industrial society?
    (a) Religion.
    (b) Mass media. Associated Examining Board

7. **Either,** (a) Outline and discuss the distinctive sociological features of a neighbourhood.
    Or, (b) Discuss the features which distinguish the culture and social structure of rural communities from those of urban society. Welsh Joint Examining Board

8. Urban living and rural living are different mainly because of contrasts in the social environment rather than physical environment. What are the major differences between these social environments?   Associated Examining Board

PART IX
THE POLITICAL SYSTEM

FORMS OF GOVERNMENT

24.2 TOTALITARIAN GOVERNMENT

Totalitarian governments are the usual forms of government both in the past and in the modern world. Essentially a totalitarian state is a country controlled by one man – 'an autocracy', or a group – 'an oligarchy'. Because the power of any state rests ultimately on its armed forces those filling key roles in totalitarian states are very often members of the military.

Usually totalitarian leaders try and legitimise their position by claiming to have taken power to save the state from danger and they often promise that when the danger is past they will return power to the people although they rarely do so.

Totalitarian states often do have parliaments and elections but have either a limited franchise, so that only those who are likely to support the status quo have a vote; or, more often, restrict the election to representatives of only one political party or to parties representing only one area of the political spectrum. It is often claimed that as the vast majority of people in the country concerned support a particular political viewpoint the only way to ensure choice is to offer several candidates from a particular political background.

In a totalitarian system those who influence or control the society or important institutions within it and who are acknowledged as superior by virtue of this influence are likely to be clearly apparent. This 'elite' can be less obvious in states claiming to be parliamentary democracies and may limit the extent to which the states concerned can be regarded as truly democratic. C. Wright Mills (*The Power Elite*, 1956) emphasises the similarity between the attitudes, values and social background of those who make up the ruling elite in the United States, and Michels (*Political Parties*, 1959) suggested that 'elites' are inevitable in any organisation structure, 'who says organisation, says oligarchy'.

268

Fig. 24.1 *British Members of Parliament: by socio-economic status*

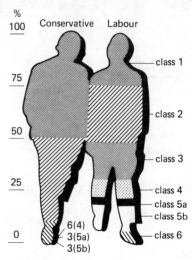

SOURCE   *New Society,* 1982

In 1950 one researcher claimed that after thirty years of communist government in Russia a ten-class social system had emerged, 'from the ruling elite (officials, scientists, top artists and writers) down through managers, bureaucrats, and three classes of workers and two classes of peasants, to the slave labourers' (V. Packard, *The Status Seekers*, 1959). Perhaps it is true to say that the major difference between democratic and totalitarian states is that in the former elites can be challenged, in the latter they cannot.

The British 'ruling circle'

The British 'ruling circle' is obvious. In most Western countries, ruling groups are an abstract entity, like Wall Street, or are groups hidden behind closed doors, as, it was alleged, the French 200 families. In Britain, the social system, reinforced by the education system, seems to take pride in presenting to all and sundry the names of the members of the ruling circle and the mechanics of their contacts. Nowhere else do 'influential' families seem to take such pleasure in advertising their existence and their size; nowhere else does the education system openly extol the combined advantages of 'breeding' and contacts.

The persistence of a small number of leading families is probably unique, as is the existence of the public schools. It is perhaps natural in a country which did not have any revolution for almost three hundred years, although the absence of revolution has in turn to be explained. It has perhaps to be accounted for by the absence of military occupation and of the political collapse which often ensues; large scale immigration might also have modified the social and political equilibrium, but no such immigration ever took place. The aristocracy had the wisdom to accept new families within its ranks: in return, it succeeded in not suffering the disgrace of being relegated to a museum-like isolation. Social values have continued to recognize the supremacy of the aristocracy. That social supremacy may be challenged; it may be recognized only on the surface and not deeply felt. Yet by the very fact that lip-service is paid to the social superiority of the upper class its members enjoy initial advantages which do not exist to the same extent in other industrial nations. In most developed countries, the aristocrats who remain have to accept appearing bourgeois if they want to succeed. The British upper class may no longer have power *as a class*; its members still can claim as of right that they belong to influential circles if such is their desire. They do not have to gain places *in spite* of their background, as in some Continental countries; their background helps them. It remains for a large number of members of the upper class to use this privilege, and the general position of the group appears well-established. Since a sufficient proportion is talented enough to make a good career, the general claims of the group appear reasonable.

These points are well-known. As for pre-democratic Britain, one can still rather easily trace ramifications of influential families in the upper ranks of the Conservative party, in many financial houses of the City, even in the Foreign Office and in the services. The charts of cousinhoods and intermarriages show connexions which can extend very far. A Conservative prime minister can have a dozen M.P.s, a good number of peers, and several heads of financial houses among his 'family'.

Family connexions are essential to this tightly knit structure. The education network provided by the public schools is also of extreme importance. In the same sectors of society, Conservative party, finance, Foreign Office, to some extent the services, those who went to public schools are at considerable advantage and those who went to the best public schools have the best chance of all. An analysis of C. S. Wilson and T. Lupton conducted in the 1950s showed that Eton produced 30 per cent of Conservative ministers, of the directors of large banks, of the directors of City firms, of the directors of insurance companies. Eton and five other schools (Winchester, Harrow, Rugby, Charterhouse, Marlborough) produced between two-fifths and half of the holders of these posts.

In a formal definition, the ruling circle, if not perhaps the ruling class, is bound to exist everywhere; in a more specific analysis of British society, the 'establishment' also exists, because families and schools crystallize traditions and enable contacts to take place.

Three characteristics, as we said, are necessary to a 'ruling circle' if it is to have real political power. It must have unity of purpose, it must permanently have power, it must be able to rule in the strong sense of the word. The establishment and its inner circle seem to have the first of these three characteristics, although probably not so much because it is an establishment with an inner circle, but because it belongs to the wider group of the middle classes. Particularly if we define it as being concentrated in the leadership of the Conservative party, in financial houses, and in traditional business groups, this inner circle clearly has a certain unity of doctrine. It is conservative-minded. It wants to preserve the social system more or less as it is. It does not want to introduce reforms, except on a small scale and piecemeal. [J. Blondel, *Votes, Parties and Leaders* (Harmondsworth: Penguin, 1969).]

Author's note This 1969 extract should be compared with that from *The Changing Anatomy of Britain*, 1982, on pp. 120-2.

24.2 DEMOCRATIC GOVERNMENT

Democracy is literally 'government by the people'. A direct democracy would be a state in which everyone took a direct part in running the country by public meetings or holding 'referendums' on every issue. A referendum is a ballot in which everyone has an opportunity to express their opinion, as happened in Britain in 1975 to decide whether we should join the European Economic Community, and in Wales and Scotland (1979) to see whether the majority in those countries wished to have some form of local parliament. In ancient Greek city states, decisions were reached by public meetings of all 'citizens', but this did not include women or slaves!

In fact there has never been a perfect democracy although many countries claim the title; Rhodesia prior to 1979 claimed to be a democracy although only whites were permitted to vote. East Germany is the 'German Democratic Republic', although only political parties of a communist variety under a 'National Front' banner are permitted; the GDR would seek to justify their title by claiming that 99.86 per cent of the electorate voted for the National Front in 1976! (This communist-based National Front is not to be confused with the British 'National Front' which has fascist overtones.)

Direct democracy would clearly be impossible in a country as large as Britain so we operate a system of representation – of parliamentary democracy; in 1800 this meant that 3 per cent of the population were entitled to vote. Since 1969 every man and woman over the age of eighteen who is not disqualified by reason of lunacy, felony or being a peer of the realm is entitled to vote.

'Democracy' however involves more than just the right to vote. In a democratic situation, it must be possible to say what you like (usually with certain restrictions to protect minorities and the innocent from the malicious); to be allowed freedom of association; and to be free from physical restriction without due cause. It might also be claimed that all sides in an argument must have access to the same level of resources, both monetary and media; this last is a particularly difficult criterion to achieve.

Government 'by the people' is usually interpreted as meaning by the majority of the people, and yet few people would be prepared to accept the tyranny of the majority as democratic. For example in Northern Ireland there is a permanent majority of 60 per cent in favour of unity with England, and an equally permanent 40 per cent who want union with the rest of Ireland. For many years the minority felt that the majority were depriving them of equal opportunities in such areas as housing and employment and this frustration was a major contributory factor in the outbreak of terrorism.

Britain aspires to be a democracy but it is claimed that the press is owned by people with similar political views who are generally biased towards one political party; that the Civil Service only presents the facts that it chooses to select for ministerial decision; that the non-elected trade unions have an undue influence on political decisions; that political parties do not have equal resources to present their viewpoints, and that Governments are not elected by a majority of the people.

Power in Britain

The stability of parliamentary democracy in Britain has removed the need for direct military involvement in politics, except on rare occasions when instructed by the civil authorities to take action. Such stability allows the military to retain its traditional role in reserve, ready to repel external aggression and ready to assist the police in the maintenance of internal law and order as, for example, in Northern Ireland.

It is only in times of war and occasional civil unrest that military power is of great relevance in the advanced countries, but the possibility of the military defending the civil order adds strength to a political system.

In addition to these three centres of power – political, economic and military – other institutions exert great influence and also have some degree of power. The education system acts to spread knowledge and to train young minds, and, to a considerable extent, to ensure conformity. With the mass media, the education system controls the flow of ideas and information we consider. This gives them great control over what ideas and information are seen as legitimate.

Organized religion still exerts some power, and much authority, though over a declining proportion of the population. Pronouncements of leading churchmen are still of great importance and are widely reported.

Leading members of the judiciary have both great power and authority, for their pronouncements are also listened to with interest and are presented as authoritative. Once again it becomes clear that one cannot point to one group of people and say 'they alone have power'. In Britain power seems to be spread among many people . . . This has led some people to argue that Britain remains democratic and stable because no one group or individual has overwhelming power – there is a constant competition between power groups which prevents one group from dominating, power is diffused throughout the political system. Another view holds that the competing groups do so on unequal terms – some are able to dominate others and to impose their wills on other groups. A third argument is that most of these people in positions of power share common backgrounds and beliefs and form one, not many groups – a ruling class. This approach implies that the beliefs which hold our leaders together are stronger than their differences. Each of these approaches has strong political implications – the first tends to be supported by conservatives – those people who support the present system whatever political party they belong to. The last view tends to be that of the 'extreme' left, whose members are highly critical of the present system. The second view can be embraced by those who hold both types of political view at various times. [A. Renwick and I. Swinburn, *Basic Political Concepts* (London: Hutchinson, 1980).]

24.3 THE BRITISH SYSTEM OF GOVERNMENT

More people have voted *against* the political party that has formed the Government in Britain than have voted *in favour* at every General Election since 1945. The Conservatives actually formed the Government in 1951 even although the Labour Party received more votes, while in 1974 (February) the opposite was the case (see Figure 24.2).

In 1974 the Liberal Party received 6 million votes and returned fourteen Members to Parliament; the Conservative Party received about 12 million and returned 296 Members; the Labour Party received about a third of a million votes *less* than the Conservative Party, but won five more seats – and formed the Government! There has been considerable support in recent years for some kind of proportional representation which would more fairly reflect the support for particular political parties. In the 1983 the position was further complicated by the emergence of the SDP in alliance with the Liberals, giving an even more bizarre result (see Table 24.1).

273

Fig. 24.2 *The popular vote at all elections since 1918*

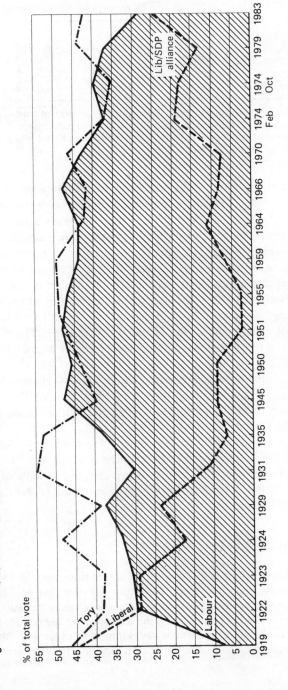

% of total vote

Tory

Liberal

Labour

Lib/SDP alliance

55 50 45 40 35 30 25 20 15 10 5 0

1919 1922 1923 1924 1929 1931 1935 1945 1950 1951 1955 1959 1964 1966 1970 1974 Feb 1974 Oct 1979 1983

SOURCE *New Society*, 1983

Table 24.1 *votes cast in General Election of 1983*

Party	Votes cast	Number of MPs
Conservative	13 012 602	397
Labour	8 457 124	209
Liberal/SDP Alliance	7 780 587	23
Scottish Nationalist	331 975	2
Plaid Cymru	125 309	2

NOTE: In Northern Ireland the numbers of MPs elected were – Official Unionist 11, Democratic Unionist 3, Ulster Popular Unionist 1, Social Democratic and Labour Party 1, Provisional Sinn Fein 1 giving a total for the United Kingdom of 650.

However the method of election is only one limitation on democracy in Britain. People at elections usually only have a choice between three or four political party nominees; these nominees themselves have been chosen from a limited number of people by a handful of party activists in the constituencies; so that MPs are chosen partially by election but also by selection. Although all party members do not participate in the selection of prospective parliamentary candidates the number of individual party members gives some indication of the limited number of people involved in the selection process. In 1979, *Labour Weekly* estimated that the total individual membership of the Labour Party was 284 000 although listed officially at 650 000. Some constituencies had only a handful of members – one had only fourteen.

Financially, there is a considerable difference between the political parties. For example, during the 1979 General Election the central campaign costs of the Conservatives were £1 300 000; of Labour £1 000 000 and of the Liberals £135 000.

R. Rose commented on the degree of democracy in Britain: 'The mechanics of the electoral system determine how a person's vote is counted, social characteristics affect how his vote is cast, and decisions of those who run the parties determine for whom he can vote' (*Politics in England Today*, 1974).

Democracy and the two-party system

The basic British doctrine of the absolute supremacy of Parliament also came under challenge. Obviously the idea that no Parliament can pass an act that binds its successor was hardly compatible with Common Market rules, or with the proposals for devolution. Another new challenge to parliamentary supremacy came with the 1975 referendum on the Common Market, and the 1979 referendums on

Scottish and Welsh devolution. Although these referendums were advisory only, they did represent a substantial derogation from the idea that the decision of parliament was final. It is hardly conceivable that parliament would ever reverse a clear-cut referendum verdict.

Collective Cabinet responsibility is another doctrine that had to be reassessed in the light of the events of the 1974–79 parliament. The 1975 referendum saw the waiving of collective responsibility over a central issue of policy for the first time since 1932. Seven members of the Cabinet openly campaigned against a basic government recommendation. The convention was again relaxed in 1977 in the vote on the method of election to the European Assembly. But collective responsibility was also under assault from a distinct increase in the number of government leaks, and the questioning of the principles of secrecy on which collective responsibility depends. One more challenge to collective responsibility came with the Lib-Lab pact and the system of consultation under which ministers sounded out official Liberal spokesmen on proposed policies in advance of announcing them to parliament or to their party.

The most obvious threat to the established certainties of British government came with the decline of the two-party system. . . Ulster loyalists and Scottish Nationalists accounted for most of the growth in third party MPs, while English Liberals accounted for most of the growth in third party votes. It is the MPs who make the difference to the working of government, and the Ulster members had plainly come to stay as an independent force. Assuming even a modest Scottish and Welsh nationalist presence it seemed that in the future 25 minor party MPs would be the minimum likely complement in any parliament; and 25 would have been enough to hold the balance of power in five of the nine parliaments elected since 1950. With proportional representation a multi-party system would be almost inevitable, together with minority or coalition governments. In the event, from 1974 these 'unthinkables' were produced under the established first-past-the-post system. It was generally realised that single party government could no longer be taken for granted, any more than the other features of British government which hinged on it.

Because of this development, doubts arose about the first-past-the-post electoral system which used to be as totally accepted as the two-party system in parliament. The snags in the voting system (particularly its unfairness on the Liberals) were thought to be a small price to pay for the responsible one-party governments it produced. Under the winner-take-all system the major parties secured full power for some of the time and full powerlessness for some of the time, instead of suffering the compromises of coalition. Most MPs still supported the *status quo*, but the question ceased to be a closed one. Critics fastened on the power that could be wielded by a single party majority in the Commons. There was growing criticism of the adversary style of politics in which increasingly a party taking over government busied itself with reversing its predecessor's policies. Some measures, if they are to be beneficial, have to be maintained beyond the lifetime of a single parliament. [D. Butler and D. Kavanagh, *The British General Election of 1979* (London: Macmillan, 1980) (adapted).]

24.4 POLITICAL PARTIES

There are now four main political parties in England with elected Members of Parliament:

1. The *Conservative Party*, which is generally thought to represent the middle class, with an emphasis on the importance of competition, private enterprise and individualism. With an income largely drawn from business undertakings and private membership subscriptions.
2. The *Labour Party*, which is generally thought to represent the working class, with an emphasis on the importance of welfare and division within itself on the degree of public ownership which should now be sought. Over three-quarters of the Labour Party's income is from the 'political levy' element of trade union subscriptions.
3. The *Liberal Party*, generally thought to occupy a middle ground between the Conservative and Labour parties and drawing its much smaller income mainly from membership subscriptions.
4. The new *Social Democratic Party*, in alliance with the Liberal Party and very much like it in terms of policies and income.

These outlines are of course very crude and would be hotly contested by some party members. However, they probably fairly represent what most of the electorate believe to be the position.

There is, in addition to the four major parties, a host of minor – usually extreme – parties none of which have any Members of Parliament. These parties include the *Communist Party*, the *National Front* and the *Socialist Workers Party*.

In Scotland the *Scottish National Party* seeking some form of Home Rule or even separation from England, and in Wales the *Plaid Cymru* with a similar platform retained two seats each in 1983.

In Northern Ireland various brands of *Unionist* candidate represented mainly Protestant voters; the Social Democratic and Labour Party attracted most Catholic votes. Various *Irish Independence Party* candidates represented more extreme Catholic opinion, while the non-sectarian *Alliance Party* attracted only 6.8 per cent of the votes in 1979.

Each party will try and persuade electors to vote for them

PRESSURE AND INTEREST GROUPS

25.1 DIFFERENT TYPES OF PRESSURE GROUPS

Pressure or 'interest' groups are groups of people who are in association because they have a common interest; and who use whatever power is available as a result of their unity of interest to put pressure on other agencies to have their views adopted.

The agencies most likely to be able to influence events are central and local government, or agencies connected with these – for example the Civil Service or a Local Education Authority. However, multi-national corporations, the Churches or any other policy-making or decision-taking body may be subject to the activities of pressure groups, or they may themselves become pressure groups and try and influence other agencies.

Pressure groups are often classified into two types: 'sectional' groups which seek to protect or promote the interest of their members or some other specified group of people as their major function and 'promotional' groups which seek to achieve particular changes or to fight specific issues.

'Sectional' groups are sometimes called 'protective' groups because they are mainly concerned with protecting the sectional interests of individuals – often their own members. They include such organisations as the trade unions; the Confederation of British Industry; professional associations such as the British Medical Association; and a variety of organisations set up to help specific groups of people such as Help the Aged, or the NSPCC.

Many of these groups have been so successful in persuading policy-makers that their views should be heeded that it has become a constitutional convention for the Government to consult them before introducing legislation that might affect their interests.

'Promotional' groups seek to promote a cause of some kind. The cause may be quite *limited* in its objective; for example the Abortion Law Reform Association was founded in 1936 with the objective of legalising abortion and was successful in 1967; or more *general*, for example, the

Viewers and Listeners Association set up by Mrs Mary Whitehouse to reduce the element of sex and violence in the media. A myriad of such promotional groups exist – sometimes very briefly – to obtain a zebra crossing outside a school; to stop an airport being built; to resist the construction of a hotel which will spoil a view or similar local or transitory aims.

There is no firm boundary between 'sectional' and 'promotional' groups. Often sectional groups will promote a particular cause – the Ramblers Association may fight to protect a footpath from closure or the Royal Automobile Club may oppose legislation that insists upon the wearing of seat belts.

Sometimes pressure groups are divided somewhat differently into economic-interest groups and non-economic interest groups such as Oxfam or the Churches. Economic interest groups are also often subdivided into (a) the labour lobby, including all trade unions that are members of the TUC, (b) the business lobby, including the Institute of Directors and the CBI, and (c) the professional lobby, including organisations representing lawyers, teachers, doctors and the like.

Big business as a pressure group

It is not only that the big firms are large enough to lobby by themselves, it is also that the very structure of business is often an adequate substitute for a formally organized interest group. What is required for interests to defend themselves is not an interest group as such, solely designed for this effect and, as it were, 'registered' as an interest group. What is required is a set of contacts through which a common policy can be defined. Small business has often remained unorganized, and it is largely subjected to the conditions of individual capitalism. Big business, on the contrary, has become more and more integrated. Personal connexions link many companies. These connexions are underlined, or caused, by large capital participations of firms in assets of others. Large industrial and financial companies do not need to create *ad hoc* interest groups: they are already organized into holdings or associated through participations in order to achieve industrial efficiency or to obtain financial support. They can use their own network to exercise pressure on the political and administrative worlds.

The purpose of these remarks is not to overemphasize the influence of business. Moreover, business is not alone in being able to use preexisting organizations for the purpose of exercising influence. Some cultural organizations, such as the churches or the universities, do exercise pressure in a similar way. They use pre-existing channels and they do not have to create an interest group before being able to lobby the State or its representatives.

The distinction between formally organized groups and informally constituted groupings is very important in practice: it circumscribes the sphere in which the representative principle plays a part and the sphere where there is pressure, but no representative principle, at work.

Interest groups are a means by which the views of the citizens come to be represented. This is why one can and one must, admittedly with the reservations already made, examine whether the views of the rank-and-file are adequately transmitted to the top within interest groups. But among informally organized groupings, in companies, churches, universities, it becomes pointless to start discussing the 'representation' of a rank-and-file. Clearly, even in an organization as hierarchical as the Roman Catholic Church, there are channels through which the views of the rank-and-file are communicated to the top, at any rate if these views are strongly held. This happens even more in a network of companies, despite the principle that those who own or control the majority of the capital can dictate their policy to the whole of the network. Yet this is not representation.

If we want to see, as we do here, whether the representative principle works well in the field of interests, we can therefore look at formally constituted interest groups only. We must not forget, however, that, while looking at representation, we are looking only at a certain number of interests and not at all of them. We must always remember that interest groups are the only means of pressure which wage and salary earners possess, while on the other hand, business, the churches, some other cultural groups, possess other means of influence. Conclusions which are reached about wage and salary earners' organizations should always be put in perspective with the conclusions which can be reached when one examines all the channels by which business can exercise pressure. The realistic comparison is not the one which compares the T.U.C with the C.B.I. alone, but the one which compares the T.U.C. on the one hand with, on the other hand, the C.B.I., the City, and other major business organizations. [J. Blondel, *Votes, Parties and Leaders* (Harmondsworth: Penguin, 1969).]

25.2 ADVANTAGES OF PRESSURE GROUPS

The view is sometimes expressed that pressure groups are a fundamental part of the democratic process. They give the individual an opportunity to participate directly in the processes of government, and to influence the 'elites' who have power in industry or elsewhere.

In the British system of government, particularly when Governments have absolute majorities in the House of Commons as has generally been the case since 1945, the ruling party is safely in power for several years and pressure groups are an important part of the process of debate and opposition between elections. S. Finer (*Anonymous Empire*, 1958) suggested that pressure groups provided a useful service in that they let ministers and civil servants know how people feel: 'Anger, contempt, or pleasure, expressed at first hand, are a valuable corrective to the bald facts of the case in an office file.'

25.3 DISADVANTAGES OF PRESSURE GROUPS

However, Professor Finer also expressed reservations about the role of pressure groups. The title of his book, *Anonymous Empire*, gives a clue to his worry: 'the lobbies become – as far as the general public is concerned – faceless, voiceless, unidentifiable; in brief anonymous'. The general public is often shut out from the discussion between pressure groups and policy-makers so that it is not possible to tell what arguments have persuaded the elite concerned to make the decisions it does.

Although most pressure groups, except the trade unions and co-operative societies, claim to be non-political this usually merely means that the organisation concerned is not affiliated to a political party. They may very well take a distinctive political *stance* which will make support from a particular political party likely. The Institute of Directors states, 'Any enemy of the free enterprise way of life, whatever his political views, is our opponent.' Clearly such a non-elected group might have considerable power behind the scenes but in Finer's words the 'general public is shut out'.

Finer's second criticism of pressure groups is that some groups carry much greater weight and influence than others, without any guarantee of intrinsic superiority. The two major motoring organisations for example campaign for the motorist, but there is no comparable organisation to campaign for the much greater number of pedestrians.

25.4 METHODS OF OPERATION

Some of the disadvantages of pressure groups are clear from the methods adopted by some of them. In 1945–6 the Labour Government wanted to introduce a Public Health Authority with general practitioners on salaries as in hospitals. The British Medical Association refused to co-operate, with the result that general practitioners remain as independent operators paid on a formula based mainly on the number of patients registered with them.

Resistance to the will of an elected Government was also successful when the Orange Lodges in the northern province of Ireland prevented, by the threat of armed resistance, six of the nine counties of Ulster from being included in a United Ireland when the Home Rule Bill was introduced in 1912. British Army officers at the main army base in Ireland, many of whom had family or political links with the northern protestants,

Pressure groups can appeal to the emotions of those in power; presenting feelings as well as facts

threatened to resign their commissions if ordered to fight the Orangemen. The First World War prevented a showdown, but the threat was remembered later and Ireland was partitioned into two states (A. Ryan, *Mutiny at the Curragh*, 1956).

The campaign that was waged to establish commercial television in 1953 with intense lobbying of Members of Parliament, feature articles by well-known personalities, and an orchestrated flood of letters to the press was described by a former Director of the BBC as 'one of the most deplorable, subversive and shocking actions in British history' (H. Wilson, *Pressure Group*, 1961).

In 1974, the National Union of Mineworkers was accused of being responsible for the downfall of the Conservative Government as a result of their strike action against the elected Government's industrial policy.

In the referendum campaign to decide whether or not Britain should join the European Economic Community £1 481 583 was spent by those campaigning in favour of entry and £133 630 by the opponents of entry.

Some objections to the operation of pressure groups are thus that financial power can influence events unfairly; that non-elected organisations can overcome the will of elected governments by withholding their services; that in the last analysis military power might not be available if a government's policy seriously conflicted with the wishes of military leaders; and that some groups have an undue measure of support in the media.

The practice of 'lobbying' MPs has resulting in some writers such as Finer referring to pressure groups as 'the lobby'. The 'lobby' is actually the entrance chamber of the House of Commons, where individuals or groups may request a meeting with a particular Member of Parliament and seek to persuade him, or her, to support their views.

The practice of lobbying is an essentially democratic one but there is more objection to the practice of 'sponsoring' a Member of Parliament or retaining one as an adviser for a particular institution such as the Police Federation or a business concern. Most trade unions sponsor an MP – this means that they contribute a sum towards the election and other expenses of that person. Parliamentary 'advisers' may receive direct payments.

Supporters of these practices point out that they provide a useful link between real life and the more insulated world of Parliament and that 'the offer of money or other advantage to any Member of Parliament for the promoting of any matter whatsoever, depending or to be transacted in Parliament, is a high crime' (Erskine May, *Parliamentary Practice*, 1844).

It is unlikely that any Member of Parliament *does* let financial considerations influence their judgement but opponents of these practices feel that such financial rewards are unacceptable. 'No MP should be paid to represent any vested interest in Parliament' (C. Mayhew, *Party Games*, 1969).

The extract below is given as an example of the kind of discussion document produced by pressure groups to publicise their cause; it is, of course, partisan. It is however also relevant to Chapter 10.

(a) The social wage

The 'social wage' is the contribution made to everybody's standard of living by the provision of public facilities and services paid for by taxes. These include the health and education services, public housing, social services and school meals. All these vital services are being subjected to drastic cuts at present, yet they are just as important to the lives of people with dependent children as the level of individual wages earned by the family's breadwinner(s). This booklet is not intended to document the cuts in detail or to examine the details of the economic policies which give rise to them: those tasks have been accomplished elsewhere. What we are concerned to emphasise here is that the cuts are hitting people with children hardest of all: if this or any future government is serious about wishing to help families, then policies of the kind being pursued at present are entirely inappropriate. In particular, cuts in personal social services are increasing the burden of women in the home, whether or not they are fortunate enough still to have their paid jobs to do as well. Yet the Government persists in pretending that family life is somehow being enhanced, and that women should view themselves with pride as the 'frontline providers'.

BRITAIN COMPARES BADLY WITH OTHER EEC COUNTRIES

Even before the present Government's cuts, social spending in this country, as a percentage of total production, was planned to be 20.8 per cent in 1980. In seven of the eight other EEC countries it was planned to rise to between 24.5 per cent and 31 per cent. Yet Britain has a higher proportion of elderly, disabled and unemployed people than the other countries, especially of over-85s, making heavy demands on health and personal social services.

PRESSURES ON THE FAMILY

A few examples will illustrate the sort of pressures now being exerted on ordinary families:

School meals: Prices have soared. In April 1979, a school meal cost 25p. The 1980 Education Act now allows each local authority to charge what it likes. The duty to provide free school meals has been restricted to children from families on supplementary benefit or family income supplement, although some LEAs are still providing them for other children. There is a danger, though, that, as the number of children paying for meals declines, the problem of stigma among children entitled to free meals will grow much worse.

School uniform grants are being cut back or even abolished by some local authorities.

School transport, where it is provided on a discretionary basis, is being cut, affecting poor families in rural areas particularly badly. The attempt to abolish the duty to provide free school transport for children living beyond walking distance was, thank goodness, defeated by the House of Lords. [This is an interesting example of the remaining power of the peers and the churches. Opposition to the abolition of statutory school transport was led by the Duke of Arundel, the senior Catholic layman; abolition would have affected rural Catholic children particularly badly in that Catholic schools cover wide geographical areas.]

(b) Cash

The widening financial gap between families with dependent children and the rest of the population is not, of course, the result simply of present government policies. By 1977, when the phasing-in of the child benefit scheme began, family support (that is, the combined value of child benefit and the Child Tax Allowances which then also still existed) was less than in 1946 when family allowances were first paid. [J. Coussins and A. Coote, *The Family in the Firing Line* (Child Poverty Action Group and National Council for Civil Liberties, 1981) (abridged).]

CHAPTER 26

VOTING BEHAVIOUR

26.1 VOTING PATTERNS

In 1872 the secret ballot was introduced in British elections, and so we can never be certain how people vote. We obviously know what the support for each political party is in each constituency, and thus we can see that support for the Labour Party is much higher in the North of England, Wales and Scotland than in the Midlands and Southern England – a pattern that has been described as a 'two-nations' style of voting. Additionally support for the Conservative Party is higher in rural areas than it is in industrial centres, regardless of the North/South divide.

J. Vincent (*Pollbooks: How the Victorians Voted*, 1967) illustrated that before the secret ballot, voting patterns tended to show that people voted by occupation and religion rather than by class. Butchers were predominantly Conservative; grocers were predominantly Liberal. Church of England clergymen were Conservative; Methodists and Catholics were Liberal.

Random sampling surveys developed in the 1950s and although we do not have the detailed knowledge available before the secret ballot, these have permitted scientific surveys of voting patterns to take place.

Do people vote by class as is often supposed? Are women more likely than men to vote for a particular political party? What influence has age or religion on voting patterns?

26.2 THE INFLUENCE OF SOCIAL CLASS AND ETHNIC ORIGIN

The influence of class on voting patterns has aroused considerable interest in that there is a presumed identity of interest between the Labour Party and the 'working class' and between the Conservative Party and the 'middle class'; yet the Conservative Party has held power for a longer period overall than the Labour Party since 1945, despite the fact that

Political party representatives outside polling stations ('tellers') have no official status – you do not have to tell them how you have voted

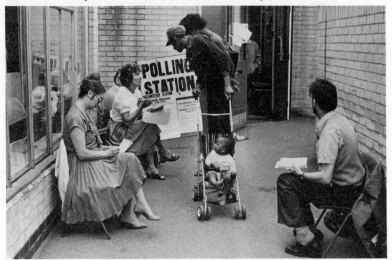

during that period the Census returns show more working-class people in the population. The working-class vote accounts for about a half of the total Conservative vote. The middle-class Labour vote is only about 15 per cent of the total Labour vote (the skilled and unskilled manual workers make up about two thirds of the electorate).

The thesis of the 'Working-class Conservative' has been the major area of study in many works; for example *Must Labour Lose?* (M. Abrams and R. Rose, 1960); *Can Labour Win?* (C. Crosland, 1960) *The Worker in an Affluent Society* (F. Zweig, 1961); and *The Working Class Tories* (E. Nordlinger, 1967).

Nordlinger identifies two main types of 'working-class Tory'; the 'deferential' and the 'pragmatist'. The deferential voter shows a strong preference to have people of a high status as their leaders rather than those of their own social class, feeling that such people are natural leaders or have been 'taught to lead'. The pragmatic voter is 'achievement orientated', they vote Conservative because they think a Conservative government is more likely to help them personally. Nordlinger found that the pragmatic voter preferred Conservative leaders to have 'achieved' their positions but that they also respected political leaders with 'ascribed' high status.

Butler and Rose (*The British General Election of 1964*, 1965) refer to a survey by the Conservative Political Centre in which 32 per cent of the working class are found to have voted Conservative while only 17 per cent of the middle class voted Labour and explained this in terms of rising standards of living, resulting in the better paid members of the working class adopting middle-class life-styles. 'A significant number of skilled workers may be called class hybrids, working class in terms of occupation, education, speech and cultural norms, while being middle class in terms of income and material comforts' who are 'more likely to abstain or to switch their voting allegiences'. Evidence for this may be seen in that the swings against Labour in the 1979 General Election were particularly high in seats where there was a large percentage of affluent working-class voters, such as Hitchin in prosperous Hertfordshire. The *embourgeoisement* thesis received further support in 1977 (K. Roberts, *The Fragmentary Class Structure*) who identified a section of the working class – manual workers owning their own houses, living on middle-class estates, opposed to trade unions, and voting Conservative. 'The bourgeois worker is a living animal', but represents a minor not a major group within the working class.

This process of *embourgeoisement* has been disputed by other studies; notably that of Goldthorpe, Lockwood, Bechhofer and Platt (*The Affluent Worker*, 1968) who found that there was no process of *embourgeoisement* among the well-paid car workers in Luton. Although Goldthorpe did find that the *less* the car workers were involved with the working-class sub-culture, the *more* likely they were to vote Conservative, Liberal or to abstain.

There also appears to be a tendency for middle-class people – such as social workers and teachers – who are directly involved with working-class people to vote Labour.

Goldthorpe found that there was a definite relationship between trade union membership and voting Labour – union members were three to four times more likely to vote Labour than to vote Conservative. The same study also found a greater likelihood of voting Labour in large plants, the environment of which increases 'working-class political consciousness'.

The importance of the environment in helping to determine voting behaviour is also emphasised by F. Parkin (*Working-class Conservatives; A Theory of Political Deviance*) who suggests that British institutions are essentially conservative and help to maintain the dominant values of the society which the Labour Party is seen as challenging. In fact while working-class Conservative voters and middle-class Labour voters are usually described as 'deviant voters' Parkin claims that the real 'deviant voter' is the Labour voter regardless of class because he is challenging the central values of British society. He points to the fact that where the norm of the area is 'working class' the middle class are more likely to vote Labour. But where middle class values are dominant the working class is more likely to vote Conservative. This view helps to explain the considerable regional differences in voting behaviour; in Wales, for example, in 1959, Labour received almost a quarter of the middle-class vote. Upward social mobility also appears to encourage people to vote Conservative, perhaps as a means of identifying with their new class. Some working-class people may vote Conservative because they support what they believe to be the Conservative Party's harder approach to law and order, capital punishment and immigration. We must also remember that, while people who are 'objectively' working class by reason of occupation may *think* of themselves as middle class, they are 'subjectively middle class,' and they vote accordingly.

The influence of ethnic origin has not yet been much studied but the evidence is that New Commonwealth and Irish immigrants are more likely to vote for the Labour Party. However, this is likely to be mainly a question of class identification as the majority of New Commonwealth and Irish immigrants have tended to be in manual employment.

The Liberal vote tends to be drawn more or less equally from all sections of the community; the Liberal vote is 'a mirror image of the nation' (D. Butler and A. King, *The British General Election of 1964*, 1965). The SDP vote also seems to be drawn from across the class spectrum. There does appear to be some evidence for Dahrendorf's claim that 'people have been liberated from their class boundaries'.

Class and politics

The rise of the Social Democratic Party has been largely discussed in relation to the crisis in the Labour Party and the decline of working class politics. But it may be that changes in the middle class are more pertinent to the appearance of the new party, both in accounting for its distinctive moral temper and in explaining the emergence, both locally and nationally, of what looks to be, at least in embryo, a new political class.

The middle class before the second world war was less a class than a society of orders, each jealously guarding a more or less self-contained existence, and exquisitely graded according to a hierarchy of ranks. The clergyman's widow, in reduced circumstances, would not make friends with the elementary school teacher, though she might have her round to tea.

Middle class identity was constituted amid a sea of social fears, with hidden reefs on which the frail barque of respectability could only too easily be wrecked. In a limited social landscape, all kinds of spectres loomed—'rude' language, 'vulgar' clothes, 'course' looks. There was the servant you couldn't trust, the daily who was sullen and resentful, the Jews who had moved in round the corner, the 'sergeant major' type who was throwing his weight about at the office. Keeping up appearances was a very condition of middle class existence, snobbery a way of life; a vast amount of energy was expended on the management of social distance and keeping intruders at bay. Class distinction became the articulating principle of British political life.

Fear of losing caste within the middle class was accompanied by real terror at the thought of falling out of it. For 100 years and more the masses—'the dangerous classes' as they were known in early Victorian England—had constituted the menacing "other" in middle class existence, the open-mouthed abyss waiting to swallow up those who lost their foothold in society. Individually the members of the working class were conceived of as pollutants; collectively they constituted the beetle-browed figures who lurked at the street corners, the harridans who fought in the pubs.

In the epoch of the October Revolution and the General Strike, such fears crystallised around the threat of the organised labour movement. Thus it was that, notwithstanding a certain lessening in economic differentials between the wars, class division became the articulating principle of British political life. Arguably it remained so up to the general election of 1959.

Class guilt 'the conscience of the rich' – was the obverse side of class fear, conditioned by the same set of contrasts. In some it was associated with a notion of moral duty—*noblesse oblige*; in others with a deliberate rejection, or partial rejection, of class identity, and an attempt to put one's talents at the service of the masses.

The middle classes of today are much more occupationally diversified, with the multiplication of professional and managerial hierarchies, and the proliferation of salaried employments. But it may be that culturally they are more compact. The vastly expanded universities have given their children a common education.

The new middle class are not, in the conventional English sense, snobs, because they don't feel anyone can threaten them. They have little sense of being privileged. Even if they are second-generation meritocrats, like the sons of Labour MPs, and have been expensively educated at the ancient universities, they believe that they owe their position not to the advantages of birth or wealth, but rather to personal excellence. The new middle class have a different emotional economy than that of their pre-war predecessors. They go in for instant rather than deferred gratification, making a positive virtue of their expenditure, and treating the self-indulgent as an ostentatious display of good taste.

From the 1920s to the 1960s, a large bloc of the middle classes voted Tory and accepted upper class hegemony, simply because they were afraid of Labour, not only on account of specific threats to their interests and privileges, but also because of that whole complex of fear and anxiety for which Labour, by its name and its constituency, was the symbol. Since the by-elections of the early 1960s, this bloc has shown signs of disintegration, and its historical rationale has increasingly come into question. [R. Samuel, 'The SDP and the New Political Class', (*New Society*, 1982).]

Voting and class

British party politics are more highly class-bound than those in most other countries. A recent comparison between four Anglo-Saxon democracies (Britain, USA, Canada, Australia) showed that of the four Britain had the highest index of class voting. Britain also has a higher class-voting index than most continental states, Scandinavia excepted. This index is constructed by subtracting the percentage of non-manual workers voting for the party of the Left from the percentage of manual workers who do so, thus revealing the gap between the classes, e.g.

% voting for Left party

Manual:	75
Non-manual:	25
Index of class voting:	+50

A high index may therefore be achieved when most manual workers vote Left and most non-manual workers do not. A lower index may result *either* from many manual workers voting Right (e.g. Western Germany), *or* from many non-manual workers voting Left (e.g. Wales), an even lower or negative index when both happen (e.g. Canada).

This makes the second qualification important. Class voting in Britain may be high, but is by no means as high as it might be. Most people, asked to locate the centre of class-consciousness in Britain would probably point to the working class; and this is correct in that class-consciousness among workers is more explicit and overt than in the middle class. The middle class, however, shows much greater political cohesion. In post-war elections the Labour Party has not succeeded in getting more than 20–25 per cent of the non-manual vote or 10–15 per cent of the business and professional classes. On the other hand at least a third of the working class consistently votes Conservative.

What is the basis of working-class Toryism? The most important ingredient is social deference, though this may take many forms. In the nineteenth century Tory Democrats like Disraeli and Lord Randolph Churchill appealed to workers on the grounds that the Tories, unlike money-grabbing Liberal mill-owners, were true aristocrats and above the class-struggle. Factory hands who would not dream of voting for Mr Gradgrind could therefore confidently follow the Duke of Omnium. Coupled with it is a respect for education, remembering that education is at least as much social training as intellectual qualification: 'The Conservatives are better suited to running the country. They're better educated – I think there is nothing better than to hear a public school man speak English.' But equally there is respect for money and business success – as indeed there was in the nineteenth century when a great many working men were willing to follow the lead of their local Liberal or Radical employers. Today money as well as birth is associated with Conservatism: 'They are business men who know what they are doing. They have been brought up to rule, to take over the leadership.' To some extent the snobbish attitudes implied by this deference are reflected in the Tory worker's view of himself. Conservative manual workers are more likely to attribute middle-class status to themselves than Labour manual workers. But this self-promotion is not the whole explanation. As often as not deference implies a desire to maintain the existing social hierarchy, to acknowledge the superiority of 'gentlemen born'.

Deference can hardly account for the whole of working-class Conservatism. Equally important is a second category, whom McKenzie and Silver call 'secular' Conservatives – predominantly younger, male, better-paid voters who happen to approve of private enterprise, value consumer affluence or dislike trade unions. They are less committed emotionally to leadership from the upper classes and take a more hard-headed and pragmatic view of Conservative capacity to govern.

Affluence may determine the form that working-class Conservatism takes; it is not, in itself, a cause of Conservatism. There is no evidence that high incomes, or the possession of consumer durables, predispose working-class voters towards the Right. The one exception is home-ownership which, at all levels of income, makes people with manual jobs feel more middle-class, and more inclined to vote Conservative than those who rent their homes. There is little support for the *embourgeoisement* hypothesis in its crudest form – that the growth of consumer affluence makes people behave, and feel, in middle-class ways. Class identification is too firmly rooted to be overturned by the arrival of a washing-machine. However, while class and party attachments may remain fairly constant, changes in living standards notwithstanding, the intensity of these attachments may diminish. Life no longer appears as a struggle for the bare necessities; the spiritual sustenance that class solidarity gives is no longer central to social existence. This possible effect of affluence, which investigators of *embourgeoisement* have so far ignored, could be of great political importance. It almost certainly accounts for the above-average drop in turn-out in industrial constituencies over the last fifteen years; without it we cannot account for the markedly greater volatility of the electorate. Above all, it goes hand in hand with the slow, but cumulatively significant, change in the country's occupational structure. [P. Pulzer, *Political Representation and Elections in Britain* (London: Allen & Unwin, 1972).]

26.3 THE INFLUENCE OF SEX, AGE AND RELIGION

Sex, age and religion are not major factors influencing voting behaviour in Great Britain. 'Class is the basis of British party politics; all else is embellishment and detail' (P. Pulzer, *Political Representation and Elections in Britain*, 1972). Of the three, sex differences may have had the greatest influence up to the General Election of 1983 (see chart on page 300), women being more likely than men to vote Conservative. This may be because a greater proportion of women work in offices and service industries which up to now have not been substantially unionised; where there is more direct contact with management leading to more identification between the two sides; and where the ambience is more middle class. It has also been suggested that women are more cautious, whether by environmental conditioning or physical characteristic, with the result that they vote for the party most likely to maintain the status quo.

Older people tend to vote Conservative more than younger people, no doubt because as we grow older we become less likely to welcome change. However, the lowering of the voting age to 18 did not result in any substantial advantage to the Labour party as many people then expected, the new generation of voters in general following traditional patterns based on class and area of residence. There does seem a tendency for younger voters to be less likely to retain the rigid party loyalties of their parents. One survey of people voting for the first time in 1974 found that 20 per cent of them voted Liberal and 5 per cent Nationalist (which would seem to indicate a 30 per cent level of support where there was a Nationalist candidate). This compared with 20 per cent voting Conservative and 36 per cent Labour (I. McLean, *Political Realities: Elections*, 1976).

Outside Northern Ireland, the rest of the United Kingdom is not much influenced by religious factors in deciding how to vote. Practising Anglicans are more likely to vote Conservative than are Catholics and Methodists. This is probably the result of the historical association between Methodism and Radicalism and the fact that many Catholics are Irish Immigrants and Irish immigrants are often manual workers – a class rather than a religious influence. However, there is a greater tendency for Catholics to vote Labour regardless of social class.

26.4 THE MEDIA AND OPINION POLLS

Two-party support has been declining since 1951 when about three quarters of the electorate had a marked preference for the two largest parties. There are now more 'floating voters' – people with no particular political allegiance – to be won, and when it is borne in mind that a 1 per cent election swing can alter a party's majority by thirty seats it will be understood that the influence of the media is watched carefully by the managers of all political parties. There is a clearly identifiable majority of national newspapers – both in terms of individual papers and total circulation – in favour of the Conservative Party. The fairness of the television authorities may be gauged by the fact that *both* major political parties accused the broadcasting authorities of bias at the conclusion of the 1979 elections. Tables 26.1 and 26.2 illustrate readers' perceptions of partisanship and also diversity of reports, in different papers, of the same incident. Both factual information and the comment made on it can be seen to vary widely as illustrated by the Press reports on a 'March for Jobs' rally on 6 June 1983 (see Table 26.2).

However it is by no means certain that the media has any very great power to change voting intentions. Advertising has most power when it is offering people what they want – it is unlikely to change established attitudes (section 22.3).

A study by J. Trenaman of two Leeds constituencies in the 1959 General Election found that 'no part of the political campaign . . . either on television or through other media, was found to have any direct bearing on the way in which people decided to vote or even on their attitudes towards the parties' (P. Madgwick, *Introduction to British Politics*, 1970). Existing party supporters tend to *select* news and comment in such a way that it reinforces their existing attitudes; floating voters tend to be protected from influence by their own lack of interest in politics.

Campaigns to change attitudes may be more likely to be successful *over a period of time* than will direct attempts to influence immediate voting intentions. In 1959 the Conservative Party established that the public in general associated their party with the more privileged sections of society and concentrated their national advertising campaign in showing working-class people voting Conservative. At the end of the campaign, research indicated a drop of 7–8 per cent in the association of the Conservative Party with privilege.

However the influence of professional persuaders is clearly limited. One example is that the Conservative Party spent almost half a million pounds trying to improve the public image of their leader, Sir Alec Douglas-Home, in the first few months of 1964. During that period, his public opinion poll rating dropped from 58 per cent to 48 per cent (R. Rose, *Influencing Voters*, 1967).

'Psephology' – the study of the way in which people vote – has become sophisticated since 1945 and the growth of accurate random sampling techniques has resulted in considerable accuracy in predicting results in elections. Good sampling techniques have reduced the 'margin of error' of the well known polls such as Gallup and NOP, to between two and six per cent.

Fig. 26.1 *Press bias*

Thursday, June 9, 1983

Thursday, June 9, 1983

SOURCE D. Butler and D. Kavanagh, *The General Election of 1983* (London: Macmillan, 1984).

Table 26.2 readers' perceptions of newspaper partisanship (i.e. which party the readers thought the paper supported)

	Daily Express 1979 %	Daily Express 1983 %	Daily Mail 1979 %	Daily Mail 1983 %	Daily Mirror 1979 %	Daily Mirror 1983 %	Sun 1979 %	Sun 1983 %	Daily Star 1983 %
Perceived Partisanship									
Conservative	82	85	80	80	8	5	33	64	35
Labour	3	2	4	7	75	80	33	10	24
Liberal/Alliance	1	2	2	2	1	1	1	1	4
None	1	4	2	3	3	3	8	6	13
Don't know	14	8	12	10	15	12	25	19	25
Result preferred by Editor 1983	Conservative victory		Conservative victory		Labour victory		Conservative victory		Conservative victory
CIRCULATION	1 936 000		1 834 000		3 267 000		4 155 000		1 313 000
% of readers in social class (1983)	AB C1 C2 DE 18 27 32 24		AB C1 C2 DE 26 30 26 18		AB C1 C2 DE 7 18 40 36		AB C1 C2 DE 6 17 40 37		AB C1 C2 DE 5 13 42 40

'HEAVIES', 'QUALITY PAPERS'

	Daily Telegraph	Guardian	The Times
Result preferred by Editor 1983	Conservative victory	Not a Conservative landslide	Conservative victory
CIRCULATION	1 284 000	417 000	321 000
% of readers in social class (1983)	AB C1 C2 DE 53 27 13 7	AB C1 C2 DE 48 28 15 9	AB C1 C2 DE 60 22 10 8

SOURCE D. Butler and D. Kavanagh, *The British General Election of 1983* (London).

Table 26.3 *varying press reports on 'March for Jobs' rally, 6 June 1983*

Newspaper	Estimate of number attending	Comment in news report
Guardian	Police: 15 000–20 000 Organisers: 130 000	None
Daily Telegraph	About 10 000	Ended in chaos and confusion
The Times	15 000–20000	Low turnout will be seen as blow to the labour movement
Daily Express	Police estimate fewer than 20 000 but Daily Express count suggests fewer still. Union leaders say at least 150 000	Soggy anti-climax
Daily Mail	20 000	Ended with allegations of violence
Daily Mirror	Thousands flocked in on 200 coaches and 11 special trains	Defiant end to 'gissa job' march
Daily Star	More than 150 000	Huge rally
Sun	Little more than 5000	Pathetic, rain-soaked end
Morning Star	100 000	Shook the conscience of the nation
Scotsman	About 150 000	Huge rally

British general elections tend to be decided by narrow margins and these are often within the margin of sampling error so that opinion polls are accused of innaccuracy or even of having influenced the result of the poll by encouraging people to jump on a successful bandwagon. However, in 1970 all the major opinion polls forecast a Labour win and all were wrong. This would appear to disprove the notion that people will change their voting intention in order to be on the winning side.

Opinion polls can also be used as part of the market research techniques used by the political parties to find out what the voters want. In this respect there can be two possible objections to their use: (a) market research is expensive, and the richest political parties will have an advantage; (b) there may be a temptation for politicians to gear their advertised

In 1983 the margin of error varied between 0.5 and 6.5 per cent but the Conservatives were so far ahead that all the major opinion polls were right.

Table 26.4 opinion polls during the General Election 1983

	Actual result	Audience selection	Harris	Gallup	Marplan	NOP (Northcliffe)	NOP (Daily Mail)	MORI (Daily Express/Star)	MORI (Evening Standard)
	%	%	%	%	%	%	%	%	%
Conservative	43.5 (1970 46.2)	45	47	45.5	46	47	46	47	44
Labour	28 (1970 43.8)	23	25	26.5	26	25	28	26	28
Alliance	26 (1970 7.5 Lib only)	29	26	26	26	26	24	25	26

policies to what the public opinion polls say the public want rather than to make a point of bringing their less popular policies to public attention; in fairness it must be said that there is little evidence that any political party is doing this.

Greater social and geographical mobility; a change in the industrial structure from traditional manufacturing industry as the largest employers to the service sector; and perhaps a more educated electorate has led to a much more volatile voting pattern than in the past. The loyalty of voters from every social class seems to have become more 'conditional' – they are much less likely to support a political party for traditional reasons.

This changing pattern in political allegiance has been growing since the peak of two-party loyalty in the election of 1951. In the early 1980s the change seemed to be confirmed by the rise of the Social Democratic Party.

Opinion polls

In 1970 the British opinion polls forecast a Labour win and in February 1974 a Conservative victory. They were wrong both times, and their credibility was badly dented. After the 1970 election the pollsters spent a long time licking their wounds, and devised some modifications to their calculations to take account of the fact that they had all overestimated the Labour vote. Applying these modifications in February 1974, they promptly overestimated the Conservative vote instead.

In fact, the polls' record in general election predictions is much better than it looks. They appeared to do badly only because people, especially newspaper sub-editors, expected them to be able to do things which they could not possibly do. As we have said, the impossibility of avoiding sampling error means that a percentage figure given in an opinion poll can never guarantee to be closer than 2 or 3 per cent away from the true figure. But the margin between the two leading parties in British elections is almost always slender, and often within the 4 to 6 per cent range of sampling error. If a poll shows Labour as being 3 per cent ahead of the Conservatives, the true position could be anywhere between a dead heat and a 6 per cent Labour lead. In February 1974, as a matter of fact, the polls were almost spot on; they predicted a Conservative lead over Labour of 3 per cent, and there actually was one of 1 per cent. Labour won more *seats*, because of the way the votes were distributed, but the Conservatives won more votes – very close to the share the polls had predicted.

Opinion polls, therefore, are not too reliable as tipsters for general elections, because the result is usually so close that it falls within the range of sampling error. But this is not true of inter-election periods, when there is often a yawning chasm between the parties.

The general trends in party support that are chronicled by the polls in between elections are undoubtedly fairly reliable. Like by-elections and local elections, they show a consistent pattern of the government of the day doing very badly in mid-term, and rallying as the next election approaches. [I. McLean, *Political Realities – Elections* (London: Longman, 1976).]

vote by sex and age

	Men	Women	18–22	23–34	35–44	45–64	65+
Conservative	46	43	41	45	47	46	48
Labour	30	28	29	32	27	27	33
Liberal/SDP	24	28	30	23	26	27	19

SOURCE Ivor Crewe, article in *The Guardian*, 13 June 1983.
(Based on 4.141 interviews in England, Scotland, and Wales conducted on June 8 and 9 1983.)

QUESTIONS FROM PAST O-LEVEL GCE PAPERS

1. Voting Intention by Social Class in Great Britain in 1970 and 1974.

Social Class	A		B		C		D	
Election Year	1970 (%)	1974 (%)	1970 (%)	1974 (%)	1970 (%)	1974 (%)	1970 (%)	1974 (%)
Conservative	70	63	59	51	35	26	33	22
Labour	20	12	30	24	55	49	57	57
Liberal	9	22	9	21	7	20	6	16
Other	1	3	2	4	3	5	4	5

(Adapted from *Financial Times*, 25th October 1974.)

(a) What percentage of people in social class C intended to vote Labour in 1970? 2 marks

(b) What patterns and changes in voting intention does the table show for social classes A and C? 6 marks

(c) Outline **four** explanations for the fact that some working class people vote Conservative. 4 marks

(d) If the above information was obtained from an opinion poll, what **four** factors might produce information which was not reflected in the actual election result? 8 marks

Associated Examining Board

2. Outline and comment upon the part played by any *two* of the following in British politics.
   (a) Opinion polls
   (b) Pressure groups
   (c) Television
   (d) Political parties

Associated Examining Board

3. 'Democracy involves more than just the right to vote.' Explain.

Associated Examining Board

4. Examine the factors used by pressure groups in Britain to achieve their objectives. Illustrate your answer with examples.

Oxford Local Examining Board

5. What are the major factors which sociologists use to explain voting patterns?

Oxford Local Examining Board

6. **Either,** (1) Explain, with examples, what are meant by *political parties* and *pressure groups* in society.

   Or, (b) Explain what is meant by saying that a government has the *monopoly of legitimate force.*

Welsh Joint Examining Board

7. 'Whatever politicians may say, the role of the state inevitably increases.' Discuss.

Oxford Local Examining Board

8. Examine the relationship between social class and voting behaviour in Britain. What, if any, have been the changes in this relationship since 1945?

Oxford Local Examining Board

PART X
EXAMPLES OF COMPLETE
QUESTION PAPERS AND
OUTLINE MARKING SCHEMES

ORDINARY LEVEL

NOTE: These example question papers and the outline marking schemes
that follow do not represent actual papers or schemes set by any
GCE Board. They are intended for the guidance of examination
candidates so that they can perform a self-assessment, and so that
they may have some idea of the marking methods that may be
used by examiners.

SOCIOLOGY

Paper 1

2 hours allowed including reading time

Answer any *THREE* questions

All questions carry equal marks, the marks
for parts of questions are shown in brackets

Adjusted from 1977 following the *Criminal Law Act*

Offenders found guilty of, or cautioned for, indictable offences: by sex and age

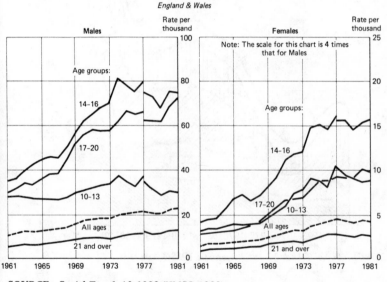

England & Wales

SOURCE   *Social Trends* 13 *1983* (HMSO 1982)

1. (a) Which age group is most likely to commit a crime?   (1)
   (b) Out of every thousand females in the population under the
        age of 14, how many were found guilty or cautioned for
        serious offences in 1977?   (1)
   (c) Identify the trends in male crime for those aged between 14
        and 16 over the period shown in the diagram.   (3)
   (d) Why are women less likely than men to commit a crime?   (6)
   (e) Account for the apparent increases in crime shown in
        the charts.   (6)
   (f) In what ways might the information given in the diagrams
        be misleading?   (3)

Unemployment: by duration

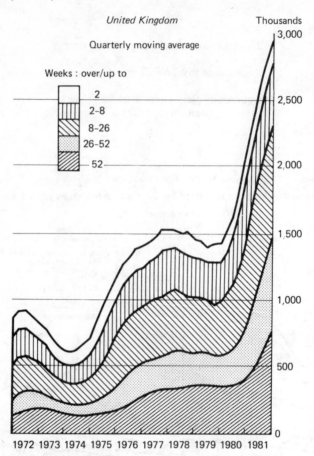

United Kingdom   Thousands

Quarterly moving average

Weeks : over/up to
- 2
- 2–8
- 8–26
- 26–52
- 52

SOURCE *Social Trends* 13 *1983* (London, HMSO, 1982)

2. (a) How many people were unemployed in 1975? (1)
   (b) What was the percentage increase in the long term unemployed (that is people unemployed for over six months) between April 1980 and April 1981? (2)
   (c) What factors account for the increase in the number of those unemployed between 1972 and 1982? (4)
   (d) What factors might result in an under or over-estimate of the degree of unemployment nationally? (4)
   (e) What measures might be taken to reduce unemployment nationally? (4)
   (f) What sociological factors need to be taken into account in calculating the social effect of unemployment on those involved? (5)

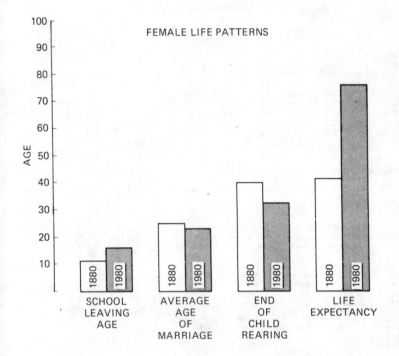

FEMALE LIFE PATTERNS

3. (a) What was the average age of marriage for women in 1980? (1)
   (b) What TWO factors have resulted in the position shown on
       the diagram for the age of death? (2)
   (c) What TWO factors have resulted in the position shown on
       the diagram for the age of marriage? (2)
   (d) How long was a woman likely to have in 1980 between
       the completion of the rearing of her children and death,
       compared with one hundred years previously? What have
       been the major effects of this change? (5)
   (e) What social and economic factors have influenced the
       status of women during the twentieth century? (5)
   (f) To what extent do women now enjoy complete equality
       with men? (5)

Trade union membership:

	United Kingdom			Millions and percentages		
	Membership (millions)			As a percentage of all employees		
	Men	Women	Total	Men	Women	Total
1951	7.7	1.8	9.5	56	25	45
1961	7.9	2.0	9.9	53	24	43
1966	8.0	2.2	10.2	53	26	43
1971	8.4	2.8	11.1	59	32	49
1976	8.8	3.6	12.4	61	38	52
1977	9.1	3.8	12.8	63	39	53
1978	9.2	3.9	13.1	64	40	54
1979	9.4	3.9	13.3	66	39	55
1980	9.0	3.8	12.8	64	38	53

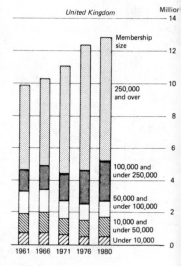

size of union

United Kingdom — Millions

Membership size

250,000 and over

100,000 and under 250,000

50,000 and under 100,000

10,000 and under 50,000

Under 10,000

1961 1966 1971 1976 1980

Manual and non-manual employees

	Great Britain		Thousands and percentages	
	Manual		Non-manual	
	Potential membership (thousands)	Percentage belonging to trade union	Potential membership (thousands)	Percentage belonging to trade union
1951	14,450	49	6,948	31
1961	14,020	50	8,479	30
1966	14,393	48	9,461	30
1971	13,343	52	10,405	34
1976	12,300	60	11,000	41
1977	12,300	60	11,300	42
1978	12,100	63	11,500	44
1979	12,100	66	11,600	45

SOURCES   *Social Trends* 12 *1982* and *Social Trends* 13 *1983*.

4. (a) What was the total membership of trade unions in Britain in 1979? (1)
   (b) What trends are illustrated in the size of trade unions during the twenty-five years prior to 1976? (2)
   (c) What percentage of all employees were members of trade unions in 1976? How many of these were men (in millions)? (2)
   (d) Account for the change in the proportion of women trade unionists between 1951 and 1979. (4)
   (e) What sort of occupational groups are most likely to be unionised, and what effect is this likely to have on the earnings, benefits and voting intentions of those involved? (5)
   (f) What have been the main changes in the occupational structure of trade unions during the period shown? What are the likely causes and effect of these changes in the groups involved? (6)

Wealth distribution: only a small change over the years

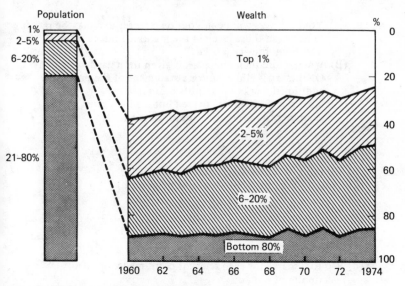

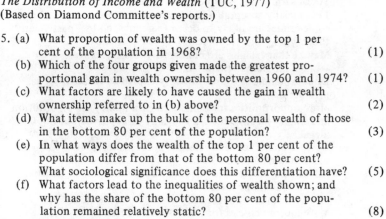

The Distribution of Income and Wealth (TUC, 1977)
(Based on Diamond Committee's reports.)

5. (a) What proportion of wealth was owned by the top 1 per
       cent of the population in 1968?   (1)
   (b) Which of the four groups given made the greatest pro-
       portional gain in wealth ownership between 1960 and 1974?   (1)
   (c) What factors are likely to have caused the gain in wealth
       ownership referred to in (b) above?   (2)
   (d) What items make up the bulk of the personal wealth of those
       in the bottom 80 per cent of the population?   (3)
   (e) In what ways does the wealth of the top 1 per cent of the
       population differ from that of the bottom 80 per cent?
       What sociological significance does this differentiation have?   (5)
   (f) What factors lead to the inequalities of wealth shown; and
       why has the share of the bottom 80 per cent of the popu-
       lation remained relatively static?   (8)

310

SOCIOLOGY 'O' LEVEL MARKING SCHEME PAPER I

NOTE: (A) Your answers will be in your own words and may be rather
longer than those given in the marking scheme where
maximum brevity is used.
   (B) Where more than one mark is given for a particular point
ONE mark is allocated for a statement of the point and
additional marks for amplification of it.
   (C) Most possibilities are covered but credit is given by the
examiner for alternative appropriate answers.

1. (a) 14–16   (1)
    (b) 10 (plus or minus 1 acceptable)   (1)
    (c) Any three of the following (one mark each):

         (i) Fairly rapid rise 1961–67
         (ii) Steep rise   1967–74
         (iii) Decline   1974–78
         (iv) Fluctuation   1974–81   (3)

    (d) Up to 2 marks for each relevant point made, up to a
         maximum of 6 marks:
         Socialisation process predisposed females to non-assertion
         Less socially acceptable for women to be in situations where
         some crimes are likely to occur (e.g. pubs, clubs – particularly
         those with a 'bad' reputation)
         May be that females are biologically less aggressive
         Women are home-orientated
         Double standards – girls' hostility expressed through sexual
         promiscuity
         More opportunities for females to earn money via prostitution
         and similar means which are socially disapproved but not
         illegal   (6)
    (e) Up to 2 marks for each relevant point made, up to a
         maximum of 6 marks:
         Advertising creates and encourages more accpetable goals
         without providing means
         More consumer goods readily available for theft, e.g. cars
         More motor vehicles for traffic-related offences.
         Link between violence and overcrowding (e.g. high-rise flats)
         Continued growth of urbanism (*Gemeinshaften/Gesellshaften*
         dichotomy)
         The influence of relative poverty
         Less restraint of adults/discipline in home and school
         (for 2 marks must be questioned)
         Possible effect of television (for 2 marks an indication of
         the kinds of people who may be influenced must be given)
         Group infouences in crowd situations, e.g. football matches
         (for 2 marks an indication that increase in violence, etc. is
         related to media publicity/labelling)
         In the case of females – former male mores are more
         acceptable.

Changing attitudes in society generally
Discussion of possible effect of working mothers (for
2 marks an indication that this influence is disputed)   (6)
(f) Any three of the following (one mark each):

   (i) More crime being reported *or* less likelihood today of
personal retribution rather than report.
   (ii) More active pursuit of offenders.
   (iii) More fairly trivial offences being categorised as serious.
   (iv) More people in the age bands likely to commit offences.
   (v) The two charts, male and female, are plotted to
different scales.   (3)

2. (a) 1 000 000   (1)
  (b) 78 per cent (75 to 80 per cent acceptable)   (2)
  (c) Any four from the following (one mark each):

   (i) A move from labour-intensive to capital-intensive
production methods
   (ii) Increasing automation and/or mechanisation
   (iii) World recession
   (iv) Government action (e.g. to contain inflation)
   (v) Rapid rise in the numbers of economically active
married women.
   (vi) Increasing automation and/or mechanisation
market
   (vii) Competition, particularly from new producers in the
Third World (e.g. textiles)   (4)

  (d) Up to 2 marks for each relevant point made, up to a
maximum of 4 marks:
Those not really seeking work registering because no
likelihood of any (e.g. early retired)
The 'black economy' or similar expression
Married women not registering because no likelihood of work
Short-time working
Overmanning
Seasonal variations
Government schemes (e.g. YTS)   (4)
  (e) Any four from the following (one mark each):

   (i) Early retirement
   (ii) Raising the age of entry to full-time employment
(e.g. raising school-leaving age or 'National Service')
   (iii) Banning or reducing overtime
   (iv) Encouraging one partner in marriage to remain at home
OR
   (v) Work sharing
   (vi) Decreasing working hours
   (vii) Increasing holiday entitlement   (4)

  (f) 1–3 marks for answers dealing with the effect of reduced
earnings on spending patterns and recreation.
4–5 marks for those dealing with above, plus loss of
status and alienation.   (5)

312

3. (a) 23 (plus or minus 1 acceptable) (1)
   (b) Any two from the following (one mark each):

    (i) Better medical attention/knowledge
    (ii) Improved knowledge and standards of hygiene/
         sanitation/nutrition
    (iii) Fewer children
    (iv) Improved standard of living (2)

   (c) Any two from the following (one mark each):

    (i) Easier economically to set up home
    (ii) Contraception/no need for immediate or large family
    (iii) Being 'in service' disappears
    (iv) Greater independence for young
    (v) Earlier maturity (2)

   (d) About 40 years (1)
       Up to 2 marks for each relevant point made, up to a
       maximum of 4 marks:

    (i) Greater opportunities for career/personal development
    (ii) Greater importance of personal relationship with
         husband
    (iii) Greater likelihood of divorce (4)

   (e) Any five from the following (one mark each):

    (i) Expanded educational opportunities
    (ii) Female suffrage
    (iii) Changing/improving work opportunities (including
          Equal Pay/Equal Opportunities)
    (iv) Reduced family size/contraception (not both)
    (v) World wars
    (vi) Greater independence based on Welfare State, etc.
    (vii) Changing husband/wife relationship (5)

   (f) 1–3 marks for answers which deal with theoretical equality
       based on educational opportunities and/or relevant legis-
       lation; also inequality based on physical attributes, including
       child rearing, life expectancy, earlier retirement for women,
       etc.
       4–5 marks for the above, plus consideration of socialisation
       process which inculcates differing attitudes; anticipated
       roles, etc. (5)

4. (a) 13.3 million (13.5 acceptable. N.B. statistics for charts may
       relate to different periods in year) (1)
   (b) The number of people in small unions decreases
       The number of people in large unions increases, or similar
       sentiments (one mark for each) (2)
   (c) 52 per cent; 8.8 million (1 for each correct) (2)
   (d) Up to 2 marks for each relevant point made, up to a
       maximum of 4 marks

    (i)   More women at work

    (ii) General increase in union activity in white-collar occupations where greater proportion are female

    (iii) Women becoming more militant/assertive

(e) Skilled manual workers   (2)

One for each of the answers below (or similar sentiments):

Will tend to increase earnings proportionately more than other groups

Will tend to obtain a greater variety of benefits such as longer holidays

Will probably vote Labour   (3)

(f) More white-collar workers as a result of economic and production changes   (2)

Former access by routine clerical workers to top posts being blocked resulting in a growing identification with manual workers   (2)

Increase in white collar trade unionists may reduce identification of 'Labour movement' with the Labour Party   (2)

5. (a) 30 per cent (+ or − 2 acceptable)   (1)

    (b) The band of 14 per cent immediately above the bottom 80 per cent (or similar e.g. 6–20 per cent band)   (1)

    (c) Two marks for *either*

        (i)   Social mobility as a result of increased educational opportunity *or*

        (ii) Increasing number of people in professional occupations   (2)

    (d) Any three from the following (one mark each):

        (i)   Houses

        (ii) Consumer durables (or 'household goods')

        (iii) Insurance policies

        (iv) Cars (as an item separate from other consumer durables)   (3)

    (e) 1–3 marks for answers which list various forms of share-holding, cash in banks and valuables such as jewellery among the major assets of the top 1 per cent of the population as compared with those of the bottom 80 per cent as in (d) above.

4–5 marks for those which add that the top 1 per cent of the population's wealth is more readily disposable in forms which permit its use for access to power   (5)

    (f) Up to 2 marks for each relevant point made, up to a maximum of 8 marks:

        (i)   Tax avoidance – inherited wealth continues as a result of (or similar sentiment)

        (ii) Wealthy groups tend to admit people of similar background to wealth-producing occupations

314

(iii) Poverty tends to be cyclical
(iv) Capital tends to produce further wealth
(v) Those without capital are unlikely to accumulate
it from income
(vi) 'Culture of poverty' inhibits effort (8)

SOCIOLOGY

Paper 2

$1\frac{3}{4}$ hours allowed

Answer any *THREE* questions. All questions carry equal marks.

1. The present population of Britain has resulted from the immigration of people from different countries with diverse racial or ethnic origins. Immigrants often experience discrimination. Discuss the forms that this discrimination may take and the effectiveness of legislation in reducing it.

2. 'People's expectations of marriage have changed, putting increased strains on the instituion of marriage. Husbands and wives are no longer content to be efficient breadwinners and housewives to one another. Rather they want to like one another and develop individually.' (*New Society*, 8/3/79)
Explain why divorce rates have increased in Britain during the last twenty years and consider the social impact of this increase.

3. Suicide accounts for about one death in every two hundred in Britain today. Outline the major factors that seem to cause suicide in society and consider what might be done to reduce its incidence.

4. Using one or more examples of a longitudinal study, consider the advantages and disadvantages of this form of sociological research and of the methods of sociological investigation used in the research concerned.

5. US, THEM and EVERYONE

'Normal politics, on the other hand, is largely about class. The images evoked are sectional: Us and Them, employers and workers. We lack, in short, a political language for talking about peacetime unity.

Social change and policy have narrowed the previous income and opportunity differentials between the classes more than on the continent. Inequality of bargaining power in industry has been more than remedied. So there's no reason to expect that the bulk of increased wealth will go to enrich a minority.

What still gives strength to class politics is . . . the continuing hold of subjective class identifications. People still find it hard to conceive of a better future for all. . . .

The balance between the classes has changed. The working class is smaller than it was and we have a new middle class which often feels itself vaguely proletarianised (its white-collar jobs may be pretty routine; it joins ASTMS or the AUT or ASSET, to fight for its own sectional interests). The battle of accents is not quite what it was, as anyone who listens to radio or to children coming out of school will know.

But the enclaves of the old ways remain, (*New Society*, 18/1/79)

What is meant by 'class'? To what extent is Britain a class-based society?

6. 'During the present century there has been widespread changes in social conditions and attitudes affecting both men and women'. (*Social Trends*, HMSO)

In what ways have social conditions and attitudes changed, and how have these changes influenced the roles played by men and women in society?

' Can you think of a word which means
- "The Perfect Woman " ? '

(*Observer*)

7. How successful have comprehensive schools been in meeting their objective of providing equal opportunities for all; what factors have made it difficult for this objective to be achieved?

8. 'Once a man has taken the dive down into the claiming class, it requires a tremendous leap to get him back into the working class again. If he qualifies for Family Income Supplement, rent rebates,

exemptions from prescription charges, free school meals and all the other selective benefits, there is no incentive for him to earn a few pounds just to lose all these benefits again. If he becomes unemployed, it will take a job with wages several pounds above the one he previously held to tempt him back into work of his own accord again. A family can join the claiming class at a stroke of a Whitehall pen, but nothing but a major increase in its earnings can put it back in the working class again.'

(Bill Jordan, *Paupers*, Routledge & Kegan Paul, 1973)

What do you understand by 'poverty'? To what extent has poverty been eradicated in Britain?

MARKING SCHEME PAPER 2

When a higher band mark is awarded the marking scheme presupposes that the information required in the lower bands has been given in addition to that required in the higher bands. Where this is not the case marking should be adjusted accordingly.

1. 16–20   Answers which evaluate the reasons for discrimination in terms of fear of competition for a variety of resources, group solidarity, stratification, etc, considers the rationalisation of prejudices, and mentions such factors as the two process of discrimination and the reasons for the eventual assimilation of immigrant groups

    13–15   A consideration of the various groups particularly during the present century in Britain which have suffered discrimination with relevant examples – stereotyping

    8–12   Consideration of covert as well as overt discrimination and the effectiveness or otherwise of legislation in dealing with a variety of forms of discrimination

    4–7   Descriptions of discrimination and reference to relevant legislation

    0–3   Incomplete list of obvious areas of discrimination

2. 16–20   Answers which consider the range of reasons for marital breakdown and relate these to appropriate changes in social structure. The social impact seen in the widest sense as influencing a variety of attitudes

    11–15   Influence of changing roles and expectations, together with consideration of social impact in terms of one-parent families and state support

    5–10   Some consideration of changing family patterns and the influence of those on divorce rates; longer life expectancy. Social impact seen mainly as possible psychological damage to children

    0–4   Simple descriptions of increasing divorce as a sign of breakdown of marriage as an institution, more extra-marital relationships, etc.

3. 15–20 A full discussion of altruistic, egoistic, anomic suicide with relevant examples and reference to differing cultural patterns

13–14 An appreciation of a wide variety of the factors which contribute to suicide with appropriate suggestions for reduction.

9–12 Social factors such as social isolation as a major reason for suicide, with reference to relevant research. Consideration of some appropriate counter-measures

7–8 Some reference to the effect of social agencies, such as religious influences.

0–6 Suicide as a reaction to adverse events, mental instability or fear. An inability to cope.

4. Up to 12 marks to be awarded for the advantages/disadvantages of a longitudinal study; 2 marks for each relevant advantage or disadvantage plus 1 mark for each relevant example illustrating these.
Up to 8 marks for critical examination of the methods used in the research(es); the fewer methods quoted the greater depth of criticism required. Credit should be given where the possible advantages of alternative methods are examined.

5. 15–20 Answers which reflect an understanding of the various definitions of class including the access to power and which accurately assess the influence of class membership in modern Britain.

10–14 Reference to ownership/non-ownership; consideration of life chances consequent upon class with appropriate examples. Degree of social mobility in Britain

5–9 Some analysis of the impact of class in terms of life style and accent with reference to examples

0–4 Simple definitions of class based on occupational groups and/or income

6. 15–20 An understanding of how the decreasing dependence of women (e.g. Welfare State) has influenced attitudes. An appreciation of the limitations of role change to date

11–14 A knowledge of the changes in family structure and the impact of these on both male and female roles. Knowledge of legal changes affecting equal opportunities

6–10 Impact of extended educational and occupational opportunities plus family size on female roles. 'Women's Lib'

0–5 Simple account of changes without reasons given or with only incomplete reference to reasons

7. 15–20 An appreciation of the difficulty of evaluating 'success'. A discussion of the problems associated with differing value systems and attitudes as between home and school; together with a knowledge of the relevant research.

10–14 Some attempt to evaluate the degree of 'success', together with reference to such factors as impact of neighbourhood upon schools and educational factors such as streaming and setting.

6-9 An assumption regarding success with difficulties such as simple class hostilities and bias being quoted.

0-5 Lack of success being regarded as the result of organisation problems such as size, interpersonal factors such as indiscipline, or economic factors such as lack of resources. Or simple claims of success.

8. 16-20 Answers which demonstrate an appreciation of the general inequality of society; including the lack of power and helplessness of the poor

10-15 An understanding of the concept of relative deprivation and the cyclical nature of poverty, including the 'Poverty Trap'.

6-9 Consideration of the degree of poverty in Britain by reference to specific groups

0-5 Simple descriptions of poverty in terms of low income

PART XI
QUESTIONS WITH SPECIMEN
ANSWERS

(All questions are taken from questions previously set by the Associated Examining Board.)

The answers are not intended to be model answers, as model answers often attempt to bring in all relevant points and are therefore unrealistic in that even an extremely able candidate would not be able to include all the information given in the time available. These answers are intended to represent example of answers which would receive Grade 'A's in the actual ordinary level examination and are intended to represent fairly the volume and level of work which an able candidate could reasonably be expected to repeat in the time available.

These answers are entirely the responsibility of the author and in no way represent the opinion of the examination board concerned.

Question 1

'Some people think of poverty as a condition in which families go hungry or starve and others as a condition relative to the standards enjoyed on average or by most people in a society.' (P. Townsend, Poverty in the UK, Penguin 1979)

(a) Which groups in society tend most frequently to find themselves in poverty in modern Britain? (5 marks)

(b) Why do the poor always tend to remain poor? (15 marks)

Question 1 – Specimen answer

(a) The groups who find themselves in poverty in modern Britain most frequently are the long-term unemployed; the old; one-parent families and families with large numbers of children, and the low paid. Other groups likely to find themselves in poverty include the chronically sick and the disabled or mentally handicapped.

(b) The reasons that the poor tend to remain poor is that there is a cyclical nature in their poverty so that it is very difficult for them to break out of the vicious circle. This circle was called the 'cycle of deprivation' by Coates and Silburn in *Poverty: The Forgotten Englishmen* – people live in a poor area and go to a school where many of the pupils are hostile to education and which may have worse facilities than schools in better areas. With no formal qualifications they have poor job opportunities and marry early, producing children who in their turn will grow up in a poor environment.

Practical considerations such as the fact that rents on council housing will be continued throughout the lifetime of the person concerned (with no real decrease as is the case with an owner-occupier buying on a mortgage); and the fact that the types of credit available to the low paid are likely to be at higher rates of interest, increase the financial problems of the poor.

H. Gans in *More Equality* suggests that poverty continues because it is needed in order that the most unpleasant jobs are done; because it increases the status of those who are not poor and because it creates jobs – in social work and the police for example.

Lewis found in a study of poor Mexican and Puerto Rican families in American that there was a low level of social organisation and a lack of interest in the facilities provided by the State, which is part of what he called 'the culture of poverty'. In Britain too there is a large number of people who do not take up the benefits to which they are entitled, either through ignorance, pride or apathy.

In Peter Townsend's study *Poverty in the United Kingdom in 1979* he found a similar low level of organisation among the poor in Britain and his solution entails abolishing the considerable income and wealth differentials that occur in Britain today. He demonstrated that the same processes that keep the rich rich, keep the poor poor, and suggested that by getting rid of excessive wealth, poverty could also be considerably reduced. Townsend said that the poor remain poor because they lack power; they do not usually belong to trade unions or join political parties.

Figures for wealth ownership vary according to the various areas of wealth included in the statistics but those compiled by the Government in *Social Trends* show that 10 per cent of the population owned 50 per cent of the wealth in Britain in 1980. This means that the remaining 90 per cent had to share what was left. The important fact is that the lower you go down the social scale, the less wealth ownership there is. The little that does remain to those in the bottom 10 per cent of the population is likely to be in consumer goods which have little resale value, and which do not bring the access to power and decision-making processes that the ownership of shares or other forms of capital bring with them.

The poor then are relatively more deprived than any other section of the population by definition but remain so because the culture of poverty makes it difficult to break out. The child from a very poor home will have little access to books or conversation likely to provide a basis for advancement at school. The norms of the area are likely to be anti-education and anti-authority. The facilities are likely to be much worse than those available elsewhere in terms of education, recreation, housing and other environmental factors.

Question 2

(a) What is meant by vertical social mobility? (2 marks)

(b) Suggest three ways by which a person can become socially mobile in modern Britain. (NOTE: A fourth way has been given in brackets in the specimen answer, but if only 3 are asked for only 3 need be given.) (6 marks)

(c) How does social class differ from either feudalism or a caste system of stratification? (12 marks)

Question 2 – Specimen answer

(a) Social mobility is the moving up or down the social scale, e.g. moving from working class to middle class or, less likely, moving from middle class to working class.

(b) People can become socially mobile by being promoted in their employment; by achieving a high standard of education and thus being enabled to enter an occupation of a higher social level than that occupied by the family into which they were born; and a woman in particular is able to enter a higher class position by marriage to someone in a higher social class than herself (also, access to a higher social class can be gained by a change in life chances caused by a windfall such as a win on the Pools).

All these changes can of course work equally in reverse although this is less usual in that there has been an increase in mobility upwards as compared with mobility downwards. This has been partially caused by the increasing number of professional and other white-collar jobs and the decrease in manual work, coupled with the improvements in educational provision. It is also related to the fact that those in higher positions have access to methods of maintaining the social position of their offspring which is not available to those in lower class positions wishing to improve the relative position of their children. For example, the child of an upper middle class person who does very badly at school and passes no examinations will not necessarily have to resort to manual work with a consequent decrease in social prestige. It is more likely that the financial reserves of the family in question will be used to purchase a business of some kind – perhaps a retail shop – which will maintain the person concerned in the position of a self-employed person.

It must also be said that nominal access to positions in a higher social class by reason of occupation or wealth will not be fully accomplished unless such change is coupled with appropriate changes in lifestyle, such as accent, mannerisms (folkways) and other behaviour appropriate to the class that has been joined.

(c) Feudalism is a system of social stratification in which each man is a tenant to someone of a higher rank until one reaches the king, who is responsible directly to God. The tenant or 'vassal' holds land or some other right from his lord. In return for this and his lord's protection, he is obliged to fight for his lord if required; accept the judgement of the lord's court, and pay money or goods to the lord from time to time. Each person is in a fixed position in the hierarchy and cannot usually escape from this unless he provides exceptional service, usually in times of war. It is also expected that people will marry within their position in the feudal hierarchy; this is called 'endogamy'.

As feudalism was mainly based on land tenure, one other way of escaping from it was to seek sanctuary in a town. It was the growth of towns and commerce (in association with the rise of Protestantism) together with more money in circulation, and political centralisation that led to the end of feudalism and the rise of capitalism, which is the basis of our system of social class. This system depends on people being able to sell goods for the highest price they can obtain and also, at least in theory, a freedom for people to sell their labour for the best price they can get for it. It is important, therefore, that people should be able to move out of their position in society if they do well, and in a social class system there is no legal or religious barrier to moving up or down the social scale. Nor is there any reason why people cannot marry outside their social class, for instance, a nobleman might marry a chorus girl whose father was a bricklayer. However, in practice, most people do marry within their social class.

Although there is movement up, it is generally to the class immediately above the one occupied previously. This is because those in higher social classes are in positions of power and therefore can protect their positions by excluding those beneath them from equal opportunities in education and job selection.

Marx thought that society would polarise into one group of very rich 'bourgeoisie' and one poor group, the 'proletariat'. This has not in fact happened. The middle class that Marx thought would die out has greatly increased and conflict tends to be less in terms of status than in access to 'life chances' including income, housing, education and health; which Max Weber regarded as the basis of 'class'.

Clearly, social class is not closed – as was the fuedal system – to mobility. However, it is by no means as open as may appear. Accent, private education, inherited wealth, and personal contacts with others in prestige positions effectively over-rides movement in line with ability, although mobility is much greater than formerly.

Possible alternative answer

If comparison was to be made with the caste system, then the answer could take the same approach as above, except that one would emphasise the religious base of the caste system, the fact that it was even more closed than the feudal system, again there being very little marriage outside the caste in which one was born; one would also mention the very large numbers of castes – some 2378 – and the many sub-castes within them, all requiring certain rituals in connection with food and excluding other groups. One might also mention that in the feudal system mobility was made possible by joining the celibate priesthood but this avenue was also closed in the caste system.

Question 3

It is sometimes suggested that work is a central fact of life – its influence on our behaviour outside work is often very extensive. Show, with examples, the ways in which this happens and attempt to explain why.

(20 marks)

Question 3 – Specimen answer

Although it is believed by some that work is becoming less important for most people because of shorter working hours and longer holidays, this can be much overstated. Many people live further away from their jobs than ever before and time gained by shorter hours may be more than compensated for in commuting time. In addition, despite the sharp increase in working hours during the industrial revolution, many people are more involved in their work today. It may be difficult for people such as teachers who may be involved in extra-curricular activities, preparation of work and marking of homework, to know precisely where their work finishes and their leisure begins. The same may be true of many others such as professional cricketers, social workers and doctors. Such people are said to have an 'intrinsic' attitude to their work, gaining satisfaction and enjoyment from it.

The job we do can affect many aspects of our non-work activities, our leisure, our relationships within the family, our involvement with trade unions and political parties, our social relationships with our attitudes generally. Two of the most widely quoted works, Jeremy Tunstall's *The Fisherman* and Dennis Henrique's and Slaughter's *Coal is Our Life* are now more than twenty years old but they do give us valuable insight into the effect of work on non-work activities.

Jeremy Tunstall's survey on fishermen relates the hard, dangerous life of the deep sea trawlerman from Hull, and the fact that he could only be on shore for a few days between three-week-long trips, to the fact that his social relationships with his mates were of greater importance than his relationships with his wife and children. The comradeship built up aboard ship was carried on into the leisure activities of drinking and club-going. The small basic wage of the fisherman established the living pattern of his family while the large sums that could be earned as 'bonus' at the end of a successful trip established a free-spending leisure style for the fisherman himself. Equally, the study of a mining community in Yorkshire identified the comradeship established by the danger and discomfort of the pit as being instrumental in establishing a leisure pattern outside work built around friendships established during working hours. The grim working conditions in the coal mine resulted in a demand for comfort and warmth when in the home.

In Peter Hollowell's *Study of a Lorry Driver* he found that the occupation resulted in home contact being limited and irregular for the 'trampers' and 'trunkers'. However, unlike the coalminer and fisherman, the lorry driver tended to be more isolated from his mates at work and therefore on his return tended to have a much closer relationship with wife and family. Indeed the most frequent leisure activity tended to be trips in the family car. Some 50 per cent of the lorry drivers' leisure activities were

326

home-centred. One commented 'Yes, it's a lonely job but you are independent.'

This 'privatisation' of the lorry driver is also apparent in other occupations where people have little socialisation during working hours, for
example, the research scientist in a laboratory or the school teacher in a
classroom meets colleagues comparatively rarely.

Peter Hollowell compared the lorry drivers with textile workers. Whereas
the lorry driver's major dislike was the ordinary road-user, textile workers
disliked the monotony and boredom of their job, together with the level
of supervision at management level. The lorry driver had a considerable
degree of independence and although the author of the study felt that the
lorry driver was 'alienated', in many ways the lorry driver had more power
over his work pattern than many other employees. This 'alienation' – a
feeling of powerlessness and being deprived of the opportunity to use
one's potential – is a major factor in establishing attitudes outside work.
S. R. Parker found in his study of bank clerks that if work is boring and
routine with little opportunity for initiative, then a similar pattern may
be established in non-work activities. However, others may feel that work
is merely a means of earning a living and that they really live during their
leisure time (an 'extrinsic' attitude).

The fact that work is a central fact of life can be illustrated by the
effect of unemployment on many people. It is during working hours that a
person's status is often established and social contacts made. Without
work, many people feel that there is no point or direction to their lives
and there has been established a correlation between unemployment and
marriage breakdowns, heavy drinking and crime.

Question 4

'. . .is the process of learning in which children and adults take on the feelings and attitudes and ways of behaving in the society around them. The
process never really stops.' (Hambling and Matthews, *Human Society*,
Macmillan 1974)

(a) What do sociologists call the process described above?   (2 marks)

(b) How does this process take place?   (12 marks)

(c) Explain, using examples, what a sociologist understands by the
term 'culture'.   (6 marks)

Question 4 – Specimen answer

(a) Socialisation.

(b) Socialisation takes place throughout our lives, but particularly when
we are young, and some research indicates that it is the first few years
of life that are most important in the socialisation process. All influences that act upon us are to some degree instruments of socialisation.
There are, however, particular institutions within any society which
help to socialise people.

The family is the first institution involved in the socialisation
process. From the moment a child is born there are set rules and set

ways of doing things. For example, if a young child or baby throws his food or deliberately knocks something over, he is punished so that he knows that what he has done is wrong. Equally children are rewarded if something they do is regarded as good. When they begin to walk or talk the parents show they are pleased and the child then knows that what he is doing is good. The pleasure may be shown by a smile which in sociological terms is an informal, positive sanction.

Children quickly learn what is expected of them in terms of behaviour. For example, by learning the gender role appropriate to their sex so that in due course they will be accepted as normal members of the society.

The home prepares the child for school life, and the degree to which it is successful in orientating the child towards the value system of the school will in a large measure determine the child's future success. At school the socialisation process continues; a willingness to conform to the school rules will be rewarded, rebellion punished. Punishment may take the form of detention in which case a negative formal sanction is being operated. The socialisation process will be more formalised and disciplined than that of the home, preparing the child for the discipline of work. In general the values of the school will be the middle-class ones of the teachers and for that reason, middle-class children will often be at an advantage in the school situation.

The peer group becomes an important socialising influence as the child grows older. The peer group are the acquaintances of the same age as the child, and the approval of the peer group will become increasingly important as the young person seeks to establish a separate identity for themselves, away from home influences. The values of the peer group may be different from the values of the home and some young people will, at least for a time, accept deviant values in an effort to gain approval. If the young man, for example, refuses to join a group of friends in taking away a car for a joy ride and as a result is excluded from the group, we say that an informal, negative sanction has come into play.

Later, in employment, new rules will have to be learned and again there will be informal sanctions of ridicule or praise and formalised ones such as an increase in pay or dismissal, depending upon whether the behaviour at work is approved or disapproved of.

Throughout our life we have to learn what roles are expected of us. If we learn well, we are rewarded; if we learn badly, we are punished.

(c) A culture is a group of people who have broadly similar beliefs and behaviour. The term 'culture' usually refers to the way people dress and behave, but it also includes the way that people think because this in turn will influence their actions. So within a culture we would expect people to have broadly similar speech, dress, food and behaviour. They may share the same religion, certainly they will have broadly similar moral standards.

Even within one society there will be different cultures. Some sociologists believe that there is a distinctive youth culture; that teenagers dress in the same way, buy the same things and listen to the

328

same music – although the degree to which there is a separate youth culture is disputed.

Within any society there are likely to be several sub-cultures in which groups of people have distinct modes of behaviour. There may, for example, be a deviant sub-culture of people who believe that stealing is not wrong and that opposition to the police is normal. Groups of Hell's Angels may deliberately seek to break the rules of the general society.

Question 5

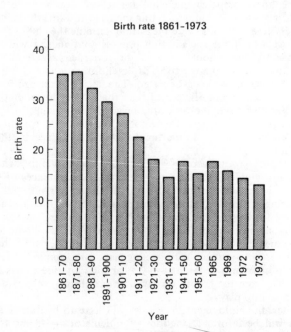

Birth rate 1861–1973

(Source: J. B. Meredith Davis, *Community Health, Preventive Medicine and Social Services*, Baillière Tindall 1975)

(a) What, according to the table, was the average annual birth rate between 1951 and 1960? (1 mark)

(b) What is meant by the term birth rate? (3 marks)

(c) Identify *two* trends in birth rate changes over the period shown in the diagram. (4 marks)

(d) Account for the changes in the birth rate during the period covered by the table. (12 marks)

Question 5 – Specimen answer

(a) Between 1951 and 1960 the average annual birth rate was 15.

(b) The term 'birth rate' means the number of live births per 1000 of the population per year.

(c) By 1880 the birth rate had begun to decline and did so steadily until 1940. A drop from 35 births per 1000 of the population to 14 per 1000; the second major trend is the flattening out of the birth rate from 1940 to 1973 with minor fluctuations upwards during the periods 1941–50 and 1965. The birth rate at the end of the period 1973 being just under that of 1931–40.

(d) The decline in the birth rate during the later part of the nineteenth century and the first part of the twentieth century until the Second World War was the result of several factors. Firstly children became more of a liability than an asset. The Education Acts from 1870 onwards brought about compulsory and free education which meant that children could no longer work and bring money into the family – they were an expense rather than a source of income. Knowledge and methods of contraception had improved, particularly with the introduction of the 'pill' so women who do not want children do not need to have them, or they can restrict the size of their family if they wish. At the same time, an increasingly secular society takes less notice of religious restrictions on birth control. Attitudes have also altered so that the person with a small family or no children at all is no longer regarded as odd.

Other factors influencing the fall in the birth rate include greater mobility of labour, which would be more difficult if there were many children; the fact that more children survive and therefore it is no longer necessary to have many to ensure the survival of a few; and the fact that the Welfare State has taken over many of the functions previously performed by the family so that, for example, it is no longer necessary to have children to ensure that one will be looked after in one's old age.

In the second half of the twentieth century there was an increase in the birth rate following the end of the Second World War and the return of members of the forces eager to start a family which had often been delayed by the war, although this is not clear from the diagram as the period covered is both during and after the war. Later in the 1965 period there was a further slight bulge in the birth rate because the children born some 20 years earlier started to have families of their own; since that date the decline in family size has continued until by 1973 the birth rate was at about the replacement rate for the population.

Question 6

'The chances of the child of an unskilled worker being a poor reader at seven are six times greater than in the case of an upper middle class child, who arrives at school tuned in to educational demands . . .' (Jilly Cooper, *Class*, Methuen 1979)

(a) What do you understand by the expression 'tuned in to educational demands'? (5 marks)

(b) What other factors have sociologists suggested to explain the differences in achievement between the two types of child mentioned?

(15 marks)

Question 6 – Specimen answer

(a) The expression 'tuned in to educational demands' suggests that the middle-class child arrives at school having been socialised to understand the reasons for education. He carries with him his parents' norms and values which are likely to be in accordance with those of the school; he is likely to appreciate the need for education in order to achieve the advancement that his parents regard as desirable. The middle-class atmosphere of the school and the fact that the teachers will be middle-class either by birth or by educational achievement is likely to make the middle-class child feel that he belongs. The working-class child on the other hand is unlikely to have the aspirations of the middle-class and has been socialised to expect the teachers to be hostile; what has been called the 'them/us dichotomy'. The working-class child is also unlikely to have had a background of books or basic teaching in reading.

(b) There are basically two factors influencing the performance of a child at school: home factors and school factors. Of these, home factors are the most important because they tend to be the most influential. It has been suggested by Glass that children from small families, and older children in the family, tend to do better at school than those from large families; large families have tended to be working-class. The resources of families are important as middle-class children are more likely to be provided with a room of their own for private study, books, and access to external stimulation such as holidays abroad.

It has been suggested by sociologists that middle-class children are socialised and educated from early years in a way which makes them understand the value of education and to fit in to the value system of the school. Middle-class children are more likely to practise deferred gratification, where they put off 'going out' and sacrifice short term gain in order to gain more rewarding jobs in the long term. Because middle-class parents have themselves achieved success, their aspirations are handed on to their children.

Bernstein and others have also formulated a theory that middle-class and working-class people speak a different language. That the middle-class are more likely to speak the elaborated code in which all necessary thoughts are expressed verbally whereas the working-class child is socialised in the restricted code where language is less formal but also less exact. It is the elaborated code that will be used by middle-class teachers and therefore they are more likely to be understood by, and to understand, middle-class children and will therefore regard them as successes and the working-class child as a potential failure.

This labelling of working-class children is likely to become a 'self-fulfilling prophecy' particularly if they are placed in lower streams; research shows that lower-stream children are likely to develop at a slower pace than those in higher streams even if they are initially of the same ability level.

In addition to the factors immediately applicable to the home or the school are the peer groups. Hargreaves found in a secondary modern school that there tended to be two groups: the academic, characterised by hard work and cleanliness, and the delinquent, characterised by little work and a reaction against uniform and other discipline. In general, the two groups tended to split on class lines and the children in the non-academic group established themselves into a group which reinforced the roles that they had adopted.

It has been suggested that the advent of neighbourhood comprehensives may have increased the likelihood of some working-class children failing to achieve academically, in that they are no longer removed from the sub-culture of the neighbourhood in which academic achievement is derided.

PART XII
A COMPARISON OF ORDINARY
WITH ADVANCED LEVEL

OMPARISON OF O LEVEL AND A LEVEL SOCIOLOGY, WITH EXAMPLE OF A QUESTION AND ANSWER AT A LEVEL

SOCIOLOGY AT ADVANCED LEVEL

Many people fail Sociology at Advanced level because they underestimate the syllabus. This is particularly true of mature candidates who may be misled by apparently straightforward questions into assuming that they can pass with a good general knowledge of current affairs – which is not true at either Ordinary or Advanced level.

In order to illustrate the sort of standard required for a good pass at 'A' level, a specimen answer to a typical question on the differences between life in rural and urban communities is given. It will be noted that, as well as being longer than an 'O' level answer, it contains more references to specific sociological studies; theoretical sociology and sociological concepts; together with a more sophisticated analysis. (From 1983 the urban/rural dichotomy has become more prominent in the AEB 'O' level syllabus, e.g. 'Discuss the major differences between living in a large urban area, and living in a rural area' – this specimen answer therefore has a dual function in pointing out that such a question requires more than a general discussion of differences in shopping, entertainment and employment opportunities, even at 'O' level.)

Example question

Why do urban areas have higher crime rates than rural areas?

Example answer as for an 'A' level paper

There is evidence to show that the statement made in the question is correct. In the 1980 edition of the Government publication *Social Trends* a special article on the inner cities describes the considerably higher crime rates pertaining in these compared with elsewhere.

More recently, *Regional Trends* (1983) shows that the higher figure for reported crime is in the North-West of England where the bulk of the population live in conurbations (in 1981, 7 crimes for every 100 people in the population), the lowest figure for Britain was in the South-West, a mainly rural region (4 crimes for every 100 people in 1981). In the same year the highest rate for recorded robberies was in the South-East which includes London and its dormitory areas where the urban ethic pertains (75 robberies for every 100,000 people in the population) which was 6 times greater than the corresponding figures for East Anglia and Wales.

There are some fairly obvious reasons why crime should be greater in the urban areas. There are more articles readily available for theft; the anonymity of the cities makes it less likely that offenders will be recognised by those who know them. It is easier to steal and vandalise the property of strangers (studies of supermarket thefts indicate that their impersonality is a contributory factor in shoplifting because it is not felt that the theft directly hurts another individual). Living conditions in urban areas are crowded and McClintock, in his study of crime in London between 1950 and 1960, suggested that the amount of violent crime may be directly related to the degree of overcrowding. Reynolds made a similar suggestion following his observations of wild chimpanzees as compared with those in zoos when he found that wild chimpanzees rarely attack each other but caged ones frequency do.

The less-desirable areas for living in the centre of cities provide a cheap refuge for the old, unemployed, immigrants, unskilled workers and the socially rejected. They are likely, therefore, to be areas where many who conform to Merton's category of 'innovators' are likely to live. These may accept the goals of the society, but resort to illegitimate means of attaining them because they are denied access to legitimate means. The inner cities have been described as being in a 'spiral of decline' in which declining living standards force out all the more able, and increasingly suck in the dispossessed.

The higher crime rates in urban areas, however, cannot simply be explained by the greater availability of goods to steal, greater poverty, more overcrowding or a greater proportion of the 'criminally inclined' although these are all factors in the process. If the mores and values of the society condemned criminal action then most people would adhere to that moral code.

Theoretical sociological explanations can be found in slightly different forms in both the works of Toennies and Durkheim. Toennies used the terms *Gemeinschaft* and *Gesellschaft* to describe the ethos of country and town respectively. He suggested that the term *Gemeinschaft* which equates to that of 'community' was applicable to rural areas where the relationships between people are direct, profound and all-embracing. This compared with *Gesellschaft* which he equates to 'society' which pertained in urban areas and in which such relationships were indirect, superficial and related to only part of the lives of the people concerned. Toennies saw the modern world moving towards *Gesellschaft* in which there would be a lack of social ties and increasing social disorganisation, including crime.

Durkheim took a similar view to Toennies and emphasised the increasing degree of what he called *anomie*, the state of normlessness, in modern society. However, while Toennies generally saw *Gesellschaft* as fundamentally detrimental to the human condition, Durkheim felt that the chances of *anomie* were counterbalanced by an advance in terms of freedom and individual liberty within the urban condition. Although suicide and attempted suicide is no longer a crime in Britain, it was until about 30 years ago and one of Durkheim's major works illustrated how *anomie* was a major factor in suicide. He found that countries with a Catholic ethos had much less suicide than countries with a Protestant ethos and he related this to the fact that rigid beliefs and norms were not laid down for Protestants to follow. This connection between social displacement and suicide was reinforced by Peter Sainsbury's study *Suicide in London in the 1950s* which identified the major areas of suicide as 'bed-sitter land' with much lower rates in the areas with stable, long-established populations.

The urban/rural dichotomy was illustrated by Frankenburg in *Communities in Britain* and comparisons between rural Wales and such urban areas as Liverpool and Sheffield illustrated how the personal relationships of the people concerned were radically affected by the nature of their community.

However, urban areas are not all the same, and, equally, rural areas are increasingly influenced by the norms and values of the town. Nevertheless, the theory of Toennies is supported by other studies which indicate that the greater the concentration of *Gesellschaft*, the greater the incidence in crime. For example, Shaw and McKay of the 'Chicago School' found that crime decreased as one moved through five concentric zones from the centre of Chicago.

The worst area for crime was the central one which they termed the 'zone of transition'. Here social disorganisation was indicated by delinquency, prostitution, gambling, illegal drug use, high alcoholic consumption, violence and broken families. These are not all criminal activities, but are indicative of the rejection of the norms and values of the society whilst the behaviour itself is likely to lead to crime. Large towns do not, of course, always have their main criminal zone in the centre but in most large towns there is such a zone.

Wirth, in his essay 'Urbanism as a Way of Life' (1938), effectively expresses the same view as Toennies and Durkheim. Rural communities have mainly primary group contacts, and their relationships are intense, personal and permanent as compared with urban communities. Here, contact is mainly with strangers, that is, secondary group contacts, and these relationships are superficial, anonymous and short-lived.

Some sociologists have criticised Wirth (and by implication Durkheim and Toennies) by suggesting that the difference is not really between urban and rural, but between industrial and pre-industrial forms of living. A stronger criticism is that they do not sufficiently recognise the existence of urban villages, for example, the Bethnal Green of thirty years ago (Young and Willmott, *Family and Kinship in East London*) or the Cypriot community in North London. However, although these are areas with a considerable degree of primary group contacts and crime rates are certainly lower, the urban ethos still persists. For example, Willmott himself described the considerable level of delinquency in Bethnal Green in his other book *Adolescent Boys of East London*.

It can be said, therefore, that crime is one manifestation of social disorganisation and where this social disorganisation is at its most intense, crime will be highest. Social disorganisation is likely to be greatest where there is a lack of social control developed, because of the anonymity of individuals within the area which in turn permits the development of a delinquent subculture. Such a situation prevails in its most extreme form within the inner cities.

PART XIV
GLOSSARY

GLOSSARY

(Also see the index, as many of the terms and concepts listed are defined in more detail in the text.)

alienation An individual's feeling of social isolation; leading to a feeling that his life or work is meaningless and that he has no power over his own destiny.

anthropology A comparative study of mankind, particularly of biological and social development.

anomie A lack of confusion of values within a society or group. For example, there may be socially approved goals but no way in which some people can achieve these.

attitude A consistent approach and a predictable response towards particular views and situations.

automation A replacement of men by electronic and mechanical devices so far as control of the work processes is concerned (i.e. not just physical labour).

bias A tendency towards a particular point of view (which may subconsciously influence researchers, invalidating their results).

bipartite (or bilateral) A system of education in grammar and secondary modern schools.

birth rate The number of live births per thousand of the population per year.

bourgeoisie Private owners of the means of production. May be used in a general way to describe the middle classes.

bureaucracy A type of organisation which has formal rules and a hierarchy of officials backed by trained experts. A feature of bureaucracy is often rigidity. In modern society bureaucratic features dominate both capitalist and socialist societies.

capitalism An economic system in which the concentration and control of the means of production (capital) is in the hands of private owners. Private profit is the goal and this stimulates competition.

case study An examination of a particular group or organisation by which it is hoped to gain an insight into similar entities. The subjects of case studies may be families, social groups, small communities, etc.

caste A system of social stratification based on religion in which there is a hierarchy of social groups with positions fixed and no mobility. Castes are hereditary, endogamous and occupationally based.

class A broad category of people within a society who have similar social and economic status. Although primarily based on economic factors such as ownership or occupation, class also encompasses attributes such as life-style and attitudes.

concept A word or words expressing a point of view reached by concentrating on certain aspects of a subject.

community A community is a collection of people, such as part of a town or village, who share common values and experience a feeling of belonging to one another. Increasingly used to denote a community of interests unconnected with a specific geographical area (e.g. 'gay community').

conformity Behaviour that fits in with the expectations of a group.

conjugal Relating to marriage – conjugal roles may be joint (the partners sharing duties and responsibilities) or separate (segregated).

conurbation A densely populated urban area in which a number of towns have merged.

control group A group similar to another group which is the subject of experiment, but not subjected to the variable under examination. It serves as a comparison with the experimental group.

culture Social characteristics, including behaviour ideas or beliefs that are shared within a group and transmitted through the socialization process.

custom Established modes of thought and action.

death rate The number of deaths per thousand of the population per year (unless a specific alternative period is given).

deferential voter A working-class Conservative voter who feels that higher social groups are more fitted to govern.

deferred gratification Postponing immediate reward in the expectation of future benefits.

delinquency Refers to the breaking of the legal or moral codes of a society. Often used to refer to less serious breaches of the rules of society, particularly by the young ('juvenile delinquent' – young law-breaker in Britain between the age of 10 and 17).

demography The study of the size, structure and distribution of a population.

dependent age groups Those who are either above or below working age and who are economically dependent on the working population (either through state benefits or relatives).

deviance Behaviour that does not conform to the expected pattern.

divorce rate This indicates the number of marriages which are dissolved in a particular country in any given year. The 'divorce rate' can be assessed in a number of different ways and care should be taken to ascertain the method of calculation. The base may be the proportion of divorces to marriages in a given year (for example, in 1969, 12 couples were divorced for every 100 couples who married in that year, giving a 'divorce rate' of 12 per cent). The base may be the number of couples who were divorced per 1000 existing marriages (giving a rate of 4 in 1969). The rate may be calculated on the number of divorces per 1000 of the population (giving a rate of 1 in 1969). The rate has also been calculated as the number of divorces per thousand married women aged 20–49 (6 in 1969).

elite The most powerful groups within a group or society – a group which has considerable control and influence.

embourgeoisement A theory that the working class are adopting middle-class life-styles, attitudes and goals.

emigration The movement from one country to another on a permanent basis.

empiricism An outlook based on experience rather than a set of values.

endogamy An insistence that marriage must be to people within one's own kinship or social group.

environment All the physical factors and emotional influences that surround the members of a particular group or individual – particularly important area of study is how environment influences intelligence or determines behaviour.

estate A system of social stratification based on inherited rights and duties, legal rather than religious. As the law is man-made, estate systems are less rigid than caste systems but more closed than social class, e.g. feudalism in Europe.

ethnic group People with a common nationality or racial background who share a common culture (see **culture**). There is usually a degree of voluntary identification between members of an 'ethnic group'.

exogamy An insistence that marriage must be to people outside one's own kinship or social group.

family A group of people whose relationship is based on shared kinship. From a practical point of view an *extended family* includes the nuclear family and other relations who are in regular contact, the *nuclear family* consists of the husband, wife and their unmarried siblings (children sharing a common mother and/or father).

fertility rate The number of live births in any one year per thousand fertile women in the population (counted as women between the ages of 15 and 44). The 'fecundity' rate is the number of children who could theoretically be produced in any one year by the fertile women in the population.

folkways Socially approved behaviour which is informally sanctioned but not regarded as of great importance within a society (e.g. dress, 'good manners', etc.).

gender Refers particularly to the social differences between men and women; such as differences in dress, occupation or leisure activies; and to the personality differences associated with being feminine or masculine; such as being emotional or aggressive. Gender can be distinguished from sex, which should stand for the biological differences between male and female; such as differences in genitals or in the ability to bear children.

generation gap A term used to indicate a supposed difference in the behaviour and values between one generation and another.

heredity The characteristics which are inherited biologically from one's parents.

hypothesis A suggestion that there is a relationship between certain facts that can be tested later.

industrialisation The process by which production becomes mechanised and factory-based.

infant mortality rate The number of deaths per 1000 live-born babies in a given population in any one year.

interest group An organisation of people which exists to promote or protect a common interest.

labelling The process by which a person is identified in a negative way, e.g. as a deviant, in one respect and will then receive special attention because of this 'label' so that the person comes to see themselves in the way that they are described by the label.

life-expectancy The average number of years a member of a given group can expect to live from a particular moment in time (usually from birth, but life expectancy from any age may be gauged).

longitudinal study A study of the same individual or group carried out continuously or periodically over an extended length of time.

mass media The means of communication which can reach large numbers of people, e.g. television, radio and newspapers. Films and advertising posters are sometimes included.

matriarchal A group (e.g. a society or family) ruled by the mother.

matrilineal Descent through the female line.

matrilocal Living with or near the wife's family.

mechanisation The process by which machines are used to replace manual labour and other physical work.

methodology The techniques used to manipulate data and acquire knowledge.

meritocracy A society in which status is gained solely on the basis of individual achievement.

migration The moving of people from one area to another.

monogamy A system of marriage which permits one woman to marry only one man at one time and vice versa.

mores Patterns of behaviour which a society regards as of great importance in maintaining social order. A breach of mores will be punished either formally or informally with more severity than a breach of 'folkways'. (Essentially mores reflect the morality of a society.)

mortality The pattern which deaths follow in a society; as in 'mortality rate' = the number of deaths per thousand of a given population in any one year.

net migration The difference between the number of immigrants and the number of emigrants (may be gain or loss).

norm A standard of behaviour shared by a group and acceptable within it. ('Normlessness', a lack of norms to guide an individual's behaviour, may be the result of too few norms within a group; or too many, so that selection is difficult. Can lead to anomie.)

nuclear family see **family**.

objectivity The quality of attempting to use an unbiased scientific technique.

participant observation A situation where a research worker becomes a member of the group which he is studying and participates fully in the life of the group.

patriarchal A group (e.g. a society or family) ruled by the father.

patrilineal Descent through the father.

patrilocal Living with or near the husband's family.

peer group A group whose members have more or less equal status (as in a 'Peer' meaning someone who has similar status to others in the House of Lords). Used in sociology to mean a groups of people with similarities such as age, shared interest or status with whom an individual identifies.

polygamy A system of marriage where it is possible to have more than one spouse at any one time. 'Polygyny' is a system where a man may have more than one wife. 'Polyandry' is a system where a woman may have more than one husband.

poverty A situation in which the standard of living of an individual or group in a society below that generally acceptable. 'Absolute poverty' is a situation in which people's basic requirements for survival are not being met. 'Relative poverty' is a situation where people are living at a standard below that of other people within the society with whom they might reasonably expect to be compared – this will vary from society to society. Rowntree divided poverty in York between 'primary' being that where total earnings were insufficient to obtain the minimum necessities for maintaining physical efficiency and 'secondary' being that where total earnings would have been sufficient if some were not used wastefully.

pressure groups Groups which seek to influence those in power – such as the Government, Members of Parliament, or local government members or officials.

proletariat Those who sell their labour in return for wages.

public schools These are private, fee-paying secondary schools, attendance at which may be thought to confer a privileged position in society. The term is not used to include all private secondary schools as some of these are specifically directed towards providing for the needs of young handicapped people, while others have no claim to academic excellence.

(a) Sometimes the term 'public school' is used to describe only the 217 (in 1984) whose Heads belong to the 'Headmasters' Conference'.

(b) More usually the term is extended to include other major private schools associated with the 'Society of Headmasters' (totalling 53 in 1984).

(Both (a) and (b) are mainly for boys, although a few are mixed – in 1984 about 3 per cent of pupils in the United Kingdom were educated in these schools.)

(c) The 175 principal private schools catering for girls are also sometimes included in the term 'public school'.

(d) There are also some 104 'public schools' overseas, these are private fee-paying schools with British connections (some are also members of the HMC).

In terms of examination results many state schools achieve standards as high as, or higher than, many public schools.

In 1981 there were 4 992 000 children in secondary education in the United Kingdom and of these, 385 000 (7.1 per cent) were being educated in assisted and independent schools – of these, some 5 per cent might be described as attending 'public schools' as outlined in (a) (b) and (c).

race A designation used to denote people of common descent. Used biologically to describe an adaptation to a particular environment by natural selection. There are usually held to be three human 'races' – Negroid, Caucasoid and Mongoloid – but the concept is of dubious value as there is as much physical variation within races as between them.

role The part that a person appears to play in a group and the pattern of behaviour that is expected from a person in a particular position (may be 'ascribed', that is, given, e.g. 'father'; or 'achieved', that is, chosen, e.g. 'doctor').

role conflict A situation in which the carrying out of one role interferes with the carrying out of another, e.g. a working mother may have conflicting duties as between her children and her employment.

sample A representative small section of a larger population.

sampling frame The list of people from which a sample is selected.

sanction A penalty or reward intended to encourage or discourage particular forms of behaviour.

secularisation A term used to describe a general decline in religion, both in its practice and in the significance of religious thinking; and to describe the process by which religious groups and institutions become more concerned with non-religious activities, e.g. as status enhancers or as centres of social activities such as youth clubs or meeting places for young mothers.

self-fulfilling prophecy The process by which someone is defined in a particular way and thus comes to behave or achieve in the way anticipated (e.g. a teacher expects a child to under-achieve and transmits this opinion to the child who accepts a negative self-image and thus under-achieves).

socialisation The learning of the values of the group to which one belongs and one's role within the group (sometimes restricted to the learning processes of childhood).

social stratification The permanent or fairly permanent way in which people are ranked within a society by virtue of their inheritance, power and wealth.

social mobility The movement up or down a social hierarchy (often called 'vertical social mobility'). 'Inter-generational mobility' = a movement up or down the social scale when compared with the class position at the start of their career as compared with the position at the time of the survey. 'Intra-generational mobility' = a comparison of a person's class position at the start of their career as compared with the position at the time of the survey. 'Sponsored mobility' = obtaining high status by reason of family background or other factor not directly related to ability or effort. 'Contest mobility' = obtaining high status on the basis of ability and achievement.

status A person's position within a given social situation (sometimes used in the same way as 'class' or as a position within a hierarchy). Status must be recognised by others and accorded a level of esteem. May be 'achieved', i.e. reached by personal effort: or 'ascribed', i.e. inherited.

urbanisation The process by which towns and cities grow and become more important as features within a society. (Louis Wirth, *Urbanism as a Way of Life*, claims that the size and density of population is the main determinant of much social behaviour.)

values The general principles governing conduct within a given sphere in a society, generally accepted by the group as a standard by which conduct can be judged.

white-collar worker Used either to denote a routine clerical or other non-manual worker; or as an alternative term for 'middle class'.

INDEX

For entries marked * see also Glossary.

A
Abel-Smith, B.   110, 115
abortion   214, 225
Abortion Act (1967)   179, 278
Abrams, Mark   103, 224, 287
absenteeism   136
absolute poverty   107
advertising   294
*alienation   11, 50, 59, 62-3, 66,
         135-6, 142, 152, 156, 220,
         224
Alliance, the   296, 298
Alliance Party   276
Aliens Act   198
achieved
   role   8
   status   97, 100, 287
anomie   11, 45, 187, 231, 246
anthropologist   30
Arapesh   6
Argyle   133
aristocracy   269
armed forces and politics   267-8,
      271, 281, 283
army officers   119-20
ascribed
   role   8
   status   97, 100, 287
Asian immigrants   198
attitudes   250-1, 294
autocracy   267
automation   143, 152-6
   effect of   135, 184

B
Babylon   7
Baldwin, Stanley   243
Banks, J.   177
Barnett, A.   200
Belson, W.   222, 224
Becker, H.   212, 216
Bernstein, Basil   79, 80-1, 86
Beveridge Report   184

birth control   178-9
*birth rate   44, 49, 125-6, 176-80
Blondel, J.   270
blue collar workers   146-7
Booth, Charles   106
Bott, E.   245
Branca, P.   165
Box, S.   233
Bullock Report   150
burden of dependency   184
Burgess (and Locke)   40
Butler Act   70
Butler, D.
   and Kavanagh   276, 120
   and King   289
   and Rose   287-8
British Medical Association   281

C
Campbell, Anne   218, 223
cargo cults   260
*capital   100
Carter, N.   84
*caste   98, 99, 100, 259
Catholic Church   255-6, 259-60,
         280, 285, 293
celibacy   99
census   102
   in UK   14, 18, 19, 175-6
   enumerators   19
Chicago School   187
child benefit   108, 285
children
   influence of television on
         222, 224, 250
   rights of   47, 168
church
   attendance   255, 256, 257
   membership   255, 256
   pressure groups and   278
   State and   259-60
   voting and   286
civil law   225